NASHVILLE PUBLIC LIBRARY

FOUNDATION

*This book added
to the library's collection
through the generosity of
the **Joyce Family Foundation***

DISCARDED
From Nashville Public Library
NPLF.ORG

LITTLE RED

THREE PASSIONATE LIVES *through the*
SIXTIES *and* BEYOND

LITTLE
RED

DINA HAMPTON

PUBLICAFFAIRS
New York

Copyright © 2013 by Dina Hampton.

Published in the United States by PublicAffairs™,
a Member of the Perseus Books Group

All rights reserved.

Printed in the United States of America.

No part of this book may be reproduced in any manner whatsoever without written permission except in the case of brief quotations embodied in critical articles and reviews. For information, address PublicAffairs, 250 West 57th Street, 15th Floor, New York, NY 10107.

PublicAffairs books are available at special discounts for bulk purchases in the U.S. by corporations, institutions, and other organizations. For more information, please contact the Special Markets Department at the Perseus Books Group, 2300 Chestnut Street, Suite 200, Philadelphia, PA 19103, call (800) 810-4145, ext. 5000, or e-mail special.markets@perseusbooks.com.

Book Design by Trish Wilkinson
Set in 11 point Minion Pro

Library of Congress Cataloging-in-Publication Data

Hampton, Dina.
    Little Red : three passionate lives through the sixties and beyond / Dina
Hampton. — First Edition
        pages   cm
    Includes bibliographical references and index.
    ISBN 978-1-58648-093-6 (hardcover : alk. paper) — ISBN 978-1-61039-197-9
(e-book) 1. United States—Biography. 2. Little Red School House (New York,
N.Y.)—Alumni and alumnae—Biography. 3. Davis, Angela Y. (Angela Yvonne),
1944– 4. Hurwitz, Tom. 5. Abrams, Elliott, 1948– 6. Women political activists—
United States—Biography. 7. Cinematographers—United States—Biography.
8. Political consultants—United States—Biography. I. Title.
E840.6.H36 2013
920.72—dc23
[B]   2012040645

First Edition

10 9 8 7 6 5 4 3 2 1

For my mother,
Maria Corbett Goldberg

CONTENTS

PROLOGUE

In the early- to mid-1960s, a remarkable crop of graduates emerged from a progressive private school with less than four hundred students in the heart of bohemian Greenwich Village, New York. These young people entered college at the peak of the transformative era that would come to be known as "The Sixties" and would continue to impact the course of United States history in the second half of the twentieth century and beyond. The name of the school is Little Red School House and Elisabeth Irwin High School.

This book focuses on three graduates of the era. Tom Hurwitz, class of '65, son of an artistically and politically radical filmmaker, became a key player in the New Left in the 1968 occupation of Columbia University and in the GIs against the Vietnam War movement in California. Angela Davis, class of '61, first achieved nationwide prominence when she went head-to-head with California governor Ronald Reagan after he tried to remove her from the state university system because of her membership in the Communist Party. She then became an international cause célèbre when she landed on the FBI's Ten Most Wanted list, accused of murder and kidnapping in connection with the 1970 Soledad Brothers prison uprising in California. Elliott Abrams, class of '65, rebelled against the radicals that ignited the '60s revolution and became a member of the inner circle of the equally radical neoconservative movement that came to power with the Reagan administration on the 1980s—and a major figure in the Iran-Contra scandal that threatened to scuttle it.

The founder of the school was a remarkable woman named Elisabeth Irwin. Born in 1880 to well-to-do parents in Brooklyn, Irwin attended Smith College and then moved to Greenwich Village in 1903, joining artists, educators, radicals and social reformers who would create the first flowering of the Village's bohemian culture. Pursuing a career in psychology and social work, Irwin became inspired by the pedagogical theories of philosopher, psychologist and educational reformer John Dewey, who, railing against an educational system based on rote memorization, believed that an interactive school experience was crucial in turning out emotionally integrated adults equipped to fully participate as citizens in a democratic society.

In 1921, Irwin established the first in a series of model schools within the New York City public education system in Public School 64 on the Lower East Side of Manhattan. There, she began to put her theories to the test. Irwin believed, for instance, that children should learn to read on their own timetable and be spared the "torture" of "irksome drills."

"The amount of nervous strain which a child endures in trying to learn to write before he is ready is more than a growing organism should be subjected to. It is one of the most egregious of all our inherited educational errors," she wrote in *Fitting the School to the Child*. She was equally radical in her views on teaching mathematics, likening a teacher misguided enough to teach students to count in the first grade to a "master [who] teaches his dog to sit up and beg." Underlying these theories was a bedrock belief that a school "should above all things be a place for children to get the habit of being happy."

At the height of the Great Depression in 1932, at which time the city withdrew its support for the experiment. As a result, Irwin and a group of loyal parents, many of them educators, artists, writers and performers, formed Little Red School House, a private school on Bleecker Street in Greenwich Village. In the early years, the school day would begin with an assembly in the ground-floor meeting hall, with the children sitting cross-legged on the floor and teachers and parents standing around the perimeter of the room. Guests like legendary blues singer Leadbelly, Paul Robeson, or Pete Seeger might stop by to perform, or a local policeman or fireman might visit the school to talk with the children.

Social studies formed the core of the curriculum, with emphasis placed on the exploration of oppressed cultures. Little Red children studied Native Americans long before it was politically correct to do so. Ten-year-olds studied Jewish history from the ancient Hebrews to modern times. Instead of textbooks, students read from primary sources (the Bible was used, though without religious interpretation), and they would travel to area libraries to research selected topics. Students were encouraged to apply their research to written reports as well as to plays, dances and poetry.

In eighth grade, a good part of the year's social studies curriculum was given over to what was then called "negro" history, including trips to Harlem to visit prominent African American artists and writers. "We want to rid ourselves of the tawdry stereotype to be found in the ordinary work of fiction, movie or radio script, where the Negro is portrayed as a clown, a lackadaisical, shiftless good-for-nothing, or the abjectly devoted menial," wrote a teacher in 1942.

Little Red was one of the first schools to extend the educational experience from within the four walls of the classroom to the outside world. The field trips were wildly ambitious. Students were taken the Phelps Dodge plant in Queens to meet with striking workers and bussed to upstate New York to spend weekends with farming families and to the New Jersey bogs to pick cranberries with migrant workers. They were taken to meet the workers laboring in the steel mills and coal mines of Pennsylvania. Students in the 1950s and '60s vividly remember riding down a mineshaft elevator, the light disappearing above them until they were in total darkness, warding off their growing terror by singing "Dark as a Dungeon." And graduates recall the senior trip to Walden Pond, where they stood by the water at sunrise, listening as their teacher read selections from Walt Whitman and Henry David Thoreau.

Irwin and the founding parents envisioned a student body of mixed social, racial and economic backgrounds, but the move to Bleecker Street put an end to that utopian dream as the $125-a-year tuition was prohibitive for many poor parents. Moreover, many working-class and immigrant parents wanted their children to join the ranks of the middle class. To them, that meant a traditional education; they had little use for Irwin's work-should-be-play notions. So despite the best of intentions, Little Red became populated with the mostly white children of artists, professionals and educators.

On October 16, 1942, Irwin died, at age sixty-two, from breast cancer. Weeks before, a high school bearing her name opened a few blocks south of Little Red. "The school will not always be just what it is now," Irwin wrote. "But we hope it will be a place where ideas can grow, where heresy will be looked upon as possible truth and where prejudice will dwindle from lack of room to grow. We hope it will be a place where freedom will lead to judgment—where ideals year after year are outgrown like last season's coat for larger ones to take their place."

———————

Ten years later, Little Red and Elisabeth Irwin (or "EI" as the high school was almost universally known by its students) boasted a parent body that constituted a roll call of New York's artistic and intellectual figures. These included playwright Arthur Miller, who moderated his son's eighth-grade discussion of *Death of a Salesman*; Woody Guthrie; John Hammond Sr., a record producer who, in his long career, discovered talent ranging from Leadbelly to Bruce Springsteen; Moe Asch, owner of Folkways Music; and blacklisted actors Herschel Bernardi and Jack Gilford. School veterans still talk about the bawdy midnight shows where the parents, along with friends of the school like Zero Mostel, Harry Belafonte, Josh White and Jack Gilford would entertain at a Little Red benefit downtown after finishing up their performances on Broadway and night spots. Also on the parent roster were screenwriters Walter Bernstein, author of *Fail Safe* and *The Magnificent Seven*; Abe Polonsky, writer and director of the boxing classic *Body and Soul* and the film noir *Force of Evil*; and Abel Meeropol, who, under the pen name Lewis Allen, wrote the heart-stopping anti-lynching song *Strange Fruit*.

A short list of notable alumni of the era includes Toshi Seeger '36, activist and wife of Pete Seeger (who frequently performed for the children); Victor Navasky '50, publisher of *The Nation*; the late folk singer Mary Travers '55; author and anti-communist ideologue Ronald Radosh '55; editor and author Daniel Menaker '59; singer John Hammond '60; actor Robert DeNiro '61; Peter Knobler '64, who was editor of the counterculture music magazine *Crawdaddy*; Paul Solman '62, editor of Boston's alternative *Real Paper*; and Michael Meeropol '60 and Robert Meeropol '65, sons of Julius and Ethel Rosenberg.

The "Little Redders," many of whom entered the school at the age of four and graduated from Elisabeth Irwin High School in the mid-1960s, grew up in a counter-culture hothouse steeped in progressive pedagogy and radical politics. In 1950s America, when prosperous conformity was the American ideal, Little Red School House encouraged its charges to scrutinize, question and resist the inequities of American society. "It was a glorious little island," remembers Tom Hurwitz. As such, it was an epicenter of the 1960s movements that still exert an influence on our national dialogue.

As the 1960s recede into the history books, two stereotypes have emerged in the popular imagination as to what became of that era's rebels. The Sell Outs, so the narrative goes, were mostly white kids from middle-class families who made a lot of noise, fought for a lot of causes and partook ecstatically of the drugs, sex and rock and roll the era had to offer. Then, sometime in the late 1970s, they put on suits and joined the world of their parents, becoming dues-paying members of the establishment they once professed to despise. In the popular imagination, Jerry Rubin, co-founder of the Yippies, who later became a successful Wall Street businessman, exemplifies this type.

By contrast, the Burn Outs destroyed themselves and the lives of others—often the working-class stiffs they claimed to be championing—in their sincere but tragically misguided fervor. Decades later, they are dead or serving time in prison. The beautiful, charismatic Kathy Boudin comes to mind. The daughter of attorney Leonard Boudin, whose clients included Paul Robeson and Fidel Castro, and the niece of influential journalist I. F. Stone, Boudin joined the radical Weathermen and was one of the survivors of the 1970 Greenwich Village townhouse explosion caused by a botched bomb-making attempt. Boudin then went underground, emerging eleven years later to take part in the infamous 1981 Brinks robbery in which a guard and two policemen were killed. Boudin spent twenty-two years in prison before her parole in September 2003. Looked at in this light, the sixties can be dismissed as a self-indulgent burst of post–World War II excess.

But the three 1960s alumni of Little Red School House and Elisabeth Irwin High School whose stories I tell in this book have a different and more complex tale to tell. Unlike their revolutionary colleagues from high schools across the country who first discovered activism in college, Hurwitz, Davis and Abrams, like so many other Little Redders, were imbued from their earliest years with the belief that they could change the world for the better. Decades later, they still believe they can.

No matter what high school we attended, we all have powerful memories of our youth, when all experiences are new and our sense of invincibility gives us the courage to take risks. As we grow older, we take stock: Which dreams did we realize? Which dreams are no longer dreams at all? In Anton Chekhov's play *Three Sisters*, three women spend their lives yearning to go to Moscow—only a train ride away—yet they never leave their home. These Little Red alumni bought their tickets and got on the train. This is the story of where it went.

PART ONE

CHAPTER ONE

Red Diaper Baby

TOM HURWITZ, 1947–1965

Tom Hurwitz's rarified cultural pedigree was bestowed on him in the first week of his life. He made his film debut days after he was born, February 5, 1947, in his father's documentary, *Strange Victory*. In the documentary, about the shameful treatment of black World War II soldiers returning home from the front, Tom is seen in a maternity ward as his father, Leo, gazes on adoringly. Then, balladeer Woody Guthrie wrote a song celebrating Tom's birth titled "Tommy Dudley Hurwitz."

Six years later, Leo drove Tom from the family's Upper West Side apartment all the way downtown to Bleecker Street for his first day at Little Red School House. In the hyper-concentrated island of Manhattan, where one need not venture beyond a ten-block radius to access life's necessities, sending a child to school eight miles away was unusual. But in 1953, the Hurwitzes were a family under siege and Little Red was one of the few schools in which Tom's parents felt he would be accepted.

———

In the 1930s, an idealistic group of cinematographers and photographers formed the Film and Photo League. Its members, including Leo Hurwitz, Elia Kazan, Paul Strand and Ralph Steinglitz, shared an intense disdain for Hollywood-produced pap. Later called Nykino, the League was backed by

Communist International, an international communist organization whose mission was to "awaken the working class, to support its political activities through meetings and boycotts, and to establish a film and photo school that would produce and exhibit politically committed photographs, newsreels, and films." In a country experiencing the first wave of devastation from the Great Depression—and especially in the intellectual and artistic circles of New York City that would come to be known as the Old Left—to be a Communist was not terribly unusual. Many saw Marxism as the utopian antidote to the class divisions and economic inequality that plagued the capitalist nations of the world. Communists and fellow travelers of the era were proud to be part of a group that stood against fascism and racism and that championed the labor movement and equality for blacks and women.

"Any self-respecting young person was a member of the Communist Party," said Tom's mother, Jane Dudley, decades later. Many in Leo and Jane's circle were certain that the Soviet Union, under the rule of Josef Stalin, had realized Karl Marx's utopian vision of a world in which poverty and inequality had been eradicated. It was only a matter of time until America underwent such a transformation. As artists, they wanted to speed that day along and to do that, many were willing to be guided by Soviet agents. As screenwriter Walter Bernstein, a future Little Red parent, put it: "The Communists had led the antifascist fight. They had led the fight against racism and colonialism. They had dared and sacrificed the most. . . . And they not only had a vision of a better, more humane world, they knew the way to get there."

At first the League's output consisted of hastily edited news footage chronicling labor unrest and beleaguered working families shown at union halls, workers' clubs and during strikes. But such efforts were not creatively challenging, and although Leo and his colleagues were fervent in their political beliefs, they were artists first and foremost. Using the raw footage, they began to craft full-length features, virtually creating the documentary as a cinematic art form. The League's first major effort, *Hunger*, recorded a massive march of unemployed people from New York to Washington in 1932. "Our cameramen were class-conscious workers who understood the historical significance of this epic march for bread and the right to live," said Samuel Brody, one of the group's founding members.

In 1936, the group reconstituted itself as a non-profit organization called Frontier Films. Its mission statement read: "There are many aspects of American life ignored by the film industry. In the stirring events that overflow our newspapers . . . in the vivid reality of our everyday lives . . . in the rich and robust traditions of the American people . . . This is the subject matter that needs to be dramatized in America's most popular medium of entertainment. It is this America—the world we actually live in—that Frontier Films will portray." Under the auspices of the Farm Resettlement Administration, established by President Franklin Roosevelt as part of the New Deal, they made *The Plow That Broke the Plains*, which portrayed the plight of western sharecroppers. Frontier Films lasted until 1941, when its members, including Leo, dispersed to devote their talents to the war against fascism in Europe that would soon become World War II—but not before producing what would stand as Leo's masterpiece, *Native Land*. Co-directed by Paul Strand, co-written by Ben Maddow (Leo's best friend), narrated by Paul Robeson and with a score composed by Marc Blitzstein, the film artfully juxtaposes newsreel footage and scripted dramatizations to address brutal union-busting activities by corporations and the spies they employed. After the war, Leo served as the first head of news and special events for the CBS television network, pioneering the use of multi-camera production as the fledgling industry found its feet. Commercially and artistically, his career was on an upward track.

But the populist ethos that had been widely accepted, if not adopted, by mainstream America during the Depression years was giving way to a more guarded world view. The House Un-American Activities Committee (HUAC) was established in 1938 to ferret out American fascists and Communists. With the advent of the Cold War, HUAC's focus shifted exclusively to exposing Communists—real and imagined—in the government, the arts and academia. In 1947, HUAC established a subcommittee to look into subversive activities in the entertainment industry. That year, the "Hollywood Ten," including screenwriters Ring Lardner Jr.

and Dalton Trumbo, were cited for contempt of Congress when they refused to answer the now-famous question: "Are you now or have you ever been a member of the Communist Party?" For more than a decade after, when actors, directors, screenwriters—anyone who worked in front of or behind the cameras in the film or television industry—was called to testify, they were faced with three choices: "Invoke the First Amendment . . . and risk going to prison for contempt of Congress like the Hollywood Ten; to invoke the Fifth Amendment, with its privilege against self-incrimination, and lose their jobs; . . . or to cooperate with the Committee and name names and hope to continue working," wrote Victor Navasky in *Naming Names*. Those who chose to "name names" either from direct knowledge, out of desperation to find favor with the committee or as a way of settling old scores, rendered those who were named unemployable by the heads of movie studios and television networks who were unwilling to run afoul of the committee. The Blacklist destroyed careers, and in some cases, lives.

By the time Tom entered Little Red, Leo was firmly established on the Blacklist in no small part because his name had appeared in *Red Channels: The Report of Communist Influence in Radio and Television* in June 1950. Then, in April 1952, Elia Kazan—the brilliant stage director who had cofounded the Group Theater in the '30s and then migrated to Hollywood where he directed such masterpieces as *A Streetcar Named Desire* and *On the Waterfront*—appeared for the second time in front of HUAC. In the first session, he had named "those he said he knew to be members of the Communist Party between the summer of 1934 and the spring of 1936 when he quit the party and severed all connection to it. This time around, Kazan named Leo—even while admitting that he had no certain knowledge of his party affiliation.

The one-two punch was enough to hobble Leo's television career. He was fired from CBS and, unable to raise money to make the documentaries that were his passion, took whatever piecemeal gigs he could find. As the family's finances dwindled, Jane, who had been a principal in the Martha Graham dance troupe, became the chief breadwinner by giving dancing lessons.

In this fraught atmosphere, sending Tom to a public school, where teachers were required to sign a loyalty oath denying any Communist associations or leanings, was out of the question. There were a few left-leaning private schools close to home on the Upper West Side: Ethical Culture, New Lincoln and Walden (Jane's alma mater), but Little Red, eager to claim the child of a Martha Graham dancer, offered the family a scholarship. That, combined with Leo's admiration for Elisabeth Irwin's progressive educational experiment, sealed the deal.

Weeks before Tom started Little Red, a signal event in the Cold War occurred—and close to home: On June 19, Julius and Ethel Rosenberg, first-generation Russian Jews who lived on New York's Lower East Side, were executed by electric chair at Sing Sing Prison, having been convicted of conspiracy to commit espionage. It was the first time in U.S. history that civilians charged with that crime were executed.

It is hard to overstate the sense of dread the execution of the Rosenbergs instilled in the Old Left parents of Little Red, indeed in progressives of all stripes throughout the country. Today, with access to documents declassified after the fall of the Soviet Union in the early 1990s, it is clear that Julius was involved in espionage activities, although Ethel's complicity remains in question. But at the time, to anyone even moderately to the left of center, the Rosenbergs were innocent victims, martyrs to the cause of democracy and social justice, their deaths foreshadowing the power of an ever-more repressive U.S. government.

"The stakes were high," wrote Little Red alumnus—and New Left activist turned conservative ideologue—Ron Radosh, who co-authored *The Rosenberg File*, the 1997 book that brought the evidence of Julius Rosenberg's guilt to light. "For if the Rosenbergs were innocent, the Old Left was correct; America had been on the edge of fascism, and it was the United States, not the Soviet Union that threatened the peace and sought to repress those who believed in freedom and democracy."

In the hours before the executions, many Little Redders accompanied their parents to Union Square to stand vigil. When the deaths of the Rosenbergs were announced, it was the first time many students remember seeing their parents cry. If, after all, the government was capable of

the cold-blooded murder of two of their own, then any of them could
be next.

The teachers of Little Red School House and Elisabeth Irwin High
School were no less controversial than the parent body. Many had landed
at the school because they had run afoul of New York State's Feinberg Law
regarding public employees and subversive activities. The statute autho-
rized public school administrators to dismiss employees who, after notice
and a hearing, were found to advocate the overthrow of the government
by unlawful means, or who were unable to explain satisfactorily membership in certain organizations determined to have that aim.

Bob Leicester, who served as social studies teacher and who was the
school's director for a time, came from Midwestern Republican stock but
had been converted to progressive politics by his wife-to-be, Agnes, and
had run for Congress on the American Labor Party ticket. The charismatic Leicester had vivid but varying effects on Elisabeth Irwin High
School students. Some found him intimidating, others warm and cheerful.
All agreed he had a forceful personality.

English teacher Norman Studer started at Little Red School House in
its first year and taught seventh and eighth grades until he left the school
in 1951. In 1938, he founded Camp Woodland in the Catskill Mountains,
which "linked urban-based radicalism with the 'naturally' democratic traditions of rural America," according to *Raising Reds*, Paul C. Mishler's account of left-wing summer camps. HUAC investigated the camp, calling
Studer to testify on the last day of camp in 1955. He took the Fifth Amendment and returned that evening to a hero's welcome.

Science teacher Milt Unterman had been a shop steward for the United
Auto Workers in Baltimore. He, too, was called to testify in front of HUAC
and took the Fifth. "I gave them nothing," Unterman said.

Earl Robinson, a songwriter who composed the union anthem "Joe
Hill" and "The House I Live In," a song about racial tolerance popularized
by Frank Sinatra, came to Elisabeth Irwin in the 1950s and taught music
there until the mid-1960s.

Harold Kirshner was a hugely influential, if controversial, teacher at
Elisabeth Irwin. Short and balding, he would come to school atypically

dressed in a shirt and tie. The students knew better than to call him by his first name—it was "Mister Kirshner," and then, when he obtained his Ph.D., "Doctor Kirshner"—at least to his face.

A dyed-in-the-wool Marxist, Kirshner was a rigorous teacher, all the students agreed. Victor Navasky credits him for the top grades he achieved at Swarthmore College. Navasky remembers asking a friend what Kirshner had taught at his previous place of employment, the radical Jefferson School in Lower Manhattan, and receiving the light-hearted reply: "Oh, a street guide to Moscow."

But other students were appalled by what they saw as Kirshner's absurdly lopsided interpretation of history. Radosh, one of the handful of prominent political conservatives the school produced, incredulously remembers Kirshner teaching even earth sciences from the perspective of dialectal materialism. Years later, Tom's classmate Elliott Abrams was similarly astonished.

By the time Leo and Jane entered their "red diaper baby" at Little Red, many progressives who had joined the Communist Party in their youth had grown disillusioned with the Soviet Union. Leo was among them, perhaps not so much on ideological grounds but due to his unwillingness to be dictated to by any authority figure. Nonetheless, for those willing to face facts, there was much to deplore. The first major test of faith for Old Left acolytes for whom anti-fascism was a core tenet, came on August 23, 1939, when the Hitler-Stalin pact was struck. In it, the two dictators agreed that Germany and Russia would not attack each other or support any country that attacked either of them. Considerable mental gymnastics were required to rationalize the deal until Germany's invasion of the Soviet Union on June 22, 1941, made the issue moot. The second test came when the world learned of Soviet leader Nikita Khrushchev's "secret speech" denouncing Stalin at the 20th Congress of the Communist Party on February 25, 1956. In it, Khrushchev detailed the atrocities that Stalin had perpetrated on his own people, a reign of terror under which some 20 million Soviet citizens were killed or sent to labor camps.

"Leo had no love lost for Stalin after '56," said Jane.

But even if Leo and his set had become disenchanted with the Soviet system by the Blacklist years, many still believed passionately in the causes they had taken up under its banner. Regardless of their political beliefs, some were to save their own careers by informing on their friends and relatives. The lyrics to "Which Side Are You On?" the famous pro-union song, now took on an ominous new meaning. People in the once-united Old Left artistic community were split into two camps: those who named names and those who refused to do so.

For Leo, naming names was unthinkable. It was crucial to be on the righteous side and at all costs to shun the ultimate anathema of the Left: selling out. Over the years, that phrase assumed different meanings for Leo. In the 1940s it meant "going Hollywood"—forsaking the gritty, socially relevant filmmaking of the New York School. Now, the crucible was whether you had the guts to hold out against government pressure to rat out your friends. Leo's close friend Ben Maddow, after much agonizing, named names—including Leo's—and the two never spoke again.

Leo Tolstoi Hurwitz came by his independent nature honestly. His parents, Solomon and Eva, were Eastern European Jews who emigrated to the United States in 1896, settling on the Lower East Side of Manhattan. Sol, an intellectual and sometime teacher in the Old Country, had a difficult time providing for his family in America. There was limited demand for itinerant philosophers in the New World. He worked mostly in factories but was constantly getting fired for his union-organizing activities. Sol did, however, have some success, though not in the monetary sense, writing for a Yiddish radical paper, *Freie Arbeiter Shtimme* (*The Free Voice of Labor*).

If Sol was hopeless in the workaday world, he had an unerring instinct for attracting people with a fascination for ideas and an appetite for disputation. The long wooden table in the family's dining room on Messerole Street in Brooklyn, where Sol, Eva and their eight children now lived, was a hub of conversations at dinnertime and long into the evening. The children, many named after revolutionaries and anarchists, were included in these discussions and were expected to develop their own thoughts and belief systems.

"It was a family of judgments," according to Tom. "Business was dirty, and activity of the intellect was to be applauded. But not activities of the intellect that were too mainstream, that were too popular, that make you too much money. The best thing to be is well respected in a very small circle."

Sol and Eva's last child, Leo, was born in 1909. As the youngest, he was adoringly pampered by his older sisters. By the time Leo graduated from Harvard University on full scholarship, he had grown into an unconventionally handsome but undeniably charismatic man. While at college, one of Leo's sisters introduced him to one of her prize pupils: Jane, a dark-haired beauty, the gently reared daughter of an old-line Episcopalian family. They married in 1933 and embarked upon a glorious bohemian New York life where the dance, theater, music, art and political scenes were all of a piece. Best of all were the frequent impromptu parties in which Woody Guthrie was a mainstay as were Leadbelly, Pete Seeger and, along with Jane, other members of the Martha Graham Dance Troupe. Afterward, some might drop in to hear whoever was playing at Greenwich Village's Café Society, the first integrated nightclub in the United States its motto: "The wrong place for the right people." John Hammond, a record producer and future Little Red parent, supplied remarkable performers to the club and, as master of ceremonies, introduced Billie Holiday, who debuted "Strange Fruit" there to a hushed crowd.

As a young man, Tom looked at his parents' wild ride through the Depression era with envy. With his liquid brown eyes and full lips, and his wiry brown hair brushed into submission and parted on the side, Tom was by turns a dreamy and stubborn youngster who, like his father, couldn't bear to concede a point. In some ways, he was a typical child of the 1950s. "He owned a suede leather jacket with fringe and a Daniel Boone fur hat with a tail round the back," said Jane. "And [he] had the biggest collection of [toy] guns of every sort. When I spoke to my analyst about it he said, 'let him have them—and he won't want to have any of that any more when he grows up.'"

But unlike most children of the era, Tom was in a continual state of anxiety about his parents' safety. His fear was magnified when Michael and Robert Meeropol joined the school in 1955. Rumors circulated among the class of '65 that Robert and his brother were actually the sons of the executed Rosenbergs. Tom remembers squashing the speculation, knowing full well that it was true. The death of the Rosenbergs was an ongoing, unspoken terror that pervaded Tom's childhood. One day, he summoned up the courage to broach the subject with his father.

"Could they get you and mom?" he asked.

"No," his father reassured him. "We're artists."

Although Leo's response was not particularly on point, Tom was somewhat comforted by this response. But throughout his childhood there lingered a fearful suspicion that when politicians referred to "enemies of the free world" they were talking about his parents—and, by extension, about him.

Tom's fears were stoked by the FBI men who approached Jane and Leo from time to time on the street, even knocking on their apartment door once, asking obliquely, "Do you have anything to say to us?" One weekend, the family rushed back to the city from their summer cottage in Cape Cod after a friend called warning them that a raid on their apartment was imminent. Back home, Leo burned all his communist literature. No such raid occurred.

But Tom's fear for his parents did not keep him from participating in political causes. He and his classmates spent many Saturdays picketing the midtown Woolworth's protesting the five and dime's segregated lunch counter policy in its southern stores. Picketing Woolworth's was an "unofficial requirement at EI," recalled Regina Nadelson, class of '62. "EI teachers, students, even the occasional parent showed up to join in, chanting slogans, admonishing shoppers not to enter Woolworth's doors, the straggly line with its gaily painted signs circled eagerly in front of the store. . . . The mornings ended with hot chocolate at a coffee shop. . . . where long conversations about civil rights—and less pressing problems—lasted well into the afternoon."

On his own, Tom ventured uptown to Harlem, picketing the 125th Street store with the Committee to Defend Martin Luther King Jr. and the NAACP. In Harlem, he also heard King and Malcolm X speak.

But in one respect Tom stood apart from the mores of his family and school. From his earliest memories, he was drawn to Christianity. To this day he remains mystified as to why. It did not come from his mother, whose parents were secular Protestants, and certainly not from his father, who was, as Tom put it, an "orthodox atheist" and looked with disdain on any organized religion. As a child, Tom loved the Negro spirituals he would sing with his classmates under the tutelage of Charity Bailey, the school's only African American teacher. Early on Sunday mornings, he would surreptitiously watch early-morning religious television broadcasts like *Lamp unto My Feet*. In his neighborhood, which contained a mix of ethnicities, he would walk by storefront Baptist churches and stop to listen to the spirituals. "Although I grew up in New York City, which was overwhelmingly Jewish, in my heart in many ways, I was secretly Christian," Tom said.

When he was eight, Tom and his classmate Miles Mogelescu decided they wanted to join the Cub Scouts. Leo looked with disfavor on his son joining an organization that he viewed as both militaristic and religious, but he made no overt objection. Two days a week after school, until he was eleven, Tom would attend scout meetings held in a church near Little Red. He loved reciting the Lord's Prayer at the end of each session, but his happiness was mixed with apprehension as he imagined his father's reaction.

In truth, there was room for only one god in the Hurwitz family and that was Leo himself. Tom learned that there was no way to win a debate with Leo, who would dispassionately question and then systematically dismantle any argument in exacting Talmudic fashion. Leo didn't get angry with any interlocutor more than an all-knowing deity would become irate at the questions of a misguided mortal. "Were you ever wrong?" Tom once asked his father. The answer came immediately: "No. I made mistakes on some small things. But on the big things I was always right."

Once a week, young editors would crowd into the living room of the family apartment on West 93rd Street to receive critiques of their work from Leo. Tom loved those gatherings. He loved the film projector, the smell of it—oil mixed with dust. He loved to watch Leo lace the film through the machine in preparation for a viewing and later rewind the film, his fingers deftly stopping the spinning reels, while avoiding the sharp metal spikes. Tom would go to sleep to the sound of grown-up voices in the next room and the whirring of the projector.

In seventh grade, Little Redders "moved up" to the Charlton Street building for middle school. According to tradition, each student in the class was assigned a big brother or sister to ease the transition to the higher grade. Tom drew a senior named Angela Davis who had arrived at Elisabeth Irwin the year before from Birmingham, Alabama. Tom was impressed and a bit intimidated by the beautiful and soft-spoken young woman, but Angela evidenced little interest in engaging him. She dutifully toured Tom around the building, went through the student handbook with him and then left him to his own devices. "I'm not sure if she sensed my shyness or if it was her shyness, but we said hello for the first couple of months and then we just let it go," Tom remembered.

When Tom turned thirteen, in 1960, the movement against nuclear testing was in high gear, and he and cousins became involved in the student chapter of the Committee for a Sane Nuclear Policy, known as SANE. For Tom, attending student SANE peace marches and meetings was a way to experience something like the excitement his parents encountered in the 1930s and '40s—and to feel "a loving nostalgia for political activity, when life really meant something." That year, the first regional meeting of student SANE was scheduled to ratify its national constitution. On a Friday afternoon, with great excitement, Tom joined 250 other teenagers from New York's most rigorous public and private high schools in a midtown meeting hall often used by union groups. But at the opening reception, the participants were informed that SANE wanted the student chapter to include an anti-Communist oath in its constitution. The turn of events quickly broke the conference into pro- and anti-oath factions. The pro-oath contingent argued that since Communists were undemocratic it was illogical to include them in a democratic organization.

Red diaper babies like Tom took a vehement stand against the proposed oath. For a progressive organization like SANE to demand such a thing of its members was beyond reprehensible to those who had experienced the effects of McCarthyism firsthand. Friday afternoon and all day Saturday the two sides wrangled. Despite Tom's young age, he was newly versed in "Roberts Rules of Order" and had acquired some chops in intra-party fighting from his participation in the Student United Nations. As Tom ran through the hallways from one caucus to another, arguing and persuading, he discovered a talent for thinking logically and tactically on his feet and winning people over to his point of view. By Saturday evening, due to lobbying from Tom's faction, the issue of a loyalty oath was separated from the rest of the SANE student constitution and an up or down vote on its inclusion scheduled for the next day. Tom and his friends went home that night in high spirits, all but certain that they would prevail in the next day's vote.

But when they returned the next morning they were met by shocking news: not only would no vote take place but SANE, displeased by the resistance to the proposed loyalty oath, had summarily disbanded its student contingent. Furious, Tom returned home, crushed. It wasn't that they had fought and lost, he told a sympathetic Leo; he could have accepted that. But his side had played fair, only to see the process shut down before the question could even come to a vote. Tom dramatically vowed that he would never again join a political organization.

In 1961, as stigma of the Blacklist started to ease, CBS hired Leo to supervise the filming of the Adolf Eichmann trial in Jerusalem. Eichmann was the Nazi bureaucrat who had masterminded the logistics of transporting millions of Jews and other "racially impure" persons to concentration camps across Nazi-occupied Europe. After Germany's defeat, Eichmann fled to Argentina, where Israeli security agents captured him. Tom and his mother joined Leo in Jerusalem in June as the trial was in progress and stayed until the trial's end in August. Leo directed and edited half-hour segments of the trial that were televised each week in the states and would later use that footage to make a feature documentary.

One fall day in 1963, Leo interrupted Tom, now a junior, as he was doing homework.

"Hey, Tommy, do you want to go on a walk?"

"Not really," Tom replied.

"I think we really need to," his father said.

Strolling through Central Park, Leo told his son that he and Jane were ending their thirty-year marriage. Tom was blindsided by the news. His parents had never fought openly, although sometimes at night Tom could hear terse whispered conversations coming from the kitchen.

In fact, the split had been a long time coming; Leo's infidelities throughout the marriage had caused Jane significant anxiety and distress. By 1963, Leo had been involved for years with his young assistant, Peggy Lawson. Unbeknownst to Tom, his parents had come very close to divorcing three years earlier, but the discovery of Jane's breast cancer had put the process on hold. Now, with Jane's cancer in remission, Leo had made the final decision to end the marriage. He moved in with Peggy at 617 West End Avenue, where they lived until her death.

Leo and Jane's divorce came through the next year. It was a devastating event for Jane, who was single for the first time in her adult life at the age of fifty-one. She began to focus on her dance career. In addition to being a principal dancer with Martha Graham, Jane was also a noted choreographer. She frequently drew inspiration from the social issues of the day— some of her early efforts were titled, "In the Life of a Worker," "Songs of Protest," "Under the Swastika" and "Women of Spain." She had co-founded two dance troupes in the 1940s and '50s, the New Dance Group—an outgrowth of the earlier Workers' Dance League—and the Dudley-Maslow-Bales Trio. Now, Jane began to teach at universities in the United States, Europe and Israel. In 1970, she would move permanently to London, becoming the head of the modern dance department at London Contemporary Dance School until her retirement in 1998. She never remarried.

Tom's reaction to the split was to withdraw from the family emotionally and physically. "I spent much, maybe most, of my time sleeping at friends houses that year," said Tom. It helped me avoid the emotions of my parents."

———————

The EI class of '65 was consumed by the politics of the day. Petitions circulated through the class at the rate of two per week: Fair play for Cuba!
Ban the Bomb! Civil Rights Now! In the basement cafeteria, heated lunchroom debates often broke out between Tom and classmate Elliott Abrams
who, although a liberal, was far to the right of most in the class. The students would gather around the combatants, cheering Tom on as Elliott
pugnaciously defended his views in a verbal prizefight. These arguments
became the stuff of '65 lore, rehashed with glee at reunions through the
decades. As the 1960s progressed, American culture seemed to become
slightly more in synch with Tom's world, as loud, rude and irreverent
voices from the music world, in comedy and in print emerged in reaction
to the post-war complacency of the 1950s. At EI, Tom and his clique, sar-
donically named the "Brain Trust" by Bob Leicester, were avid fans of
Lenny Bruce, the British rock and roll invasion and *Mad* magazine, with
its cheerfully cynical take on American culture and politics. Tom and his
crew's condescending attitude was not reserved only for those outside EI.
Although Tom admired some of the teachers, Harold Kirshner for one, he
was unimpressed by the tired Old Left platitudes of the faculty. Sure, they
championed the rights of the oppressed peoples of the world—as long as
they didn't have to deal with them directly, Tom thought. There were, after
all, precious few black kids who actually attended the school—his big sister, Angela Davis, had graduated—and the only African American in-
structor was Charity Bailey, the Little Red music teacher. With the lofty
sense of superiority only a very clever teenager can possess, Tom observed
that although the teachers championed the cause of civil rights, it would
take more than benevolent good wishes from white liberals for blacks to
achieve equality. "The teachers didn't know black people. They wanted
them in the abstract, not near the school. At assemblies, the student body
would stand to sing the Negro national anthem, 'Lift Ev'ry Voice' in place
of 'The Star Spangled Banner,' but no one had been above 96th Street."

Tom gave the old guard their due. In their youth they had stood up for
what they believed in and had suffered the consequences. But their day,
Tom felt, was done. He and his friends were looking for a mode of dissent

that was energetic, muscular and free of what years later would be called "political correctness."

In eleventh grade, Tom and his crew drew a series of scabrous cartoons expressing the vitriolic anger bubbling below the surface of the dissident yet nonviolent school culture they disdained. There was an image of an innocent-looking EI student wearing a loden coat pulled open to reveal knives and guns in the inner pockets. On a less political note, another drawing depicted the World Health Organization raiding the lunchroom. Tom recalls with shame a drawing featuring Blanche Schindelman, a polio-stricken teacher whom he disliked, dressed as a Nazi pinup girl, her malformed arms shaped into a swastika. There was also a sketch that portrayed blacks as cannibals with bones through their noses, meant to expose the hypocrisy and complacency of the teachers who idolized "good Negroes" like Martin Luther King Jr., Floyd Patterson and Jackie Robinson.

The cartoons made the rounds throughout the term and were eventually bound into a folio. One day, it was given to Tom to take home, but he left it on top of his locker, where it was discovered by a maintenance man, who gave it to Bob Leicester, then the assistant director.

The next day, the Brain Trust was summoned to Leicester's office to face him and English teacher Ed Suvanto. "As existentialists, you know that we are all defined by our acts," said an outraged Suvanto. "This is your act."

Tom, always loathe to concede a point, responded: "You mean getting arrested at the World's Fair wasn't my act?"

"You were just doing that to be accepted," Tom remembers Suvanto saying. Leicester took a less philosophical tack. Surveying the group with disgust, he said: "I'll be damned if I pass down my mantle to this." Tom left Leicester's office furious and indignant. "How dare they take it upon themselves to decide what my defining act is!" he thought.

In his senior year, Tom was arrested at the 1964 World's Fair in Queens. Along with some schoolmates, he had participated in a sit-in at the Pavilion of States as a protest against those that practiced segregation. Tom spent the night in Hart Island prison on Long Island Sound, sitting up in his bunk in the dorm-style cell with about fifty others, mostly African

Americans, listening to them tell jokes and sing freedom songs. A proud Leo was waiting for Tom the next morning outside the jail.

Tom felt the enormity of his action. He had read and heard about the Freedom Riders—black and white—who had risked and in some cases lost their lives that summer, traveling to the south to desegregate stores and restaurants. In June, twenty-year-old Andrew Goodman and twenty-one-year old Michael Schwerner—both white, Jewish New Yorkers—had been brutally murdered in Meridian, Mississippi, along with twenty-one-year old African American James Chaney, who was from Meridian. Now Tom was finally joining the battle. In doing so, he was taking his first step outside the shadow of his father's Old Left and coming into his own.

As his senior year at EI came to and end, Tom was dejected to discover that he been turned down by his first college pick, Harvard University—a rebuff made more bitter by the fact that his lunchroom debating opponent Elliott Abrams had gotten in. A bright moment at the end of senior year came when he was selected to write an essay about the class for inclusion in the yearbook. It was considered an honor to be chosen for this task, and Tom was especially touched because he had not always been well liked. A friend had clued Tom in to the fact that many of his classmates thought he was arrogant and some were even afraid of him. Chastened, Tom spent his senior year making a conscious effort to change, apologizing to people he had particularly offended and trying to overhaul his attitude in general. In the essay, Tom even paid a sort of tribute to Elliott: "We had marched, picketed, and petitioned for years, and now the class had its first spokesman of the right," he wrote.

Tom spent the summer of 1965 traveling through Europe. In the fall, with no clear idea of what he wanted to do in life, he would begin his freshman year at Columbia University, an Ivy League university in northern Manhattan.

CHAPTER TWO

Transplant from Birmingham

ANGELA DAVIS, 1943–1961

At the end of summer 1959, Angela Davis stepped through the arched white stone doorway of 40 Charlton Street, accompanied by her guardian, Mary Ellen Melish. It was a week before formal classes were to begin at Elisabeth Irwin High School, but Randolph "Rank" Smith, the school's patrician director, felt it was important that this newcomer have a chance to acclimate to the building before the classes began as she would certainly have enough to contend with adjusting to her new classmates.

Angela, a reserved African American young woman from Birmingham, Alabama, had large expressive eyes and high cheekbones. Her only irregular feature was a gap between her two front teeth that could be seen when she smiled, but on this late-August day—and for much of the two years that would follow—that smile would not often be in evidence.

Smith's warm but reticent manner at first put Angela at ease but she had to mask her amazement as the old gentleman asked her to call him and the rest of the faculty by their first names. Addressing an adult, much less a teacher, in such a familiar manner would be an unheard-of impertinence back home. Smith gave Angela a tour of the school, introducing her to the teachers who were in the process of setting up their classrooms. The first teacher she met had a beard, wore a vividly colored short-sleeved shirt, beaten-up jeans and sneakers. Perhaps, Angela reflected, her mother's fears that EI would be full of beatniks would prove correct.

Angela knew that she would have to clear tremendous social hurdles at her new school as one of its only black students. "I knew I would have to be open and guarded at the same time," she wrote in her autobiography. "I would be watchful—prepared for any early sign of slight or hostility." Equally challenging was the fact that she would begin eleventh grade at a significant academic disadvantage to the rest of the class of 1961. At the lower school, Little Red, founder Elisabeth Irwin's laissez-faire methods of teaching prevailed. But at the high school, scholastic requirements were markedly more rigorous, often meeting or exceeding college-level work-loads. Near the end of each school year, for instance, history teacher Harold Kirshner would assign a one-hundred-page research paper to se-niors that would have them "setting up a cot at the 42nd Street library," as he proudly recalled.

But Angela was not completely unprepared for life in New York. For several summers as a child she had taken the long train ride from Birm-ingham to the old Pennsylvania Station on 34th Street with her younger siblings Fania and Benjamin and mother, Sallye, who was working on her master's degree in education at New York University. Angela adored the city. Here, she was free of the brutal Jim Crow laws that prevailed in the South. But being free to sit at the front of a bus, drink from any water fountain and buy a hot dog wherever she pleased only reinforced her ha-tred of the racist regime that prevailed at home. "Most Southern Black children of my generation," she wrote, "learned how to read the words Colored and White long before they learned Look, Dick, Look." Sallye and her husband, Frank, had been one of the first couples to move their family to Center Street, Birmingham's first integrated block. The area was nick-named "Dynamite Hill" due to the frequent bombings by racists egged on by notorious police chief Bull Connor, who would threaten—and often deliver—violence every time a black family moved onto the street.

As the daughter of college educated, politically active parents, Angela was keenly aware of the oppression she was subject to, and resisted from an early age. Angela was twelve when Dr. Martin Luther King Jr. spear-headed the Montgomery bus boycott in 1955. In solidarity, Angela and her

friends would take seats in the front of a Birmingham bus ignoring the furious protestations of the driver. Black people could not shop at the department stores on the city's main street. But one day Angela and Fania
entered such a store posing as French exchange students. They took malicious pleasure in the obsequiousness with which they were waited on and
exulted in the shock of the staff when they revealed their true identities.

But in New York, Angela felt free. She could attend cultural events un-
encumbered by the restraints of overt racism. After returning to Birmingham at the end of one these summers, Angela wrote, "I wish I was a bird,
and then I'd fly back to New York," in a poem for her fifth grade English
class.

As Angela grew older, life in Birmingham became increasingly unbearable. Making the transition from the city's Negro middle school to its Negro high school, she discovered "a series of beaten-up wooden huts . . .
unpainted wooden floors, ancient walls covered with graffiti" and an "archaic pot-bellied stove in the corner" in stark contrast to the modern,
well-equipped white schools. The curriculum was as shabby as the school
itself, with out-of-date and politically skewed textbooks in which the Civil
War was referred to as the "War for Southern Independence."

Angela's family moved in the genteel world of "Black Bourgeoisie."
Although most of these were active in the civil rights struggle—most were
members of the NAACP—they also sought to replicate the social mores of
privileged upper-middle-class whites. As Angela approached her mid-
teens, many of her friends were "coming out" as debutantes. Her mother
offered to host such a party for Angela, but she indignantly declined, as
did her sister. Both considered such an event a frivolous waste of time and
money.

Angela's idea of "coming out" was getting out of Birmingham altogether. Exploring her options, she hit upon two possibilities. The first
would speed her way to fulfilling her childhood dream of becoming a pe-
diatrician: an early entrance program at Fisk University in Nashville, Tennessee. The second option, via a Quaker-sponsored American Friends
Service Committee program that placed scholastically promising black
children in northern high schools, would send her to Elisabeth Irwin High

School. Angela was accepted by both programs. Fondly recalling her summers in New York and worried that she would chafe at the strict social
structure of the Black Bourgeoisie culture in vogue at Fisk, Angela chose
to head north. On their annual trip to New York, Sallye took her daughter
to meet the family she would be living with during her tenure at EI.

Everything seemed settled for Angela's move to the city in the fall. But
when the family returned to Birmingham, Sallye balked at the prospect of
being separated by such a distance from her eldest daughter and pressed
Angela to reconsider her decision and the pre-med program at Fisk. Angela was almost ready to give in to her mother's wishes when her father in-
terceded. Frank, who had himself attended Fisk but was unable to put his
education to use in the segregated south and instead ran a garage, now
spoke up in support of Angela's decision. To this day Angela isn't sure why.
Perhaps he sensed that his daughter was too spirited and unconventional
to fit into the circumscribed social life of the Southern university. Perhaps
he believed she would have more room to grow intellectually and culturally in New York. In any case, Frank, usually a man of few words, had a
long talk with his daughter, describing his experiences at Fisk and supporting her hopes to move to New York. Working in tandem, Angela and
her father calmed Sallye's fears and in August of 1959, the Melish family
met Angela at Penn Station.

The Davis family had known the Melishes by reputation long before
they met. The Rev. John Howard Melish established his Episcopal ministry
at Brooklyn Height's Holy Trinity Church in 1904, where he fought for
housing for the poor and was active in feminist issues, labor reform and
the anti-corruption cases of the day. In 1938, his son, William Howard,
joined his father as assistant pastor, striving to establish racial and economic diversity in the parish. The younger Melish helped found the National Council of American-Soviet Friendship in 1942 and four years later
became its chairman. The organization promoted an alliance between the
United States and the U.S.S.R. with the common goal of fighting fascism.
In 1948, the U.S. attorney general listed the organization as subversive and,
in the resulting press coverage, the younger Melish was described as a "fellow traveler of Communism."

In the face of this adverse publicity, the vestry of the church asked William Howard to step down. When he refused, the vestry voted to remove him from the church he had served for nineteen years. Years of litigation followed, championed by ardent anti-Communist the Rt. Rev. James P. DeWolfe, bishop of the Archdiocese of Long Island. DeWolfe had written: "[Communism] threatens not only intellectual integrity and physical freedom; it numbs men's souls. It is Communism which is the opium of the people, not Christianity. It says, in effect, 'Give us your freedom and we will make you Gods.' Instead, it has made its followers slaves."

In 1951, the courts upheld the bishop's ruling, and the elder Melish was officially removed from his post. His son, however, continued as standing rector. That state of affairs went on until 1955, when DeWolfe renewed his efforts to unseat William Howard. The controversy continued to receive national and international attention as bills were introduced in the New York state legislature to legitimize the vestry's actions. After a long series of contentious court battles, the bishop ordered the church closed and the Melishes, followed by many of their parishioners, moved their ministry to the nearby Grace Church, where they continued to put their progressive theology into action.

The Melishes' principled stand had made them heroes of the Left, which saw them as martyrs to the Communist hysteria that had overtaken the nation. Even those who disagreed with their socialist leanings believed they had been treated poorly. "Certainly, the test of a man's faith is what he is willing to risk for it. By that standard, the Melishes do not come out too poorly," wrote I. F. Stone in his influential self-titled weekly newsletter.

When Angela arrived at the Melishes' nineteenth-century six-bedroom brownstone on the corner of St. Marks and Kingston Avenues in Brooklyn, father and son were still fighting court battles and the family received hate mail and phone calls. William Howard no longer presided at the church, but he was still very much a social activist focusing his energies on the Southern Conference Educational Fund and working with civil rights leaders as the movement quickly built momentum. His wife, Mary Jane, ran the

Brooklyn Heights Youth Center, administering social programs for teens out of a storefront. The Melishes had three sons: John, the eldest, who was away at college; Bill, a senior at Elisabeth Irwin; and Jeff, a seventh grader at Little Red. Bill and Jeff escorted Angela to school every morning until she felt comfortable riding the subway on her own.

Wary and shy, Angela began her junior year at EI. Ed Suvanto, an English teacher at the school from 1958 to 1979, remembers Angela only for her unremarkable qualities. "She was very pleasant," he said. "One thing that kind of surprises me is that I knew the students so well that I generally had some memory of things they'd written, but in Davis' case I didn't. She dressed very well and was a sturdy student, but I didn't spot her as a world beater."

Well dressed and quiet—that was the way Angela struck many of her classmates. She was a bit of a mystery, and not one they were particularly eager to solve. "Davis was . . . hard to penetrate," said classmate Ellen Fried Sklar. "I don't think many people got to know her. I've never figured out if we didn't reach out enough or if it was her."

In truth, although Angela's ethnic and geographical background contributed to her outsider status, any teen arriving at Elisabeth Irwin two years before graduation would have faced a daunting social challenge. Here was a group of thirty-some teenagers, most of whom had been together since they were four years old. They shared a school, a neighborhood, politics, culture, religion (or lack thereof) and perhaps most importantly, an us-against-them feeling toward a society hostile to their convictions. An EIer of the era described her cohorts as "tough, intellectual, cynical and with-it—as only [a] certain breed of middle-class New Yorkers who think of themselves and their world as the exact center of the universe can be."

The class of '61 was intensely serious. Like their parents, many of the students held an invincible belief in the coming Socialist revolution. It was a bit unclear when the revolution would arrive and how an international workers' utopia would be established, but arrive it would, and in their lifetimes. The '61ers were in sync with the pervasively left-leaning atmosphere of the rest of the high school. During air raid drills, instead of standing in the hallways, their heads covered with textbooks as in the rest of the country, EI students would congregate in the cafeteria to sing "Down by the Riverside" and other anti-war songs.

But the class's political radicalism did not extend to their social lives. Looking back, many felt they were socially inept and sexually backward—"social morons," as one student put it. The girls of '61 disdained makeup and showy dress, opting for the regulation beatnik-black. Robert DeNiro is remembered as the leather-jacketed class rebel in the James Dean mold—refreshingly different from the more "nerdy" '61ers. "Everyone had a crush on him," said a classmate. DeNiro, in fact, was a self-made "tough." His parents were both well-regarded Greenwich Village artists whose bohemian credentials were equal to those of any of the school's parents.

Still, Angela made friends. She became close with Flo Mason, and their friendship would continue through their college years. She and Kathy Boudin were friendly, but then Kathy, who had been at Little Red from age four, seemed to be best friends with just about everyone in the class.

Regina Nadelson would spend hours with Angela at the nearby Howard Johnson's. Years after they both graduated, Nadelson would visit Davis in prison to interview her for a book called *Who Is Angela Davis?* In the book, Nadelson took a jaded view of the community's attitude toward the stranger in its midst.

"White liberal New Yorkers were faced with a problem in Angela (and a few others) which they were at a loss to solve: she fitted none of their stereotypes," Nadelson wrote. "[They] held notions about the South and black people that were not only fanciful and provincial but plainly prejudiced. The South was far away, a jungle of poverty and misery inhabited by novelists, sheriffs, red-necked whites and poor black people who were just waiting for Northern whites to descend on them with schemes for a better life . . . well spoken, well bred, well dressed, and from a solidly middle-class family, Angela was different. . . . There was no need to sympathize with Davis, no way to work for her or raise funds in her cause. . . . It was impossible to send her away once the benefit party ended."

Although Angela had braced herself for outright hostility, she had not foreseen her hosts' "tendency to be over solicitous of their few Black acquaintances," as she wrote in her autobiography. Angela did not question the community's desire to eliminate racism and knew that bringing her to the school was an earnest action toward that end; but from day to day, she questioned the motives behind any overtures extended to her. Were invitations to visit her classmates' homes prompted by genuine friendship or feelings of obligation, guilt or attempts to display their liberal largesse? There were times when she would arrive at a classmate's apartment to discover a black retainer in the family's employ. The family would invariably call her a "housekeeper," but to Angela, that was merely semantics. The "housekeeper" was in fact a servant, and that made her acutely uncomfortable. Between the community's bafflement about how to deal with this newcomer and Angela's natural shyness and consciously wary stance toward her hosts, there were limited opportunities for meaningful connections. Angela felt a constant sense of unease.

She was not alone. Such feelings of not belonging, of never knowing quite where one stood, were shared to varying extents by the handful of her fellow African American schoolmates. Judy Jackson, class of '61, grew up in Morningside Heights near Columbia University. The daughter of a social worker and a production manager, she entered Little Red in fourth grade and stayed on through graduation. Jackson, like Angela, did not feel a part of the class. "I had no idea what they were doing outside of the school," she said. "I would study, go to school, go home." Jackson, however, never ascribed her feelings of isolation to race, but to her uptown address. One spring afternoon in her senior year, Jackson was sitting in the smoking room (which had yet to be abolished by school-wide vote) with other members of her class. The teens were talking earnestly about their acceptances and rejections from the colleges to which they had applied. A male senior turned to her and asked which college she had gotten into. Proudly, Jackson reported that she had been accepted into a prestigious university. "It must have been because you sent your picture in," said the boy. Jackson smiled and the conversation continued, but she was stunned. As the years went by, Jackson would come to see her entire school experience through the lens of that exchange. She had never given her race much thought when she was in school and assumed that her classmates did not either.

Superficially, everything was non-competitive, but looking back there were clearly fault lines buried not far beneath the surface. Under a little stress, she thought, that's when the race issue emerges.

Unlike Jackson, Harold Yates, one of two African American boys in the class, was keenly aware of the racial, economic and cultural differences between him and his classmates. He was unimpressed by his classmates' complaints about their suffering at the hands of an intolerant society. It didn't add up to much, he thought, when stacked up against the oppression of his own people. Yates also took a skeptical view of the mandatory social service that students were required to perform. He detected more than a whiff of condescension in the way the school sent its students out to minister to the less fortunate children at settlement houses throughout the city. After all, he and his family were among the working-class poor upon whom the EIers were so beneficently conferring their kindness. Yates also cast a dubious eye on the school's romance with oppressed cultures. One year the school invited members of the Viceroy gang from Spanish Harlem to spend a few days with EI students. He was mortified when the students asked some of the young men to sing "doo wop." It would be interesting, Yates mused, to invite members from the Harlem Lords or the Sportsmen, two of the less affable gangs that hung around his Harlem neighborhood.

If Angela could never be wholly comfortable in her classmates' world, once in a while she would bring them into hers. After school and on weekends, Angela volunteered at Mary Jane Melish's social club, working with neighborhood teens in Flatbush. Angela had a talent for communicating with kids from the local Brooklyn street gangs with grandiose names like the Pharaohs, the Ambassadors and the Apaches. She and Flo Mason also gave the younger neighborhood children reading lessons.

One memorable Saturday, Angela took classmates Mason, Jackson and Bridget Leicester to visit the club. That evening, they toured the neighborhood, escorted by four Puerto Rican boys who were club members. For all their bohemian "trappings" the teenagers, Leicester said in retrospect, were sheltered girls and it was a revelation to follow Angela as she showed them around the—to them—exotic Brooklyn streets. "We went into a bar and I saw a transvestite," recalled Leicester. "Puerto Ricans and transvestites—what a night!"

When Angela wasn't working at the social club or at school, she took advantage of the city's cultural offerings. She was a regular at the Museum of Modern Art and at theaters, where she saw such avant garde plays as Jean Genet's *The Blacks*. She also spent time with her younger brother who had followed her path north and was attending high school in New Jersey, and with her friends from her childhood summers in New York—Margaret and Claudia Burnham, Mary Lou Jackson and Bettina Aptheker—all daughters of esteemed Communist Party members.

Back at school, the college application process was looming. Unlike the rest of her classmates, Angela had no background in foreign languages. To compensate, the school arranged for her to be tutored by the school's French teacher, Francine Prose. Angela discovered she had a natural facility and love for the language and quickly caught up with her classmates.

Mary Van Dyke, the tiny, rather fierce drama teacher, had a daunting reputation. With her favorite students, though, she could be gentle and supportive. Years before, Mary Travers had been a hell raiser and often the bane of the faculty. But Van Dyke took a liking to the girl and championed her cause on the numerous occasions when she got into trouble. Despite Van Dyke's advocacy, Travers was eventually expelled. A few years later, she achieved fame as lead singer in the folk group Peter, Paul and Mary.

A decade later, Van Dyke befriended Angela, encouraging her in drama class and even inviting her to dinner at her Bank Street house on several occasions.

But it was the school's history teacher who would have the biggest impact on Angela. She found Harold Kirshner intimidating, but was drawn to his perspective on history. In his classroom, the past was not a series of dusty names and dates to be memorized, but an web of economic, political and social forces—or "EPS" as he referred to his method. Kirshner effected a life-altering transformation in Davis when he assigned Karl Marx' and Frederick Engel's *The Communist Manifesto* to his class. Although Angela had grown up around seminal players in the CPUSA (the Communist Party of the United States of America), she had an epiphany while reading the manifesto. It brought into clear focus the violence and racism she had seen and experienced.

"It hit me like a bolt of lightning," Angela wrote in her autobiography. "What struck me so emphatically was the idea that once the emancipation of the proletariat became a reality, the foundation was laid for the emancipation of all oppressed groups in the society. . . . Like an expert surgeon, this document cut away cataracts from my eyes. The eyes heavy with hatred on Dynamite Hill; the roar of explosives, the fear, the hidden guns, the weeping Black women at our door, the children without lunches, the schoolyard bloodshed, the social games of the Black middle class. . . . [I]t all fell into place. What had seemed a personal hatred of me, an inexplicable refusal of Southern whites to confront their own emotions and a stubborn willingness of the Blacks to acquiesce, became the inevitable consequence of a ruthless system which kept itself alive and well by encouraging spite, competition and the oppression of one group by another."

In addition to ameliorating the confusion and bitterness in her young soul, Marx and Engel's work painted a glorious picture of the utopia that would exist when the ruling class had been overthrown and a true egalitarian society emerged. Angela began to attend a Communist youth club formed by her friend Bettina, whose father, Herbert Aptheker, was a noted historian of the Communist Party. About fifteen teenagers would meet weekly in the basement of Aptheker's brownstone behind the old Ebbets Field, home to the Brooklyn Dodgers. Inspired by "Advance," as they called the group, Angela took a class with Herbert Aptheker at the American Institute for Marxist Studies to further explore the *Manifesto*.

But there was one day each week when Angela's compartmentalized worlds intersected. Every Saturday morning Elisabeth Irwin students, along with students from progressive high schools and organizations all over the city, would converge on the midtown Woolworth's, chanting, "Two, four, six, eight, Woolworth's doesn't integrate." As enjoyable as those Saturdays were, for Angela, they also gave rise to disturbing thoughts and feelings. In Birmingham, Angela's family and friends were being arrested at lunch counters, knocked down by Bull Connors' fire hoses and attacked y dogs. Although picketing Woolworth's gave Angela the comfort of feeling at least tangentially connected to the struggle, it also seemed a woefully inadequate gesture. Angela castigated herself: She ought to be actively engaged in the struggle in Alabama, not walking up and down a street in New York carrying a sign. Watching the evening news in the Melishes' living room after dinner and seeing the violent images of the Civil Rights movement playing out in the South was almost too much for her to bear and she would rush into her bedroom so they wouldn't see her cry. The psychic tension took a toll on her health—she suffered from undiagnosed severe headaches and stomach aches. One evening she was in so much pain she collapsed in Mary Van Dyke's apartment.

When her misery became intolerable Angela called her parents and begged them to send the train fare so she could go back to Birmingham. But Sallye, once so opposed to her daughter's leaving home, wouldn't hear of Angela coming back before she graduated.

In her senior year, Angela applied to a number of colleges, eventually accepting a full scholarship to Brandeis, a historically Jewish university in Waltham, Massachusetts. It was an impressive accomplishment. Although not in the Ivy League, Brandeis was one of the finest liberal arts universities on the East Coast.

For Angela, one of the high points of the 1961 school year was her participation in her first major peace march. Walking across the George Washington Bridge from New York to New Jersey, along with her fellow Elisabeth Irwin students and teachers and thousands of other anti-nuke protesters, singing peace songs and carrying banners, Angela felt elated. She also happily participated in the senior play, Thornton Wilder's *The Skin of Our Teeth*, a fantastical allegory of humankind's struggle to survive oppression and its own folly. Van Dyke cast Angela in the supporting role of the Fortune Teller. Looking back, Angela believes Van Dyke's casting her in the one "racialized" role in the play was emblematic of the school's unacknowledged discomfort with black people.

In May 1961, Sallye Davis made the long trek north to see her eldest daughter graduate from high school. On the big day, family and friends of the class packed themselves into the auditorium, sitting shoulder to shoulder in the old church pews. Sallye looked proudly on as the graduating seniors—all thirty-two of them in caps and gowns—accepted their diplomas. Days later, Angela and her mother boarded a train in Penn Station bound for Birmingham. In the fall, Angela would begin her freshman year at Brandeis, once more taking her place as one of the few African Americans living in a sea of East Coast Jewish liberals who were well meaning to be sure, but profoundly oblivious to the realities of her life.

CHAPTER THREE

The Contrarian

ELLIOTT ABRAMS, 1948–1965

On a September morning in 1961, Elliott Abrams took the IND subway line from the 179th Street station in Queens to the Spring Street stop in Greenwich Village. Elliott had a slight frame, short black hair parted sharply on the side and a prominent nose; his heavy brows sat above eyes that seemed to have a perpetually wary look. Elliott tended to speak quickly with a slight lisp. Altogether, the effect was one of keen intelligence with what some took to be a hint of superciliousness.

Climbing the subway steps, Elliott found himself on the Avenue of the Americas (universally known by New Yorkers as Sixth Avenue, despite its name change in the 1940s). Walking north on the wide, tree-lined avenue, Elliott made a left on Charlton Street. Halfway down the block he spotted a group of teenagers greeting each other and talking in an animated fashion. Nervously, he joined them.

Elliott's neighborhood, Hollis Hills, was in a suburban, middle-class section of Queens. His mother, Mildred, was a schoolteacher and his father, Joseph, was an immigration lawyer. Elliott was intensely proud of his idealistic dad and the work he did, yet at the same time, with a class consciousness that he possessed from an early age, he was convinced that the prestigious white-shoe Wall Street firms looked down on his father's work.

Like many other families in their neighborhood, the Abrams were New Deal Democrats—they had, after all, named their first son Franklin. Both boys attended the area's public schools. When it came time for Elliott to enter high school, Franklin, who was already attending Harvard University, reported to his parents that the public school system had not prepared him well for college and advised them to send his younger brother to private school. Some friends of Elliott's mother recommended Elisabeth Irwin High School.

Entering the double doors of the building, Elliott followed the crush of teens climbing three flights of stairs to ninth grade homeroom. There, he found himself among the thirty-odd students that comprised the entire ninth grade. In this small class, Elliott immediately sensed the bond between the students, many of whom had played and studied together for years. The boy from Queens looked different from his classmates. With his short hair, pressed chinos and shirt and tie, he stood out against the other more casually dressed boys, many of whom wore jeans or corduroy pants with pullover shirts. The girls, too, looked markedly different from their public school counterparts, some wearing roughly woven ponchos and leather sandals, and carrying battered, oversized leather shoulder bags.

But as the weeks went by, Elliott's sense of discomfort dissipated as his intelligence and biting wit earned him friends. His popularity was such that in Elliott's freshman year, his classmates trekked all the way out to his family's Queens home to attend a party, smoking marijuana in the Abrams' basement late into the night. Elliott participated enthusiastically in the class's other extracurricular activities, joining an after-school discussion group, for which he scoured Upper East Side bookstores in search of a dozen copies of *The Communist Manifesto*, despite the quizzical looks he received from the booksellers. That first year, he also participated in a demonstration in front of the FBI building to protest the agency's failure to protect civil rights workers in the South. Two FBI men came out at one point to see what all the commotion was about.

"Why, it's just a bunch of kids," one said to the other.

Another time, he accompanied some of his classmates to hear a speech by Corliss Lamont, the founder of the National Emergency Civil Liberties Committee, on the subject of free speech. When Elliott told his father about the expedition the next day over breakfast, Joe was appalled.

"What's going on here?" he exclaimed. "That man is a Communist!" Joseph warned his son that he must be careful to draw the distinction between liberals and Communists.

In most American high schools in the early 1960s, the Abrams family's politics would have put Elliott to the left of his classmates. At Elisabeth Irwin, he was the equivalent of a rock-ribbed Republican. Culturally, Elliott was also out of step. Like most of his classmates, he was Jewish. But unlike most of his classmates, who either came from secular families or were the products of mixed marriages, Elliott's family was observant and kept a kosher home. Just the year before, in eighth grade, Elliott had spent a year on the bar mitzvah circuit attending the coming of age ceremonies of his thirteen-year-old friends. At Elisabeth Irwin, religion was a non-issue. "There was no such thing," said Elliott. "It would be like asking me in 1962, 'what's your position on vegetarianism?' I assumed that everyone was an atheist."

As the months went by, Elliott began to react to what he perceived to be the knee-jerk, left wing orthodoxies of the school. Browsing the magazine racks in the library, he saw progressive publications like *I. F. Stone's Weekly* and *The Nation*. Why, he asked Isabel Suhl, the sweet-faced librarian, could the school not achieve some balance in the publications it displayed? Why not stock a magazine like *The National Review*?

"The culture is dominated by right-wing politics," Suhl replied. "We don't need to get more of it in the school."

In Elliott's view, history teacher Harold Kirshner personified the school's stilted politics. He was, Elliott allowed, a rigorous and dedicated teacher, but his analyses of historical movements seemed patently absurd. Why did countries acquire colonies? According to Dr. Kirshner, because countries needed economic markets. "Who the Hell in those impoverished colonies was in a position to buy anything?" Abrams wondered incredulously. In 1964, the word around school was that Kirshner had voted for Lyndon Johnson in the presidential election—the first time, so the whispers went, that he had ever cast such a mainstream vote for fear that a victory for conservative Republican Barry Goldwater would bring fascism to America. In Elliott's opinion, that fear was a bit overblown.

Increasingly appalled by the school's ideological slant, Elliott began to vocalize his own political views. He debated with his classmates in the basement cafeteria. His chief opponent was Tom Hurwitz, his equal in intellectual precocity and love of a good fight. The impromptu discussions often ended in shouting matches between the two. A hot topic in these lunchroom debates was Cuba and its leader, Fidel Castro, who had come to power in 1959. Most EI students saw Castro as a romantic revolutionary who was bringing economic and social justice to his people. Elliott viewed him as just another standard-issue Communist dictator.

"I remember him despising Castro," said Tom. "He couldn't stand his verbosity and his long speeches and his beard. . . . It was just horrendous [to Elliott] that such an undignified person with such uncivilized trappings should fly in the face of our rich democratic traditions."

Most of the time, Elliott kept his own counsel, wearing a mysterious smile on his face. "It would be going too far to call it a sneer," Tom later said. "It was a grin." But Elliott had no trouble voicing his beliefs, discovering that he actually enjoyed drawing fire for his views.

But Robert Miller (Arthur Miller's son), thought that Elliott's combative stance was put on mostly for effect. "He was very facile, funny and bright," he said. But Miller's mother, Mary, wasn't convinced. She wondered how Elliott could be so different from his mild-mannered and liberal parents.

To be sure, Elliott was not completely alone in his skeptical take on the school's prevailing ethos. As far as classmate Julian Zukmann was concerned, EI, which prided itself on being a bastion of independent thought, was intolerant of any opinions diverging from the norm. "At an assembly, a kid refused to stand to sing the Negro National Anthem," Zukmann said. "A teacher came down the aisle of the auditorium, pulled him out of his seat and dragged him out. He subsequently left the school. There were murmurings about the incident but no full cry." Zukmann admired the way Elliott addressed such injustices head on. "I didn't confront them the way Elliott did. I was probably too scared," he said. Cathy Michaelson, two years behind Elliott in school, attended Little Red and Elisabeth Irwin from kindergarten through twelfth grade. She looks back at her experiences with bitterness. "The school was staffed by "mediocre diehard liberals," Michaelson said. "If you didn't agree with the political mantra of the school it was like, 'What's wrong with you?'" Michaelson, a straight-A student, also resented what she perceived to be an unspoken bias against striving for academic excellence. "I was surrounded by kids who made me feel like I was wrong because I wanted good grades. . . . You weren't supposed to be competitive if you were a good person—a good liberal person. The political overtone of the place poisoned everything." Like Zukmann, Michaelson admired Elliott for giving voice to the misgivings that she was too timid to express at the time.

Sara Fishko (class of '67), the daughter of the president of the powerful, left-wing International Printing, Graphics and Communication Union, certainly fell on the left end of the school's political spectrum. Yet despite—and also because of that—Fishko was intrigued by Elliott, and the two dated for a time. Fishko loved to engage Elliott in arguments, enjoying his wordplay and wit. She was aware that a lot of her classmates couldn't stand him, but she saw him as an idealistic Democrat. "For me, it was like growing up in the Midwest and having never met a Jew," Fishko recalled. "He was brilliant and taking his ideas in another direction." For all their differences, Fishko thought, they were both basically on the same side.

Lisa Fein Gilford, daughter of celebrated character actor Jack Gilford, was also in the pro-Elliott camp, remembering him as "generous, kind, funny and insanely smart." Although he didn't speak a lot, "he had a dry wit," she said. Gilford has fond memories of hanging out with him at Curry's coffee shop on the corner during free periods, laughing over french fries and Cokes, and accompanying him to a Beatles concert. Gilford lost touch with Elliott after they went to college, but contacted him in the late 1980s when he was serving as assistant secretary for foreign affairs in the Reagan administration. A dance troupe she was bringing to America to perform was stranded in London due to a bureaucratic snafu. "I called him and said 'I need your help.' Elliott made a call. Ten minutes later it was done."

Any intolerance the faculty may have had for Elliott's retrograde political views did not affect their recognition of his academic excellence. In his
senior year, he was named to the coveted post of co-editor of *Info*, EI's student publication. One Saturday each month, Elliott, co-editor Larry Hendel, Susan Gill and Sara Fishko met at Joe Abrams' midtown law office to
assemble the issue, first typing the articles and then pasting them onto the
master copy with rubber cement. Press-on letters were used to form the
headlines. The final product emerged wet from the office's state-of-the-art
Photostat machine.

"He used to stand at the window of his father's law office and make
these speeches," said Hendel. "It was an intimidating place with fancy electric typewriters and big swivel chairs. Elliott would, like, trip out on it.
Once he went to the window and said, 'Look at all the little, tiny people
down there. Some day, I'll have control over them all.'" Although Elliott
smiled as he made this pronouncement, Hendel suspected that his co-
editor was speaking "half in jest, wholly in earnest."

As an editor of *Info*, Elliott penned editorials in which he took predictably controversial stances—at least to his readerships' rarified sensibil-
ities. In one, Elliott defended the building of bomb shelters, a seemingly
benign opinion, but at EI the prevailing belief was that the government
was promoting those shelters in order to incite fear and anti-Soviet fervor
in the United States. In another editorial, Elliott considered whether liberals should cooperate with Communists in order to achieve common goals
like civil rights. No, he concluded, liberals would lose credibility as a result
of such collaboration, and attacks from the Right would undermine their
cause. Cold War liberals, Elliott had come to believe, were more dangerous
than conservatives.

That editorial caused a furor. "All of us thought it was a reprehensible,
bizarrely radical position," said Fishko. "We accused him of being a Mc-
Carthyite." *Info* followed up on that theme by publishing a letter from a
distressed ninth grader. Under the headline, "E.I.: Narrow-Minded Liberals?" fourteen-year-old Jo-Ellen Beder complained that she and others
were ridiculed when they strayed from the school's ideological orthodoxy.
"Recently," she wrote, "I saw a large group of classmates, some of them the

ones I respected most, writing all over Goldwater posters, putting moustaches on his pictures, and swastikas and other 'brilliant' little exaggerations all over the paper. Sure I'm against Goldwater, but this is a horrible way to say you disagree with someone else's honest opinion. EI teaches presumably liberal thinking. It may be considered liberal politically, but this certainly is not a liberal approach to learning."

Drama teacher Mary Van Dyke, always sensitive to those students a bit out of step with the rest, now took a shine to Elliott. In addition to giving him private lessons to overcome his lisp, she cast him in the senior play, *Idiot's Delight*.

In the spring of his senior year, Elliott joyfully learned that he had been accepted to his brother's alma mater, Harvard University. Intensifying the sweetness of the accomplishment was the fact that none of his classmates who had applied to the prestigious institution, including Tom Hurwitz, had made the cut. In many ways, Elliott's four years at Elisabeth Irwin had been exhilarating ones. He had been introduced to a world of arts and culture and had made what he was sure would be enduring friendships. But now that he had tested his mettle among provincial Greenwich Village ideologues, he was ready to enter an institution that trafficked in a true marketplace of ideas.

PART TWO

CHAPTER FOUR

The Making of a Revolutionary

ANGELA DAVIS, 1961–1969

Set in an idyllic pastoral setting on 235 acres outside the small town of Waltham, Massachusetts, nine miles west of Boston, Brandeis University was founded in 1948 and named after the distinguished Jewish Supreme Court justice. In 1961, the year in which Angela arrived as a freshman, the liberal arts university was composed of about 1300.

In size and location, the school could not have been more different from the institution from which Angela had graduated a few months before. But in other ways, it was Elisabeth Irwin writ large: a small, progressive school with a predominantly left-leaning Jewish student body. Despite having had two years to adjust to that particular slice of American society, Angela found herself feeling more lonely and isolated than she had at EI. In high school, her feeling of being the perpetual outsider was tempered by the fact that she had a social life outside the school with her friends from Advance and via the youth center in Brooklyn run by Mary Lou Melish.

At Brandeis, Angela knew no one and was disinclined to make new friends. There was a radical contingent on campus—activist Abbie Hoffman had graduated just a couple of years earlier—but the school was overwhelmingly composed of white students railing against the values of their middle-class suburban parents. "Who was there at the all white middle-class Brandeis for Angela to emulate? The others could discharge their anger into a 'cultural revolution,' identify with the beats and find security in a new lifestyle," wrote Angela's high school friend Regina Nadelson. "It was quite another thing to turn on your parents when their struggle was part of the as yet almost unbegun struggle for the freedom of a still-oppressed class."

Angela took refuge in her studies. When interacting with her fellow students, she consciously adopted an aloof persona, wearing jeans—unheard-of garb for a female college student at that time—to classes and even to school dances. She also kept her distance from the university's small Communist contingent, feeling condescended to by the leaders who tried to recruit her.

Angela stayed in touch with her best friend from Elisabeth Irwin, Flo Mason. Together they formed a plan to attend the Eighth World Festival for Youth and Students in Helsinki, Finland, that summer. To earn money for the trip, Angela worked three jobs: at the library on campus and at a coffee shop and an ice cream parlor in town. The trip proved to be well worth the money Angela had worked so hard to earn. She was thrilled to be among the congregation of Communist youth from all over the world. Angela was especially inspired by the Cuban delegation's revolutionary fervor and noted with approval the inclusion of women in the country's militia. At the close of the conference, members from each country's delegation entertained on the main stage. When the Cuban performers finished their presentation, they formed a conga line that was joined by the hundreds of people in the audience. The joyful procession snaked through the building and out onto the street.

Angela's sophomore year at Brandeis began on an ominous note when FBI agents approached her and questioned her about the Helsinki festival. "Don't you know what we do to Communists?" one of them asked. That question took on added weight a few weeks later when, on October 22, 1962, President John F. Kennedy informed the country that the U.S.S.R. was building nuclear missile sites in Cuba, 90 miles off the coast of Florida. Kennedy ordered a naval blockade around the island to prevent the Soviets from delivering more military supplies and demanded immediate dismantlement of the missiles. The resulting standoff seemed poised to trigger the nightmare conclusion to the U.S.–Soviet conflict that Americans who came of age in the 1950s had spent their childhoods dreading: a nuclear conflagration.

Brandeis students reacted to the crisis with varying degrees of panic. According to Angela, a good portion of them simply packed their things into cars and left—some for the perceived safety of Canada. Angela observed the exodus with contempt. "They were not interested in the fact that the people of Cuba were in terrible jeopardy—or even that millions of innocent people elsewhere might be destroyed if a nuclear conflict broke out," she wrote.

As it happened, famed African American author James Baldwin was delivering a series of lectures at the school when the crisis erupted. Announcing that he could not, in good conscience, continue, he instead participated in a rally put together by the remaining students and faculty urging President Kennedy to defuse the crisis by recalling the blockade. One of the speakers was a professor who would become a mentor and a pivotal figure in her life: Herbert Marcuse. Born in Berlin in 1889, Marcuse was a Communist and a philosopher, a member of the Marxist Frankfurt School of Social Theory. With the rise of the Nazi Party in the 1930s, he fled to the United States and worked with the U.S. government during World War II, researching Nazi and Fascist ideology to plan for the post-war occupation and "de-Nazification" of Germany. By the fall of 1962, when Angela heard him speak, Marcuse, with his craggy face topped by a thatch of white hair, was comfortably installed as a professor in Brandeis' philosophy department, where he espoused an ideology that combined elements of Marx and Freud.

Ten days later, the crisis was resolved and life returned to normal on the campus. But in those brief days of political mobilization, Angela had connected with foreign-exchange students who were active in the protests. Shedding her diffident demeanor, Angela formed a circle of friends and even started dating a German student, Manfred Clemenz, an intense and intellectual young man sporting a mustache and beard.

Angela, whose love of the French language began at EI, spent her junior year abroad in Paris, studying contemporary literature and language at the Sorbonne. Just days after she arrived, on a Sunday morning, September 16, 1963, one of the most infamous events of the civil rights era occurred. A bomb that had been planted in the 16th Street Baptist Church in Birmingham exploded, killing four young girls attending Sunday school.

The next day, walking with her fellow students, Angela passed by a news kiosk. Grabbing a copy of the paper, she stood shaking in the middle of the street as she read the news. Concerned, her companions gathered around her. "Carole . . . Cynthia . . . They killed them. I know them. They're my friends," was all Angela could manage to say as she held out the newspaper for them to see. Angela's family had been friends with all the families of the murdered girls. One of them had been a student of Sallye's; another had been her sister Fania's best friend.

No one seemed to know what to say. After a long silence, one of the students spoke up.

"It's too bad it had to happen."

Perhaps her fellow students did not know how to respond to a situation so far removed from their lives. Perhaps the expression of such raw emotion from the usually reserved Angela made them uncomfortable. Whatever the reason, what seemed to Angela to be perfunctory expressions of condolence in the face of such barbarity and—the way they viewed it as an isolated if regrettable incident—struck her as obscene. "The people around me . . . could not understand why the whole society was guilty of this murder—why their beloved Kennedy was also to blame, why the whole ruling stratum in their country, by being guilty of racism, was also guilty of this murder," she wrote, continuing, "This act was not an aberration. On the contrary, it was logical, inevitable. The people who planted the bomb in the girls' restroom in the basement of the 16th Street Baptist Church were not pathological, but rather the normal products of their surroundings. And it was this spectacular, violent event, the savage dismembering of four little girls, which had burst out of the daily, sometimes even dull, routine of racist oppression."

Weeks later, when Kennedy was assassinated in Dallas, on November 22, 1963, it was Angela's turn to remain relatively unmoved amid the distraught and sobbing expatriates who gathered at the American Embassy to express their grief. "How many of them had shed tears—or had truly felt saddened—when they read the *Herald Tribune* story about the murders of Carole, Cynthia, Addie Mae and Denise?" she bitterly reflected.

Despite its awful beginning, the year abroad was a wonderful experience for Angela. As always, she was a dedicated student, reveling in her studies at the Sorbonne. For once, though, Angela enjoyed her free time, spending her evenings in cafés with students from other countries, chain-smoking Gauloises cigarettes as she participated in intense discussions about the Algerian conflict with Colonial France and other world affairs. Angela continued her relationship with Clemenz, who had returned home to Frankfurt, visiting him periodically. Their relationship became so intense that at one point there was talk of marriage, much to the displeasure of both sets of parents. When she got word of the potential match, Sallye Davis turned to Rev. William Howard Melish for counsel. Melish, who had met Clemenz briefly at Brandeis, advised restraint, saying that active opposition would inevitably drive the young paramours closer together.

Angela had entered Brandeis with the intention of gaining a degree in French studies, but she now considered changing her concentration to philosophy. After auditing one of Marcuse's lectures, she shyly approached the professor, asking him for help in forming a reading list that would give her a firm footing in the discipline. Impressed by Angela's intellect and seriousness of purpose, the elderly professor invited her to meet with him weekly to discuss her readings. "Poring over a seemingly incomprehensible passage [of Kant] for hours, then suddenly grasping its meaning, gave me a sense of satisfaction I had never experienced before," she said.

This time both Sallye and Frank traveled north to watch Angela graduated from Brandeis magna cum laude. Angela then loaded her belongings into her parents' car for the long trip back to Birmingham. Driving through Tennessee in the middle of the night, the Davis family was stopped by a local policeman. Finding a case of liquor Frank had purchased to take home to Birmingham, the lawman curtly instructed them to follow his car to the police station. But instead, he led them to a dark alley where the policeman emerged from his squad car and opened a garage door, ordering Frank to follow him inside. Terrified, Sallye begged her husband not to go. But Frank, at least outwardly, seemed unfazed.

"There wasn't the slightest trace of fear in my father," Angela proudly wrote. "He went on in while we waited on tenterhooks in the car. After what seemed like hours, he came out with a wry smile on his face. Starting up the car, he told us, chuckling 'All the man wanted was the liquor and twenty dollars.'"

In late summer 1965, Angela returned to Europe, this time to Frankfurt, to study with her mentor Marcuse's colleague Theodore Adorno at the Institute for Social Research at the Goethe University. As Angela boarded the boat for Germany, riots broke out in Los Angeles in the poor, African American neighborhood of Watts on August 11. The inciting incident involved a California highway patrolman trying to arrest an African American driver. That sparked a confrontation between the police and blacks who were enraged about police brutality and discriminatory housing and hiring practices. A week later, thirty-four people, twenty-five of them black, were dead, according to the *Los Angeles Times*, and more than a thousand had been injured. More than six hundred buildings had been damaged or destroyed. The Watts riots would stand as Los Angeles' most destructive until the Rodney King riots in 1991.

Arriving in Frankfurt, Angela looked for accommodations she could afford on her $100-a-month stipend. She found them in an abandoned, unheated factory near to the university that a group of students—many of them political activists who belonged to the German Socialist Students' League—had commandeered and transformed into a counterculture squat. True to William Howard Melish's prediction, Angela's relationship with Clemenz had fizzled shortly after they were reunited in Germany, and she began dating another Factory resident, Tommy Mitscherlich, the son of a prominent German psychoanalyst. Angela. celebrated May Day—International Workers Day—in Frankfurt with family friends Esther and James Jackson, the latter of whom was the international affairs director of the CPUSA. Talking with them brought to mind her high school days in New York, when FBI agents would trail her and her young friends, hoping they would lead them to high-profile party members. At these occasional meetings with family friends, Angela was relaxed and happy

The disciplined reserve with which Angela dealt with most of the outside world belied the disorganized fashion in which she handled the logistics of her day-to-day life. Eating properly, clothing herself and getting to appointments on time proved baffling to her. Angela's room in the Factory was a chaotic tangle of books and clothing. One afternoon, a fellow Factory dweller visited Angela in her room only to find her rushing about frantically in an effort to locate a lost object, knocking over the makeshift bookcases, causing books to fly in all directions. In Germany, the headaches and mysterious stomach ailments Angela had suffered in high school returned, along with her terror of the dark, which first manifested itself when Angela was a child in Birmingham when each night brought the very real possibility of violence. To deal with those issues, Angela began a course of psychotherapy with Mitscherlich's father, Professor Alexander Mitscherlich. Angela found the process an uncomfortable one but stuck with it. Twice a week in his office, Angela could let down her guard and confide to a scholarly elder about the turmoil inside of her. Gradually, Angela found that the psychoanalytic process helped reconcile the constant tension between the intellectual, political and emotional aspects of her life. Adding to her growing sense of ease was the fact that she was no longer a lone African American among white people. In Frankfurt, she was one of hundreds of foreign students. Angela's social and political lives began to coalesce as she involved herself in political activities with the German Socialist Students' League, a large tent organization for leftist anti-authoritarians of all stripes railing against the conflict in Vietnam and supporting Third World struggles against colonialism. Angela threw herself into the League's activities, writing and attending meetings and demonstrations.

By the summer of 1967, her class work completed and her grant money running out, Angela was eager to return to the States. On her way home, drawn by the presence of her mentor, Herbert Marcuse, Angela stopped in London to attend a five-day seminar on the Dialectics of Liberation, In attendance was "an eclectic mix of Marxists philosophers, sociologists and psychologists, radicals, hippies and members of the Black Power movement."

Among the latter group—by far the smallest—was Stokely Carmichael, He had been a Freedom Rider in the summer of 1961 and was a leader in the Student Nonviolent Coordinating Committee (SNCC). Now however, he advocated for Black Power, a term he was said to have coined, which advocated developing self-sufficient black communities and businesses. In 1966, in a speech at the University of California at Berkeley, he said: "Negroes have been walking down a dream street talking about sitting next to white people; and that does not begin to solve the problem; that when we went to Mississippi we did not go to sit next to [Dixiecrat Governor of Mississippi] Ross Barnett; we did not go to sit next to [Alabama sheriff] Jim Clark; we went to get them out of our way; and that people ought to understand that; that we were never fighting for the right to integrate, we were fighting against white supremacy."

In London after the speech, Angela was approached by people in Carmichael's contingent who had identified her as a sympathizer with the Black Power movement by virtue of her Afro—an uncommon sight in those days. Intrigued, Angela stayed on in London for a few weeks with a cadre of black intellectuals and activists and, for the first time, took a prominent role in organizing in black neighborhoods. As a young woman in Birmingham, Angela had defiantly crossed the color line with her sister, Fania. But for the last eight years Angela had been ensconced in the world of ideas, all the while berating herself for not putting herself on the line to combat oppression—particularly that of her own people. While this was exhilarating, Angela was troubled by the group's isolationist stance and their rejection of socialism. "Because the masses of white people harbor racist attitudes, our people tended to see them as the villains and not the institutionalized forms of racism," she wrote. "It had been clear to me for a long time that in order to achieve its ultimate goals, the Black Liberation struggle would have to become a part of a revolutionary movement, embracing all working people."

———————

Angela returned to the United States in the fall of 1967. In order to pursue her graduate studies, Angela, now twenty-six, made a major geographical move. The year before she started Brandeis, she had spent part of the summer with a wealthy aunt in Los Angeles and had fond memories of her visit. But there was another draw: Herbert Marcuse had left Brandeis University and secured a tenured seat at the University of California at San Diego. Following him there, Angela acted as his assistant. She made quick work of her master's degree, completing it in one year, and in 1968 began work on her Ph.D. dissertation, *Kant's Analysis of Violence in the French Revolution*. As a graduate candidate in philosophy, Angela had evolved from an attentive but quiet student into one who participated enthusiastically in classroom discussions. Her mentor–mentee relationship with Marcuse flourished.

Eager to continue the community work she began in London, Angela co-founded a black student union on campus and then established ties with community groups in San Diego. She soon found a cause to rally around: An African American sailor named Eddie Lynn, stationed at a naval base in San Diego, had been threatened with court-martial for disseminating a petition accusing the Navy of discrimination against blacks and accusing President Johnson of condoning racism in the military. In the process, Angela emerged, almost by default, as the leader of the group; from her few weeks in Europe, she had gained organizing experience that her current comrades lacked.

Angela also established community-organizing ties in Los Angeles, frequently making the 120-mile trip north to Los Angeles in her Ford station wagon. Two years after the riots, the Black Liberation movement was thriving, but it was also severely splintered. In November 1967, Angela attended a conference, held in a Watts church, comprised of a variety of black activist organizations. Some promulgated strengthening black culture, others advocated black separatism. The most extreme faction argued for the eradication of whites. Tensions between the groups were so pronounced that a gunfight between two factions broke out on the first day of the conference.

Among the many factions present, Angela most identified with the Student Nonviolent Coordinating Committee, represented at the gathering by James Foreman and the Black Panther Political Party, a member organization of the umbrella organization, the Los Angeles Black Congress. The BPPP was unconnected with the more militant Black Panther Party for Self-Defense founded by Huey Newton and Bobby Seale in 1966.

The BPPP was represented at the conference by Franklin Alexander, a tall, handsome African American man in his twenties, and his wife, Kendra, who could have been Angela's sister down to the slight gap between her front teeth. The Alexanders and Angela quickly became friends. At their request, she attended a meeting of the BPPP and soon became a member.

It was at this time, both on campus and in Los Angeles, that Angela began to experience a new kind of discrimination, one that she would encounter with dismaying frequency in the years ahead. Although her commanding presence and intellect inspired something akin to awe in her male compatriots, it also fostered resentment. Her seriousness of purpose, likewise, was perceived as unfeminine, as was her style of dress. Sentiments like, "Hey, take off your glasses and get some new rags" were not uncommon. Working with the BPPP, Angela encountered male chauvinism as she and her female colleagues took on leadership roles.

Angela's devotion to the tenets of Marxism—first fostered in Harold Kirshner's class years before—had endured, but she had not become an official member of the Communist Party USA. Now she began to give the matter serious consideration. Again at the invitation of Franklin and Kendra, Angela attended a meeting of the Che-Lumumba Club, an all-black branch of the CPUSA, at the Los Angeles home of Franklin's older sister, Charlene Mitchell. The leadership of the CPUSA had been reluctant to allow the formation of such a group, but thirty-eight-year-old Mitchell, a member of the party's Central Committee, had fought hard to establish it. Like Angela, Mitchell had become politicized at an early age, picketing segregated movie theaters and bowling alleys with blacks and whites as a teenager and joining the CPUSA at sixteen.

In the late 1960s, "the Black Power movement was strong, and anyone who was in anything that was mixed or white was not welcome in terms of their views," recalled Mitchell. "For example, at that time there were no white people left in SNCC, not in L.A.—it had become a black organization. Anyone could support it but they were not members of SNCC. . . . CORE [Congress of Racial Equality] was that way as well. . . . There [was] a tendency of whites to take over."

Mitchell was looking forward to meeting Angela, having heard much about her from Franklin and Kendra and from her and Mitchell's brother Deacon Alexander, whom Angela was dating. Knowing of Angela's doctoral studies at UC San Diego, Mitchell envisioned a scholarly, somewhat older woman and was surprised to encounter a "hip young lady."

Around this time, tensions between the Black Panther Party for Self-Defense and the BPPP, to which Deacon also belonged, reached a crisis point when the Black Panthers decided to start a chapter of its organization in Los Angeles. One day, in the Black Congress office, Angela was assaulted by a visibly inebriated Black Panther who pulled a gun on her and screamed, "The Black Party of Self-Defense demands that your motherfucking party get rid of the name Black Panther Party. In fact, you better change it to the motherfuckin' Pink Pussycat Party. And if you haven't changed your name by next Friday, we are going to off you all." Armed Panthers made similar threats to other BPPP members. It was at this juncture that Angela bought a gun that she carried with her everywhere. "I knew that if I were ever stopped by the police and searched, I could end up in jail, yet if I did not take the risk, I could very easily be dumped in an alley somewhere with a bullet in my brain."

The issue was resolved when BPPP joined SNCC, relinquished its name and established a truce with the Black Panthers—although Angela and most of her friends kept their guns because of the possibility of further clashes.

In April 1968, L.A. SNCC established the Liberation School under Angela's charge to raise the consciousness of the black Los Angeles community about the politics of struggle. And there was no lack of struggles. Young black men—politically active or not—were assaulted and even killed by police in that neighborhood with alarming regularity. Each time, SNCC mobilized, particularly after a young black man named Gregory Clark was shot to death by a police officer who had pulled him over, suspecting the car he was driving was stolen. According to facts Angela and her friends gathered, the officer ordered Clark out of the car, and after a scuffle, handcuffed the young man, pushed him to the ground and shot him the back of the head. When the shooting was declared a justifiable homicide, the South Los Angeles community was mobilized. Posters picturing the policeman with a "Wanted" sign across his face were put up throughout the neighborhood. SNCC held a mock trial in a local park, complete with defense, prosecution, witnesses, judge and jury. The trial culminated in thunderous cries of "Guilty! Guilty! Guilty!" The crowd was primed for action as shouts of "Death to the pigs!" resounded throughout the park. Franklin took control of the situation, calmly explaining that it was not the time to take action, that they were still massively outnumbered by the powers that be and that the next step was to attract more people to the struggle until they represented an overwhelming number that could not be denied.

Angela was attending an SNCC committee meeting in Los Angeles on April 4, 1968, when she heard someone scream: "Martin Luther King has been shot!" Like many other young black activists at the time, Angela was horrified at the news of the assassination of the thirty-nine-year-old minister who had spearheaded the Civil Rights movement based on a philosophy of non-violence. To Angela's generation of activists, the concept had become outdated. "My disbelief gave way to a sadness which made me feel, for the time being, very helpless . . . an amorphous sense of guilt fell upon me. We had severely criticized King for his rigid stance on nonviolence. . . . Never would any of us have predicted that he would have needed our protection," she wrote in her 1974 autobiography.

In the wake of the assassination, riots broke out in every major city in the country with a substantial black population. In Los Angeles, Angela and her comrades worked non-stop, printing fliers to organize a mass meeting at the Second Baptist Church, an activist church in the city. On the night of the meeting, three men were left to guard the SNCC office. When Angela and her fellow SNCC members returned from the meeting, the men were gone and the office had been ransacked. The copy machines were destroyed. A neighbor from a nearby restaurant rushed in with the news that fifteen squad cars had arrived at the office after Angela and her colleagues left and arrested the guards.

As the SNCC members pondered their next course of action, someone went to the stove to warm up a big pot of spaghetti and sauce. Upon being served, the group made an alarming discovery: Nails and tacks had been placed in the food. The next morning, SNCC called a press conference in the office so the media could see how the group's headquarters had been ravaged.

In the aftermath of Dr. King's murder, the L.A. SNCC office became a hub for the community. Again, the division of work between the sexes became an issue: Out of nine people on the permanent staff, three were women who worked full-time organizing as well as handling the administrative, logistical and housekeeping tasks that kept the organization running from day to day. Of the six men, only Franklin and one other man pitched in. Still, the men griped about women running the organization, some SNCC members going so far as to call the perceived power grab a "matriarchal coup d'état."

Over time, the men's complaints escalated to the point where an SNCC official was called in to mediate. When the official arrived, he brushed aside the gender issue as insignificant and focused instead on a list of complaints headquarters had with the L.A. chapter: specifically, that it was not as businesslike as its counterparts in other cities and that its members were not spending enough time raising funds from the moneyed class. Angela found herself under fire for the Marxist-informed curriculum she had crafted for the Liberation School. SNCC's leadership feared that any taint of socialism would undercut its mission, causing it to lose credibility with blacks and whites alike.

A few days after the mediator arrived, an article in the *L.A. Times* accused Franklin of being a Maoist. The story set off a panic among SNCC members. An impromptu meeting was called by the SNCC representative at which he summarily expelled Franklin and demanded that the L.A. chapter be "purged of any traces of Marxist or Communist ideology." Shortly afterward, Angela was stripped of the leadership of her Liberation School and she resigned from SNCC.

Although Angela was still an enthusiastic member of Che-Lumumba, she had not yet made a final decision on whether or not to join the CPUSA. In part, this was because she wanted to be certain its aims dovetailed with those of the Black Liberation movement. In her meticulous way, Angela set about studying the goals and the membership makeup of CPUSA, arranging interviews with top party officials. After much soul-searching, Angela decided that the Communist Party was her true home, and in July 1968 paid the initial membership fee of 50 cents. In choosing to identify herself chiefly as a Communist, Angela staked out ideological middle ground regarding one of the key issues in the Black Power movement: the place of whites in the struggle. Despite her feelings of alienation during her high school and college years as one of the few blacks among white East Coast liberals, those experiences had left their mark. "Although we rarely think of her that way, Angela Davis is a red diaper baby, writes Phillip M. Richards in his book *Black Heart: The Moral Life of Recent African American Letters*. "Her hatred of cultural commodification and of gross materialism are in many ways the rebellions of an earlier Left against a mid-century culture. . . . Her humanism is, at its heart, the product of an earlier progressive time: its nostalgia, social criticisms and visionary hopes."

In the coming years, white and black radicals would have a hard time coming to grips with Angela's nuanced position. Famed radical lawyer William Kunstler—a member of the defense team for the Chicago 8, which tried Yippies Abbie Hoffman and Jerry Rubin and others for their part in demonstrations that accompanied the 1968 Democratic convention—and later, a Little Red father—commented at the time, "[Angela] seems to be torn between the old line theory and her friendship with black people. Remember her education is all white oriented. Brandeis, Marcuse, the Sorbonne. The Party is against the young and their revolutionary activity. She must make a choice."

But Angela chose a third way. By joining a black Communist group within a larger national group, she placed the struggle of African Americans to achieve equality in America in the context of people of all races working to overthrow oppressive regimes. It was a philosophy that fused the myriad places and peoples she had encountered in her life to date.

It was an exciting time to be in the CPUSA. Angela's friend Charlene Mitchell was running for president of the United States on the CPUSA ticket—becoming the first black woman to make a third-party bid for the job (Representative Shirley Chisholm would become the first black woman to run for president on a major-party ticket in 1972). It had been twenty-eight years since the CPUSA had participated in a national election—evidence that the party had begun to move out of the shadow of the McCarthy era.

Despite the fourteen-year age difference between Angela and Mitchell, they had become close friends. Along with Franklin, Kendra and Deacon, they became her West Coast family. At this time, Angela was spending a good amount of time in her beaten-up Blue Rambler commuting from San Diego to Los Angeles, where she shared a house with Kendra and Franklin.

In the fall of 1968, the Black Panther Party for Self Defense asked Angela and Deacon to set up an office on Los Angeles' West Side. Deacon became head of the chapter and Angela revived a version of her Liberation School. Teenagers would arrive after school and stay until the building closed at 10 p.m., participating in classes and group discussions. Angela was tremendously impressed by her students, many of whom were nearly illiterate, as they painstakingly plowed through the dense philosophical tracts.

"If I still retained any of the elitism which almost inevitably insinuates itself into the minds of college students, I lost it all in the course of the Panther political education sessions. When we read Lenin's *State and Revolution*, there were sisters and brothers in the class whose public school education had not even allowed them to learn how to read. Some of them told me how they had stayed with the book for many painful hours, often using the dictionary to discover the meaning of scores of words on one page, until finally they could grasp the significance of what Lenin was saying," Angela wrote in her autobiography. "When they explained, for the benefit of the other members of the class, what they had gotten out of their reading, it was clear that they knew it all—they had understood Lenin on a far more elemental level than any professor of social science."

When a young African American man was killed in the neighborhood, shot by a liquor store owner after an argument, attendance at classes and meetings reached the hundreds. But at that point, the West Side office was purged of key staff members by the BPPP who were trying to root out the police and FBI informers in their midst. Angela believed many of those purged to be innocent. Furthermore, she suspected that many of the denouncers were themselves members of the FBI's Counter Intelligence Program, which was targeting a vast array of radical groups. News of the supposed moles revived the fear of Communists in the Black Panther Political Party, and this time it was Deacon, not Franklin, who was called to account for his political affiliation with the CPUSA. Angela felt that she had no choice but to resign.

She now refocused her activism on the UC San Diego campus. She and the Black Student Council initiated a drive to urge the university to establish a college to serve the needs of Black, Hispanic and working-class white students to be called Lumumba Zapata College, in honor of the revolutionaries Patrice Lumumba from the Republic of the Congo and the Emiliano Zapata of Mexico. To gain support for the proposed college, Angela approached the chancellor of UC San Diego, William McGill. The meeting proved unfruitful. Afterward, Angela was told that the chancellor had described her as "full of hate."

"Filled with hate?" was Angela's flabbergasted reaction. "Hate had absolutely nothing to do with it—the man flatters himself when he thinks that we would waste important energies on hating him and his cohorts. We were just extremely serious about our insistence that the university come to grips with its own racism." Rebuffed by the administration, the black student union gained the support of liberal professors, including Marcuse, and staged demonstrations that included an occupation of the registrar's office. Under pressure, the university agreed, with some caveats, to the establishment of the alternative college.

In the spring of 1969, the director of the philosophy department of the University of California at Los Angeles offered Angela a position as acting assistant professor in the philosophy department starting in the fall. Angela accepted the appointment, unaware that it would launch her onto the world stage.

CHAPTER FIVE

Propaganda of the Deed

TOM HURWITZ, 1965–1969

Tom did not enter Columbia as a revolutionary. Even after five years, the Student SANE debacle was fresh in his mind and he remained determined not to affiliate himself with any political group. Tom's ambitions for the future were nebulous. He planned to major in English. Maybe he would become a professor or a poet like his literary hero, Crane Hart. Thanks to Leo, Tom had worked as an apprentice on films as a production assistant and editor throughout high school and would continue to do so through college. But being a filmmaker didn't seem an appropriate career for a serious person—it just seemed like too much fun.

His freshman year started on a high note: The British political theorist Isaiah Berlin delivered a dazzling series of lectures on anti-Enlightenment thinkers in Germany and France. But Berlin's flashes of brilliance only threw into drab relief the uninspiring atmosphere that, in Tom's mind, pervaded the university. "[Dean] Grayson Kirk was there—undistinguished," Tom groused. "The feeling of the place was bureaucratic without the grace of Yale and Harvard, without the pedigree of Princeton. We were not to be the ruling class, we were to be the apologists for the ruling class. We knew it at the time. We compared our reading load to Harvard and Yale—it was twice as heavy. We were the explainers. They were the thinkers, we didn't have time to think." The school certainly had a sterling history. Established in 1754, its early graduates included John Jay, the first chief justice of the United States; Alexander Hamilton, the first secretary of the

Treasury; Robert R. Livingston, a drafter of the Declaration of Independence; and Gouverneur Morris, the author of the final draft of the U.S. Constitution.

Tom began the school year dispirited because his first serious love affair had ended over the summer. But in the fall, he met Debbie Robison, a pretty and sweet-natured young woman and a fellow red diaper baby from California who was attending Columbia's Teachers College. The two spent most of Tom's freshmen year in the Hurwitz apartment, which they had mostly to themselves since Jane was teaching dance at Bennington College in Vermont and was home only on weekends.

As their freshman years ended, Tom and Debbie moved into a Greenwich Village studio, where they were soon joined by Debbie's brother, Josh, and his girlfriend, Mimi. Despite the cramped quarters, the four lived harmoniously through the sweltering summer, blasting *Rubber Soul*, newly released by the Beatles, and Bob Dylan's *Blonde on Blonde* onto Sheridan Square on Sunday mornings.

As his sophomore year began, Tom traveled uptown to Columbia via the graffiti-covered IRT local, emerging at the imposing wrought iron gates of the university at 116th Street and Broadway. Tom began to enjoy Columbia. His English studies were going well—he made the dean's list—and he began to lean toward a career in academia. Under the name Tom Dudley, he hosted two radio programs on the university radio station, WKCR: *Buckdancer's Choice* on the FM frequency and *The Mojo Show* on the AM band, on which he played soul music and imitated the voice of popular deejay Wolfman Jack.

Although he maintained his politically unaffiliated stance, Tom attended meetings and demonstrations sponsored by SDS, the dominant dissident group on campus. Over hamburgers and Cokes in the Lion's Den, the dilapidated cafeteria in Ferris Booth Hall, Tom and other politically engaged students debated a host of issues while listening to the Rolling Stones, the Beach Boys and Otis Redding on the jukebox.

Sitting on the South Lawn one spring afternoon, Tom struck up a conversation with an Israeli exchange student, Amnon Igra. Tom planned to travel to Berkeley at the end of the semester to meet up with Debbie, who was spending the summer with her parents. On the spur of the moment, the two decided to hitchhike to California. When classes ended, armed with a couple of satchels and a cardboard sign reading "Columbia Students to San Francisco," the two went on the road as Columbia alumnus Jack Kerouac had done in the 1940s. Through dramatic weather, including a series of tornadoes in Iowa and Nebraska, they canvassed every political and cultural subject conceivable as they took in the country that lay on the far side of the Hudson River. In particular, they argued about Israel. While they were traveling, mounting tensions between Egypt and Israel erupted when the Israeli Air Force attacked. The Six-Day War began with Israel bombing Egyptian air fields and ended with a victorious Israel gaining control of the Gaza Strip, the Sinai Peninsula the West Bank, East Jerusalem and the Golan Heights. Igra believed his country was completely justified protecting itself. Tom disagreed. "I thought, this is the end of Israel. They will never be the same, they will be occupiers, they will turn into their opposite. They should be making friends with the Arabs."

Stopping at a bus station coffee shop in Cheyenne, Wyoming, Tom and Igra met the beautiful daughter of the owner and her friends, who talked about rock and roll, LSD and their desire to go to San Francisco—at that time the vanguard of the youth movement.

Like his grandfather Sol and his father, Tom believed that political and cultural purity could only be maintained by staying outside of the mainstream ethos. America was a melting pot, to be sure, but once you jumped into that pot, the country appropriated, pasteurized and corrupted any unconventional politics or art forms. "*Amerikanish gonniff* culture"— American thief culture—Sol used to call the process. "Like my grandfather, I probably thought you maintained a certain sort of purity by being radical, by being on the outside, by being not part of the mainstream," he said. "But now it was like this little world of bohemianism, the youth culture for the present day *Amerikanish gonniff* culture was crossing America in waves and I wasn't such an odd duck any more. We were winning and it made me feel wonderful."

On June 10, 1967, as the Six-Day War ended, a proselytizing, chain-smoking Seventh-Day Adventist dropped Tom and Igra off at Telegraph

Avenue in Berkeley, just in time for the beginning of what would come to be called the "Summer of Love." Later that month, Tom would attend the Monterey Pop Festival along with thousands of young people. The newly dubbed "hippies" congregated to listen to the performances of Simon and Garfunkel, Janis Joplin, Country Joe and the Fish, Jefferson Airplane, Moby Grape, Laura Nyro, Otis Redding, the Who, the Grateful Dead and Jimi Hendrix.

———————

As Tom, now twenty, prepared to begin his junior year at Columbia he got a call from Peter Gessner a filmmaker and former student of Leo's. Gessner asked if Tom would like to be a part of one of the dozens of film crews pooling their resources to record the March on the Pentagon, a massive anti–Vietnam War demonstration that was to take place later that fall. Tom enthusiastically signed on to do the sound for the weekend-long assignment.

On October 21, a clear autumn day, Tom stood in front of the Lincoln Memorial wielding a bulky Negra tape recorder. With him were Gessner, his camera attached to him by a body brace, and a woman assisting on the shoot. As the march started, the crew accompanied the demonstrators, 100,000 strong, as they walked across the Arlington Memorial Bridge, past Arlington Cemetery, making their way to the Pentagon. Banners bearing peace signs, Vietcong flags and depictions of the revolutionary Che Guevara—killed in Bolivia only a few weeks earlier—undulated against the cloudless sky.

At the Pentagon the protesters encountered a phalanx of soldiers standing around the circumference of the building, each armed with a rifle with a fixed bayonet. Helicopters hovered over the scene, the noise of their propellers competing with music from the rock bands playing at the event. Tom and Gessner filmed the counterculture jubilee next to a flatbed truck from which rally organizers Abbie Hoffman, Jerry Rubin and Timothy Leary held forth. At the appointed hour, Hoffman and Rubin began the theatrical centerpiece of the demonstration: an "exorcism" of the Pentagon. They led the crowd chanting incantations in order to levitate the Pentagon to "drive out evil war spirits." The Pentagon remained earthbound, but the film crew captured protesters putting flowers in the bayonets of the soldiers who stood on the steps of the Pentagon guarding the structure from the demonstrators and even the defection of some soldiers into the ranks of the protestors.

The sight stirred something in Tom. Since starting college, he had come to adopt his father's view—and that of his peers—about religion: That it was, in Marx's well-known maxim, the opiate of the people— a backward way of thinking that led to a conservative mindset. Being political and being religious had come to seem mutually exclusive to him. Now lines from a speech of Martin Luther King Jr. about concept of a beloved community came to him. "It is this type of spirit and this type of love that can transform opposers into friends. It is this type of understanding and good will that will transform the deep gloom of the old age into the exuberant gladness of the new age. It is this love which will bring about miracles in the hearts of men." Viewing the scene before him and remembering these words, Tom understood how the spiritual and political realms could co-exist inside him. In this group of people, he saw the beloved community for which he had searched. Tom stood up and said to Gessner, "I have to go get arrested." With that, he put down his equipment and took a place on the Pentagon steps with those waiting for the police to arrive.

Tom spent the night in jail. The next day, Gessner bailed him out and the crew drove back to New York. On the way, the filmmaker talked about a project he had been mulling over, one that would be based on a *New York Times* article about a street kid named Groovy who had been murdered on the Lower East Side that summer. Gessner wanted to use the boy's story to tell a larger tale about the teenagers who had fled their bourgeois families to take up the hippie lifestyle. Gessner had been in San Francisco during the Summer of Love in 1967, when the counterculture was in full cry in the city's Haight-Ashbury district. But he sensed that New York's climate—both literally and figuratively—would make it hard to recreate that communal spirit. In addition to the brutal New York winters (the winter of '67 was forecast to be particularly frigid), the Puerto

Rican community that had settled on the Lower East Side in the 1950s did not take kindly to the bedraggled interlopers flooding into their neighborhood.

The thesis of Gessner's film was that a bohemian lifestyle alone was not enough; that it was now time to begin the less romantic process of grass-roots organizing to create lasting change in society. To raise the $80,000 needed to make *Last Summer Won't Happen*, Gessner sold limited partnerships and the crew raised money from family and friends. Thanks to an ad Gessner placed in one of New York's counterculture weekly papers, the *Village Voice*, a public school teacher who moonlighted as a drug dealer donated $3,000 to the project. Three weeks later, Gessner got a call from the man asking for his investment back as he was in jail and trying to make bail. The money, of course, had long since been spent.

Tom withdrew from the fall 1968 semester at Columbia and signed on to the project. Instead of traveling north to school each day, he now walked across the Village to the Lower East Side where, decades earlier, his grandfather Sol and his family had first lived. The area seemed to have become a magnet for every activist in the tri-state area. Queens-born Abbie Hoffman was roaming the streets, as were his fellow revolutionaries Jerry Rubin and Paul Krassner. A year later Hoffman and Rubin would introduce their group, the Yippies, to America by sneaking onto the balcony of the New York Stock Exchange and tossing dollar bills onto the trading floor like so much confetti, letting television cameras record the feeding frenzy as traders scrambled to grab the cash.

On the Lower East Side, Tom got to know the members of the group Up Against the Wall Motherfuckers. Led by Ben Maria and Tom Neumann, stepson of Leftist philosopher Herbert Marcuse, the anarchist group put into practice the "propaganda of deed," the belief that it takes dramatic actions, not talk, to shake people out of their everyday lives—and is a necessary precondition to revolution. Tom also got to know the editors of *The Rat*, a popular underground newspaper, and the New York contingent of the Diggers, a San Francisco–based activist and theater collective famous throughout the neighborhood for its free food distribution program.

The shoot for *Last Summer Won't Happen* lasted from October to December, at which point Tom returned to Columbia for the spring '68 semester. Back on campus, Tom, now wearing love beads and his black, wavy hair down to his shoulders, felt he had earned his stripes as a street fighter, having spent time in the real world with people who were serious about politics and who lived their beliefs. He had attended several major demonstrations in the city—some of which had led to violent confrontations with the police—and had been arrested on several occasions. It was therefore quite a shock to find himself surrounded by SDSers whose idea of political action was challenging their fellow students' beliefs in all-night rap sessions in their dorms. "How can we get these people to *do* something?" Tom wondered.

Serendipitously, SDS leader Mark Rudd was back on campus as well, having returned from Cuba as one of a contingent of twenty SDSers. There, they had met with the Vietnamese delegation to Cuba, which included soldiers and members of Cuba's Communist Party as well as diplomats. Rudd's group had left for the island on January 31, the day the Tet Offensive was launched by the North Vietnamese to topple the South Vietnamese government in Saigon. Vietcong soldiers had attacked the American Embassy there, keeping it under siege for nearly a day.

Rudd was elated by the trip. "The three weeks we spent in Cuba were dominated by this military action on the other side of the world," he wrote in his memoir, *Underground*. "Cuba was the U.S. turned on its head . . . on La Rampa, one of the main streets of Havana, a huge neon-outlined map of Vietnam gave the latest tally of the number of American planes shot down. Posters exhorted people to work harder, *como en Vietnam* (like in Vietnam). . . . I felt as if I had gone through the looking glass: All of my beliefs that at home seemed so radical, outrageous, and even illicit were here state policy. When our tour bus pulled into a small town, people greeted us with the latest news from Vietnam, as if it had been the World Series. . . . Encounters like this mesmerized and energized me. I was in heaven."

Before his Cuba sojourn, Rudd had been a firm believer in the credo said to have been coined by SNCC: "Democracy is one long meeting." Now, Rudd allied himself with the SDS faction known as the "Action Faction," in contrast to those in the "Praxis Axis," who still thought change could be effected by continued organizing and persuasion. The two groups—tactically divergent but philosophically harmonious—put together slates for leadership of the Columbia chapter of SDS. The Action Faction, with Rudd at its head, won handily.

Shortly after classes began, Tom and Rudd, who had known each other casually before their respective leaves, ran into each other and repaired to the West End, a venerable Columbia hangout on Broadway, across the street from the campus. Over beers, Tom argued that the time was ripe for a concerted student action. America's involvement in Vietnam was reaching its zenith and the draft was culling an increasing number of young men. Soon, he predicted, the college deferments that had kept Columbia students like himself safely out of the fray would be called into question. At that point, Tom declared, the war would hit home with unprecedented force. "Something has got to happen in the spring," he told Rudd. "We've got to find a way of polarizing this campus."

Rudd, who needed no persuading on that point, urged Tom to join SDS. "I don't do political groups," Tom replied, but he did offer to become a conduit to the revolutionaries on the Lower East Side. "Anything we want to do, people from downtown would love to be involved, I promise you," Tom told Rudd.

An ideal opportunity soon presented itself. Colonel Paul Akst, administrator of the military draft for New York City, was scheduled to speak at the school on March 20. The Action Faction and the Praxis Axis were divided on how to respond to this event. The draft resistance committee believed that Akst's speech should be greeted with "probing questions." Rudd couldn't believe what he was hearing. "The SDS intended to sit politely and listen to a speech by one of the head procurers for the war, in effect a war criminal, then ask some embarrassing questions," he thought. "What wimps!"

Making good on his promise, Tom reached out to Up Against the Wall Motherfuckers and, with Rudd, they concocted a piece of political theater to foil Akst's visit. A lead player, however, was needed to enact the scenario—someone who could not later be identified. By chance, Tom ran into a hippie from Berkeley named Lincoln Pain, who was passing through town was eager for action. Tom promptly called Rudd. "I think we've got our guy!"

On March 20, Akst arrived at Earl Hall, the school's religious center, to address an audience of about 150 "jocks," the radicals' derisive name for the conservative students, many of them football players. (The jocks returned the favor by dubbing the left-leaning students "the pukes.") A few minutes into Akst's speech, a contingent of the Motherfuckers, elaborately costumed as a Revolutionary War–era fife and drum corps, appeared at the rear of the hall playing a ragged rendition of "Yankee Doodle." As the irate audience members turned in their seats to locate the source of the disturbance, Pain took aim with his weapon—a lemon meringue pie—and hurled it at Akst, scoring a direct hit to his face. Tom looked on in delight as Rudd stood up and intoned, "Colonel," he said, "you've gotten your just desserts." In the ensuing pandemonium, Rudd and Pain escaped through a back door held open by a confederate. The two men dashed down Broadway to the safety of Rudd's girlfriend's nearby apartment. Once there, Pain dove into the nearest closet. It turned out to be an unnecessary precaution since nobody was following them.

The Praxis Axis took a dim view of the stunt, calling it "unserious and terroristic," but the outrage motivating the action was spreading across the campus, fueled by a host of issues that had been simmering for more than a year.

In March 1967, SDS member Bob Feldman brought to light the existence of a under-the-radar organization, the Institute for Defense Analyses (IDA), that, in the 1950s, focused on thermonuclear weapons and ballistic missile delivery systems. During the Vietnam War, its work turned to secret weapons research that produced chemical weapons used in air strikes, most infamously, the defoliant Agent Orange manufactured by Dow Chemical. According to the State Department, approximately 20 million gallons of the toxic herbicide were dropped on Vietnam between 1962 and 1971 to clear plant life that otherwise would have provided cover for enemy forces. Columbia was one of twelve Ivy League institutions affiliated with IDA and the university's president, Grayson Kirk, sat on

IDA's board of directors. A "portly, pipe-smoking man," Grayson, had taken over the leadership of the school from Dwight D. Eisenhower in 1953. Before that he had held positions in the U.S. State Department and had helped establish the United Nations Security Council.

SDS seized upon the IDA–Columbia connection as a symbol of the university's complicity in the Vietnam War and with the military-industrial complex, a phrase coined by Eisenhower in 1961. In the fall of 1967, the leadership of SDS hand-delivered to Kirk a letter signed by three hundred students demanding that Columbia cut off all ties with IDA and any other defense organizations. It went unanswered. That year also saw the first SDS sit-in, protesting the presence of CIA recruiters on campus, and a series of demonstrations against university recruiting policies, most notably one in April during which violence erupted between eight hundred anti-recruitment demonstrators and five hundred student counter-demonstrators.

On March 27, 1968, in what would prove to be a dry run of things to come, Rudd led 150 students into Low Library—the school's administrative hub and the location of Kirk's office suite—armed with a petition signed by 1,500 students and faculty calling for the severing of the university's ties with the think tank. Upon being told that the president was unavailable, the students roamed the building for several hours and then left. In response, the school selected six student leaders to be disciplined: Mark Rudd, four steering committee members of SDS and the chair of the draft-resistance committee. "The IDA Six" were told to report to the dean for sanctioning. Rudd and the others refused to do so, demanding a public hearing. The university took no further action on that front, but in response to the petition announced a study group that would consider the matter—a move that SDS saw as a meaningless gesture.

As the war continued to escalate, student discontent at Columbia was mirrored by students at colleges throughout the country. Mainstream America was also growing weary of the conflict that was playing out on their televisions nightly, a sentiment summed up by respected CBS anchorman Walter Cronkite on February 27, 1968, when, in a special broadcast on the war, he opined that "it seems now more certain than ever that the bloody experience of Vietnam is to end in a stalemate." On March 31, President Lyndon Johnson, worn down by the country's opposition to the war but unwilling to admit defeat, announced that he would not run for re-election in 1968.

On campus, another long-simmering issue was coming to a boil—one that involved not only students but also the larger community surrounding them. By the 1960s, Columbia was one of the city's biggest landlords. Its real estate holdings north of 96th Street were especially vast, and the school was constantly expanding—a process that often involved evicting hundreds of African Americans and Puerto Ricans who lived in Columbia-owned rent-controlled apartments in Morningside Heights and Harlem. Since 1958, Columbia had ousted more than seven thousand Harlem residents from Columbia-controlled properties—85 percent of whom were African American or Puerto Rican. Community and student discontent over what they perceived as Columbia's strong-arm tactics began to coalesce in 1961 when the school announced plans to build a gymnasium in Morningside Park, a hilly prospect designed by Frederick Olmstead and Calvert Vaux (who had also designed Central Park) that flanked the east side of campus from 113th to 123rd Street and inclined eastward on a steep descent into the heart of Harlem. The scheme allotted only a nominal amount of space in the proposed eleven-story structure for use by members of the community, who, in a symbolically unfortunate feature of the plan, would enter through a back door. The proposed arrangement quickly became known as "gym crow." In December 1967, Black Power activist H. Rap Brown denounced the gym and urged Harlem to "burn it down" should it be built.

Despite the protests, on February 19, 1968, university and city officials gathered for the ceremonial groundbreaking for the gym. The next day, twelve professors, students and community activists staged a sit-in on the land, resulting in the arrest of six students. The week after, 150 people demonstrated at the site.

That, and the controversy surrounding IDA was temporarily overshadowed by the assassination of Martin Luther King Jr. on April 4. Tom was leaving Butler Library when he heard the news. Devastated, he walked down Broadway to Leo and Peggy's apartment. Everyone on the street—black and white—seemed to be expressing their grief and outrage.

As dusk fell, Mark Rudd stood with his friend J.J. Jacobs on the corner of Morningside Drive and West 116th Street, across from Grayson Kirk's mansion overlooking Morningside Park and, beyond that, Harlem. "We could see flames of dozens of fires, dark smoke clouds trailing upward. We heard the wail of fire and ambulance sirens and, rising above that, the roar of what seemed to be all the hundreds of thousands of people of Harlem screaming at once. I had never heard such a sound in my life. J.J. and I looked at each other and both said the same words at the same time: 'Let's go!' We tore down the broken steps which descended through untended garbage-strewn Morningside Park, the no-man's land between Morningside Heights and Harlem below."

On April 9, a memorial was held for the martyred civil rights leader in Columbia's St. Paul's Chapel, presided over by Vice President David Truman and attended by a thousand people. Rudd and his fellow SDSers were appalled by the event, given what they saw as the university's shabby treatment of its black and Puerto Rican neighbors and employees. As Truman started to deliver his eulogy, Rudd moved to the front of the chapel and grabbed the microphone. "Dr. Truman and President Kirk are committing a moral outrage against the memory of Dr. King!" At the completion of his fiery speech, he strode out of the chapel followed by about forty students, faculty and community members.

Tensions continued to mount. On April 22, SDS published a four-page newspaper headlined "Up Against the Wall!" in anticipation of a mass rally planned for the next day. On the front page was an open letter to Kirk by Rudd, brashly detailing the group's grievances. "Grayson," the missive concluded, "I doubt if you will understand any of this, since your fantasies have shut out the world as it really is from your thinking. Vice President Truman says the society is basically sound; you say the war in Vietnam was a well-intentioned accident. We, the young people, whom you so rightly fear, say that the society is sick and you and your capitalism are the sickness. You call for order and respect for authority; we call for justice, freedom, and socialism. . . . There is only one thing left to say . . . : Up against the wall, motherfucker, this is a stick-up." At a raucous meeting that night, a general strike was proposed for the following day.

The morning of Tuesday, April 23, Tom woke up next to Debbie in the loft bed of their studio. "We're going to have a demonstration today," he told her.

Together for over two years, the couple, while still on good terms, had hit a rocky patch. Debbie adored "Tommy"—his worldly New York ways and his charm. But although their political philosophies jibed, the style in which they expressed those beliefs differed. Debbie sought to make a better world by working at a Head Start program in Harlem. Tom, on the other hand, had become increasingly involved in the radical New Left movement, first on the Lower East Side and then at Columbia. He would often bring his friends from Up Against the Wall Motherfuckers to the apartment. As opposed to the bright and friendly Elisabeth Irwin pals who would sometimes drop by, Debbie found them a scruffy and somewhat scary lot. And since Tom's return to Columbia, the couple's studio had become a frequent meeting place for SDS strategists who would crowd into the flat after classes and often stay until the early hours of the morning, leaving little time for them to be alone. Debbie also had a nagging but unexpressed fear that Tom might be seeing other women. Weeks earlier, Debbie had visited the Bay Area and had reconnected with an old boyfriend, which had intensified her doubts about the future of her relationship with Tom. When he had a rare moment to think about it, Tom also realized that his partnership with Debbie was in fragile condition.

"This could be quite a rally," Tom thought as he donned jeans, a T-shirt and a jean jacket and tied a red bandana around his forehead. Tom stepped out of his apartment house into the cloudy spring day. Pink buds had already appeared on the spindly trees that lined the Village sidewalk. "The jocks would be out in full force," he mused. Still, Tom didn't take his motorcycle helmet—a gift from Peggy—which he had brought to demonstrations the previous winter to protect himself from harm. On the subway uptown, Tom wondered how the day would play out.

By the time he got to Columbia, a little after noon, hundreds of students were listening to a series of speeches delivered from the sundial at the center of the campus. About 100 yards behind the speakers stood Low Memorial Library, a majestic, domed classical structure fronted by a series massive columns and stairs that spanned the width of the building and flowed deep into the campus quad. The building itself, which, despite its name, housed the university's administrative offices, was locked up tight. In front of Low stood two hundred suit-and-tie-clad anti-demonstrators ten deep, some carrying picket signs that read "Send Rudd back to Vietnam" and "Order is Peace."

When Rudd finished delivering a speech, Cicero Wilson, president of the Student Afro-American Society (SAS), addressed the crowd. An impressive orator, Wilson launched into an attack not only on the administration but also on the student body for not addressing Columbia's racist policies. The presence of a black speaker seemed to disconcert the overwhelmingly white audience. The night before, Rudd and other SDS leaders had met with the leaders of SAS. Remarkably, it was the first executive meeting between the two organization. SDS's leaders were quickly coming to grips with the fact that they had been all but oblivious to the black radical power base on campus.

Now Rudd again took the sundial podium. According to the plan agreed to the previous night, Rudd would now deliver the final speech before the crowd marched into Low Library in direct violation of Columbia's prohibition against indoor demonstrations. But there was a hitch: Earlier that morning, Rudd had received a letter from Vice President Truman suggesting a meeting of the demonstrators and faculty in McMillin Theater. In keeping with the SDS tradition of arriving at decisions by consensus, Rudd read the letter to the crowd and opened the floor to discussion.

As Rudd weighed the different options with the crowd, Tom became increasingly frustrated. All the talk was diluting the students' impetus to act, he thought. Finally able to take no more, Tom leapt onto the sundial with Rudd. Before him were the demonstrators; from behind he could hear the jeering of the jocks.

"Did we come here to talk, or did we come here to march to Low?" Tom yelled. "I'm going to march to Low!" Raising his right arm and making a fist, Tom turned and began to walk purposefully toward Low. After a few strides, he looked back. To Tom's amazement, the group was following him! Rudd and the rest of the IDA Six ran to Tom, locking arms with him at the front of the newly formed brigade. Crying "IDA must go! IDA must go!" and "To Low! To Low!" they advanced upon the library.

Very quickly, however, they collided with counter-protesters, a healthy portion of whom were the physically imposing jocks. When attempts to break through the line were unsuccessful, some students began scouting out an alternate entrance. The security door on the southeast side of the building was discovered to be vulnerable, secured only by guards who were desperately trying to keep the door pulled shut from the inside. Climbing atop an upended garbage can, Rudd yelled that it would be impossible to rush the side entrance without injury to protestors or university staff. Once more he started to outline options, but the fired-up crowd needed to move and it didn't much care where. When two women from Columbia's sister school, Barnard, cried "To the gym! To the gym!" Rudd echoed the cry into his bullhorn and the protestors surged toward Morningside Park. Once at the gym site, which was guarded by a handful of policemen, hundreds of hands began to tear down the 40-foot-long, 12-foot-high fence. Three policemen were hospitalized and one student was arrested, but once the fence was down, there was only empty space to occupy.

Back the protestors went to the sundial. It was now after 1 p.m. Once again, Rudd held forth as he tried to figure out the most effective way to direct the energy of hundreds of adrenaline-hyped students. Once again, Cicero Jones took the bullhorn. The debate over where to go, what to do, continued until someone yelled "Seize Hamilton!" The neoclassical structure on the east side of the campus that housed both administrative offices and classrooms had the advantage, unlike Low, of being unfortified, so to Hamilton they went. Adding "Racist gym must go" to their litany of chants, they rushed past the statue of Alexander Hamilton into the wide lobby dominated by a sweeping grand staircase. Once inside, they demanded to see the deans whose offices were on the first floor. Then, Dean Henry S. Coleman unexpectedly appeared at the entrance of Hamilton.

"Suddenly, all heads turned toward the main entrance where . . . Acting Dean Henry S. Coleman . . . stood, flanked by the Proctor and the Vice

Dean of the College. Like the waters of the Red Sea, the crowd moved back and cleared a pathway to the wooden door marked Dean of Columbia College," the *Columbia Daily Spectator* reported.

Rudd approached Coleman, an ex-football coach, who stood there with a pipe in his hand. The crowd fell silent. "Now we've got the Man where we want him," shouted Rudd. "He can't leave unless he gives into some of our demands." The demonstrators roared their approval.

Amid cries of "Fuck you!" and "Bullshit!" Coleman and the elderly chief security officer of the university, Proctor William Kahn, locked themselves in Coleman's office, effectively becoming hostages. Three jocks who had followed the protestors into Hamilton took up sentry posts in front of the door of the office that contained the now-captive administrators.

Tom was stunned by the speed at which events were playing out. We've gone from a pie in the face to taking a hostage in six weeks, he thought. Tearing down the fence was a big deal, he thought, but this was uncharted territory.

Having finally secured a building, the atmosphere in Hamilton turned festive. Red balloons and crepe paper were somehow procured and were festooned around the lobby as Xeroxed images of Che Guevara, Malcolm X and other icons of the Left were taped to the pillars. Flanking the wooden door to Dean Coleman's office were life-sized posters of Stokely Carmichael and Malcolm X. More ominously, a placard bearing a quote from Guevara was affixed above the door: "In revolution one wins or dies." Provisions were delivered to the building: boxes of fruit, soda and snacks and, later in the evening, hot food. By then, the Hamilton occupiers were set to spend the night, equipped with blankets and sleeping bags. They had organized themselves into work crews to handle food, garbage, security and entertainment. Hamilton had morphed, as the *Spectator* put it, into a "protestors' hotel," with its guests doubling as staff—even delivering toiletries and liquor to Coleman's office. Rock groups came to play for the protestors. A few students were deputized to "liberate" a huge floor fan from Butler Library to get some air circulating in the crowded hall.

Above all this activity, on the seventh floor, steering committees caucused. SDS leaders settled upon the Six Demands to which Columbia must accede in order to end the occupation:

1. Halt construction on the gymnasium.
2. Cut all ties to IDA.
3. Rescind the ban on indoor demonstration.
4. Drop criminal charges arising from the protest at the gym site.
5. Rescind probation for the IDA 6.
6. Grant amnesty to all protestors.

As the hours passed, representatives from black organizations and community groups, including the Black Panthers, the SNCC and the Congress on Racial Equality, entered the building and started to exert control. "At one point, six black men, community people, moved toward Dean Coleman's door," recalled Rudd. "They announced to the Jocks that they were there to take over the guard duty. The right-wingers refused to move. Suddenly and without a lot of fuss they found themselves bounced out of the building; the black phalanx had taken over."

SDS's leadership was at a loss as to how to handle this turn of events. Moreover, they were frightened by rumors that weapons had been smuggled into the building. At one point, Tom ventured into a basement men's room and discovered a bag filled with rifles. Terrified, he fled. At about 1:30 a.m. a "short African American man, surrounded by three large bodyguards," walked into the lobby to thank the students for taking the "first steps in this struggle." Two hours later, a runner from the black caucus entered the smoke-filled SDS room with an announcement for those who had perhaps not gotten the message. The black occupiers had decided to expel the white students and barricade the building. Rudd and two other members of the steering committee ran to the SAS caucus room to confirm the news. "We want to make our stand here," they were told. "It would be better if you left and took your own building." The language was polite but the message was clear. At 5 a.m., Rudd led his demoralized flock out of Hamilton as a steady rain fell. "Good luck to you brothers! We're still together," shouted one of the eighty-six black occupiers left in the building.

Tom walked out with Rudd's group, dejected and apprehensive about those he was leaving behind. He was certain that the Hamilton occupation could end only in a violent standoff in which lives might be lost. He was, however, sanguine about Coleman and Kahn's safety, sure that the dean and the proctor would not be harmed under the new regime.

At 5:30 a.m. Wednesday, the ousted protestors debated which building to occupy next. Low was the obvious choice. Heading north across the campus, the group arrived at the now-deserted building and gained entrée through the side entrance they had abandoned fourteen hours ago, this time using a bench as a battering ram. Once inside, they made their way to Kirk's office, a plush suite of rooms on the ground floor. Tom was among the first to crowd into Kirk's sanctuary. Immediately, students began riffling though the dean's files, mimeographing documents, especially those concerned with IDA. As the sun came up, a student reporter outside the building handed a camera up to Tom and asked him to take some pictures. He did so, snapping a much-distributed photo of a student sitting in Kirk's chair, cockily smoking one of the dean's White Owl cigars with his legs propped up on the administrator's desk. At 7:45, police began tearing down the barricades that had been erected outside of Kirk's office. This caused most of the students, including an exhausted Tom, to make a hasty exit through the windows.

Tom went home to reassure Debbie that he was safe and fill her in on the events of the last day. After a shower and few hours of sleep, he returned to campus to find Low undefended and open to demonstrating students. The police had taken no action except to secure a painting by Rembrandt, said to be worth half a million dollars Tom re-entered the building.

The demonstration and subsequent occupation of two Columbia buildings was front-page news in all the city's papers. Outraged members of the administration and members of the faculty—many of whom were sympathetic to the students' demands—held continuous meetings trying to find a solution to the standoff to no avail. On Wednesday night, Avery

Hall was taken. At 2 a.m. Thursday, Fayerweather Hall was secured by protestors, bringing the number of occupied buildings to four. On Thursday,
day three of the occupation, Mayor John Lindsay deployed aides to the
campus to negotiate a settlement, also to no avail.

In the early hours of Friday morning, Tom, who had spent the last two
days in Low, snuck into Mathematics Hall with sixty compatriots. One of
the more undistinguished structures on campus, Math stood to the north
of the gated entryway to the school overlooking Broadway. A contingent
of students led by Rudd had taken the building hours before using a key
donated by a graduate student. Shortly after daybreak on Friday, two professors and a dean took it upon themselves to squeeze through a half-open
window on the ground floor to try negotiating with the Math occupiers.
Tom and others were sitting in the library when the delegation made their
inelegant entrance. Tom blurted out the first thing that came into his
head: "We've got ourselves another dean!" Thrilled about having their very
own hostages, the group began searching for rope with which to lash shut
the doors. As the initial excitement wore off, however, the scheme was
aborted and the men were released.

The fifth and final building to be taken, Math quickly became known as
the most militant of strongholds—at least after Hamilton. In addition to
student protesters, it also boasted veteran activists Yippie Abbie Hoffman,
Tom Neumann of Up Against the Wall Motherfuckers, and Tom Hayden, a
founding member of SDS, who was chosen to chair the commune.

Now the 150 Math occupiers, including coeds from Barnard who, despite a dorm lockdown, had managed to make their way three blocks
downtown to Math, got down to the business of organizing for the duration. "In the first hours of the occupation," Hayden wrote in his memoir,
Reunion, all of us were overtaken by the fear that an attack was imminent.
Perhaps it was the sense that we were wrong in trespassing into this academic sanctuary. But there was also the reality of counterdemonstrators
outside, many of them campus athletes and fraternity leaders, who were
loudly threatening violence. The Kirk administration had shown a blind
indifference to our demands and might at any moment request the assistance of the city police. We were outlaws, and feeling it."

Committees were formed: steering, communications, entertainment, sanitation and food. As a rule, men assumed the leadership roles while the women were relegated to making sandwiches and running the mimeograph machine that spewed out a continual stream of leaflets. "A secret committee was swiftly appointed to procure orange juice, coffee, peanut butter and jelly, and, if possible, salami and the *New York Times*. A stereo as well was imported," wrote Hayden.

Tom, now wearing red and black armbands, the former denoting his honorary SDS affiliation and the latter proclaiming his anarchist status, was voted head of the defense committee. Under his supervision, chairs and desks were commandeered from every room in the building to construct a massive barricade spanning the width of the main entrance. Sentries were posted at other vulnerable entry points: doors, windows and underground tunnels that led to Math. A Barnard student discovered a supply of liquid soap, which was set aside to be used on the stone staircases to impede the progress of police in the event of a bust.

But fears of an invasion made up only one part of the occupation experience. Math was the most comfortable of the buildings, with a large carpeted room with couches and armchairs that was used for meetings and a lounge for food preparation. Sleeping quarters were established upstairs. Students sang protest songs and danced to the music of the bands that came to play for them. At one point a man with a bagpipe climbed through the window to give an impromptu performance. By majority vote, drugs were forbidden, and that ban was largely followed. But there was, by Tom's and other occupiers' accounts, a whole lot of sex.

One favorable feature of Math was the window ledges that ran the length of the Broadway side the building. The occupiers would sit side by side, their legs dangling off the ledge, under a makeshift banner that read "Liberated Zone 5," waving to the well wishers below. Leo, who had been elected chair of the Concerned Parents Group, was one of them, as was Peggy. Jane was following the story from abroad; she was in Israel, teaching. Merchants delivered supplies to the occupiers via buckets raised and lowered by ropes from the windows. A peace demonstration marched up Broadway to cheer them on. A city bus stopped in front of the building. The

African American driver passed the hat for donations, tipped the money into the lowered bucket and drove on. A revolutionary red flag flew triumphantly atop Math.

Three and a half years earlier, the first major campus uprising occurred at the University of California at Berkeley with the rise of the Free Speech Movement, in which students fought the ban of on-campus political activities. On December 2, 1964, one of its leaders, Mario Savio, addressed hundreds of students from the steps of the school's Sproul Hall: "There's a time when the operation of the machine becomes so odious—makes you so sick at heart—that you can't take part. . . . And you've got to put your bodies upon the gears and upon the wheels, upon the levers, upon all the apparatus, and you've got to make it stop."

By spring 1968, students all over the world were doing just that. In France, Italy and Mexico students went on strike. In the United States, the intense national coverage of the Columbia occupation made it synonymous with student revolt.

On Friday afternoon, Tom was addressing a large group in the lounge when two Barnard freshmen clambered through a window. Tom noticed Susan Brown immediately, pegging the woman with long brown hair in a soft purple top and bell bottoms as the most beautiful girl in the room. After the meeting he approached her, and they sat on the window ledge talking. Susan was immediately taken by Tom's flamboyance and charm; he looked every inch the "revolutionary prince," a moniker she would later use ironically to describe him.

For the remainder of the occupation, Tom and Susan were inseparable—except for the hours when Debbie snuck into the building over the weekend for a visit. Susan also became, in effect, Tom's secretary. "It's painful to remember how subservient and passive the women were," she said.

The Ad Hoc Faculty Panel had been working non-stop since the beginning of the occupation to craft a compromise between what a *Spectator* editorial called the "intransigent insurgents and the ossified administration." Although the administration seemed disposed to give ground on many of the demands, they balked on the issue of amnesty. For its part, the strike steering committee, led by Rudd, rejected a proposal known as the "bitter pill" to establish a tripartite committee composed of administration, faculty and students to mete out penalties to the students, a position Rudd encapsulated neatly to the Ad Hoc Faculty Group Committee as "bullshit."

The weekend passed with no progress in negotiations. On Monday, the Math occupiers prepared for a bust. As Monday night turned into Tuesday, April 30, they were finishing a midnight meal when runners from the other buildings reported that police were gathering their forces around the campus. At 2 a.m. on Tuesday, the police entered the campus. The protestors ran to the top floor of Math and watched as floodlights illuminated the Tactical Patrol Force, consisting of hundreds of helmeted and visored police, their batons at the ready, as they marched onto the quad.

Blocks away, Leo had spent the night listening to live reports from the Columbia student radio station on his transistor radio all night. When he heard the police had entered the campus, he made his way to the university. Outside the gates, he met Manny Kirchheimer, a Columbia professor and a former student of Leo's. Kirchheimer and other faculty members sympathetic to the students' cause had formed human chains around the occupied buildings, but had been ousted by the police minutes before.

Hamilton Hall, still occupied by African American students and activists surrendered to police without struggle. At 2:15, Low was taken. At 2:30, Avery Hall fell and after that, Fayerweather.

Now, the police, adrenaline-pumped, turned to Math. As chairman of the defense committee, Tom took his position at the foot of the stairway in the darkened lobby, facing the main entrance as the police formed a large arc in front of the building. A voice, amplified through a bullhorn ordered them to evacuate. In response, voices from the building cried "Kirk must go!" and "Up against the wall, motherfuckers!" The police approached the building and began to dismantle the barricades that had been packed 20 feet deep. It took them fifteen minutes to do so, their rage growing as they went. When they finally broke through, the occupiers on the second floor began hurling chairs at the invaders.

"Stop!" Tom shouted, knowing such actions would only intensify the violence. Seconds later he was grabbed, dragged out of the building and thrown into a police bus. An article in the *Spectator* the next day described the scene that followed. "Students seen cursing police in the lower-story windows were suddenly yanked backward and disappeared from view. On the upper floors the police used axes to break into rooms in which militant students held out. The strikers were led or dragged down the steps— soaped to slow the police—and deposited in a pile in the grass just outside the entrance to the building."

The entire police action had taken three hours. By 5:30 a.m. there had been 712 arrests and 148 protestors and police had been injured. Leo wasn't there to witness it. When he saw the Tactical Police Force begin their assault on Hamilton, the fifty-nine-year-old took off at a sprint with the younger Kirchheimer close behind. Ducking into a vestibule a block and a half away, the men waited out the bust as Leo regaled his friend with accounts of his own brushes with hostile police in Depression-era demonstrations. The screams coming from the university grounds echoed eerily in the transistor radios carried by the spectators on the street.

After the bust, classes were suspended for the remainder of April. When the university reopened in May, Tom helped to plan and execute a general strike, bringing classes to a halt. The strike committee ran its operations out of Ferris Booth Hall. Susan, who had emerged from Math unscathed, continued to act as Tom's de facto secretary until she and the other similarly conscripted women formed a caucus to abolish the practice. Tom remembers five mimeograph machines running constantly, artists making posters and constant debates over how Columbia should be restructured or if it should be closed altogether—and how the still-unresolved issue of amnesty for the strikers should be prosecuted.

Aftershocks from the occupation continued. On May 17, community activists and then students occupied a Columbia-owned apartment building; police cleared them out within hours. On May 21, students reoccupied Hamilton Hall to protest the threatened suspension of four SDS leaders. Again, police cleared the building and the campus, this time with 138 arrests.

On June 4, Columbia held its 214th commencement despite several hundred students who walked out of ceremonies and others who held their own counter-ceremonies. Then the students went home for the summer.

As for Tom, the occupation had caused him to rethink his political identity as an anarchist. A few months before, he'd had an argument with Debbie's father. David, a stalwart of the Old Left, challenged the young man. "What are you proposing on building? You're so revolutionary, what do you want to construct?"

"Well," Tom responded, "I want to construct anarchism."

"What does that mean?" David queried. "People aren't going to follow you unless you can tell them what you're proposing to build."

Tom conceded the point. But even if the long-term—or even short-term—effects of the occupation were unclear, Tom was convinced that his side—the forces of youth and change—had achieved a huge victory by dint of the act itself. "We won," Tom exalted. "The only way to go was up."

After the initial high of the occupation and the subsequent strike wore off, Tom realized that he was emotionally and physically drained. His love life was in limbo. In early summer, Debbie had definitively broken up with him after two and a half years together and moved to San Francisco to live with her new boyfriend. Although Tom's affair with Susan continued, he was shocked by Debbie's departure and decided, much to Susan's distress, to try and attain closure in the relationship by going west to talk things out.

Tom and Debbie met in the Bay Area. After they thrashed things out, Tom spent the summer in California, first living in a commune in Mendocino County among the towering Redwoods, and then returning to the Bay Area to participate in anti–Vietnam War demonstrations before flying back to New York to begin his senior year at Columbia. Leo and Peggy picked Tom up at the airport. Without even returning home first, Tom asked Leo to drop him off at Columbia. On campus, Tom walked in on an

SDS meeting in which one of its factions—the hardline Marxist-Leninist Labor Committee—was being purged. At issue was the bitterly divisive teachers' strike that [would cause all public schools in New York's five boroughs to remain closed past the start of the 1968–1969 school year. The strike pitted the largely Jewish teachers' union against those in favor of community control of the schools—many of them black and Puerto Rican parents. It drove an intractable wedge between the historical black–Jewish alliance that had fought so hard and successfully for civil rights in the previous decades.

At the meeting, Tom watched as the Labor Committee, which had come to wield significant influence in SDS over the summer, was expelled from the organization for its support of the teachers. It was the first but not the last purge in which Tom would be involved. That meeting also marked a turning point for Columbia SDS. Until then it had been a big tent providing a home for progressives—students and non-students—of all stripes. Now, it faced competition from the Maoist-influenced Progressive Labor Party (PL), run at the time by Lynn Marcus (who later morphed into the arch-conservative politician Lyndon La Rouche). PL prided itself on being a disciplined cadre that dressed in conservative attire so as not to put off the working-class people with whom they were trying to forge an alliance. It had gained a significant foothold at Harvard, and although it was a small—if vocal—contingent at Columbia, it offered student activists an alternative to SDS.

As the fall semester began, Tom reconnected with Susan, who, although still emotionally bruised by his California sojourn, moved into Tom's studio. Although he was still technically a student, the formerly earnest English major was now a committed SDS functionary, spending more time crisscrossing the country attending meetings to end the war than he did attending classes. In early winter 1968, Tom attended SDS's national interim convention held in its birthplace of Ann Arbor, Michigan, and was inspired by the Midwest radicals he encountered. "The Midwestern SDS was just fabulous," said Tom. "They were true action freaks—they weren't tied down by the cerebral [mindset] of New Yorkers. I loved their clarity and their bravery." At that conference, and at the spring conference in Austin, Texas,

SDS continued to try and differentiate itself from PL, believing it was unrealistic to expect the workers to rise up en masse to end the war. To that end, it crafted the Military Program. With its rallying cry, "Smash the military in the schools," the program focused on organizing student protests and undermining the ROTC, the officer training program at universities, military research and all other forms of war-related activities on the nation's campuses. "PL was blindly Marxist-Leninist, following some Soviet party line from 1928," said Tom. "We wanted to do something that would really help end the war. This was when SDS was still smart. PL was forcing us to define who we were."

SDS was now at the height of its influence and power across the country. "We had four printing presses running twenty-four hours a day in New York turning out leaflets in the high schools and colleges all over the city. Hundreds of thousands of students went on strike over the arrests of the Panther 21," charged with conspiracy to plant explosives in the Brooklyn Botanical Gardens and several department stores. They were acquitted on May 13, 1971. "There were SDS reps in most high schools and colleges" in New York. Sister organizations composed of doctors, teachers, architects and a host of other professionals sprang up all over the country. *New Left Notes*, the organization's newspaper, was everywhere.

Given all this activity, it's understandable that no one in the organization realized that it was on the verge of disintegrating—certainly not Tom, who was having the time of his life. He had lost twenty pounds over the summer and wore motorcycle boots, adopting the hybrid hippie-biker look prevalent among the major SDS players, also known as "movement cowboys."

Being a movement cowboy had its perks. As Tom traveled the country, often in the company of SDS stars Terry Robbins, Ted Gold and Bill Ayres, he bedded a seemingly inexhaustible supply of movement women. "In every town there was a woman who wanted to sleep with you," Tom said. "At that point and for the next few years I didn't want to be in a completely monogamous relationship. There was just too much going on. And I didn't expect the person I was with would want to be in a completely monogamous relationship."

But Susan was miserable. She knew Tom was having relationships with other women, but the sexual revolution had made monogamy unfashionable. She felt guilty for being jealous and said nothing. During the fall and winter of '68 and the spring of '69—at which point he officially dropped out of school—Tom stayed away for weeks at a time, returning home exhausted and often ill. After recuperating for a few days, Tom would light out again, taking full advantage of the moveable feast of parties—a heady mix of political discussion, sex and drugs. Susan, stuck in New York, felt unhappy and cheated, but Tom was too caught up in the whirlwind to notice.

Susan was not the only one displeased with Tom. From several quarters, including some of his closest comrades, Tom once again began to get flak for his high-handed and arrogant ways. "Tom had a huge heart and a great sense of humor," said Josh, Debbie's brother. "But he is also tremendously arrogant and proud of himself and the firmness of his ideas. At times we had to tell him to just cool it—it wasn't necessary for him to argue with everyone. He was always rushing around, knocking things over." Many people, Josh admitted, found Tom insufferable.

At one point, Mark Rudd took him aside and tactfully broached the subject, pointing out that his behavior diminished his ability to be an effective political worker and leader. Other friends made similar comments, "not unkindly," Tom recalled. "But I didn't like that picture of myself." Tom again vowed to change his ways.

At the end of what would have been Tom's senior year at Columbia—weeks after President Richard Nixon had begun secret bombings of Cambodia—SDS hastily planned an encore of the previous year's occupation of Mathematics Hall. Tom backed the action but had misgivings. The first occupation had capped a series of events that had created momentum, making the uprising seem inevitable. "If we were smart, we would have realized that you can't always be in charge of events, that you can't hold onto the initiative all the time," said Tom. "People respond to events or the rhythm or the season—there are lots of reasons why masses of people follow you, some of which are under your control and some are not. People are not going to follow you if there's no reason to do it."

Sure enough, with little groundwork laid, what had made history the first time around replayed itself as farce. One hundred students and activists held the building but incited little student response. University administration and city officials, having learned from the previous year's debacle, reacted to this occupation in a more tactical manner. Instead of storming the building, the city issued court orders demanding the evacuation of the building. After twenty-four hours, the SDS steering committee voted to declare victory and quit the field—and eight of its leaders, including Tom, were promptly arrested and sentenced to forty days in jail.

"There's a kind of schizophrenia that takes place among fulltime radicals," Tom said. "You develop a strong defense against defeat because you're always being defeated. So the group was explaining to itself why it was not a defeat to walk out of the building."

On June 9, Tom and ten comrades entered the New York Civil Jail on Manhattan's Lower West Side. The judge allowed most of the men to be placed in the same barracks-style dormitory, which contained thirty bunk beds separated by lockers. It was in this unlikely setting that Tom and his SDS mates were able to accomplish something they had been unable to do in the outside world: organize across socio-economic lines. The dorm population was a mix poor and working class white, African American and Puerto Rican men along with Canasta-playing "Wiseguys" being held as material witnesses in organized crime–related trials.

Despite their cultural differences, the prisoners had one thing in common: time on their hands. Amid the cacophony of raised voices competing with the two televisions and numerous transistor radios, the SDSers held court, giving improvised classes in political theory and history and engaging their fellow inmates in debates about race and the state of society. Books like *The Autobiography of Malcolm X* and Eldridge Cleaver's *Soul on Ice*, which Tom and his friends had been allowed to bring with them, were passed around and provided grist for the bull sessions that would continue long after lights out. As they acclimated themselves to jail life, Tom and his friends began to emulate the style of the other prisoners, rolling cigarette packs into the sleeves of their T-shirts and mimicking their vocal patterns and slang.

The SDSers claimed some victories during their jail stay. A seasoned convict named Jimmy Dunn was at first resistant to their message about the working class uniting. But on the Fourth of July, Dunn verbally assailed the guards, his booming Irish brogue rising above the noise of the fireworks exploding over the Hudson River. "And let me tell you, friends, let me tell you that one of these days those won't be firecrackers in the street—they'll be machine guns!" Tom and his friends cheered. When a young black man was tossed into solitary confinement for talking back to a guard, the students organized a hunger strike and persuaded almost all the prisoners—even the Mafia guys—to participate. After one meal went uneaten by the prisoners, the man was released, shaking hands all around when he was returned to the dorm. By the time Tom and his friends were released in mid-July, the guards were happy to see their backs.

Tom emerged from jail to hear troubling news about the SDS national conference in Chicago, held a few weeks earlier. At that raucous, divisive meeting, a faction styling themselves "the Weathermen" ("You don't need a weatherman to know which way the wind blows," went the popular Bob Dylan song) was gaining ascendance. Led by SDS head Mike Klonsky and Bernadine Dorhn, the group had little patience with or respect for a New Left that defined democracy as a series of endless meetings. "The world was faced with a huge crime that was going on in Vietnam and we had to find a way of dealing with it," Tom said. But suddenly—quite suddenly—something seemed to snap in the collective SDS psyche. Its members were tired of working steadily and patiently for change. What good had come of it? The war was still raging on, and U.S. aggression against oppressed peoples around the world and on the home front continued unchecked. Ideologically, Tom now considered himself a Maoist. He carried Mao's *Little Red Book* with him everywhere and was not above waving it around while chanting slogans drawn from its pages.

The Weathermen philosophy was perfectly encapsulated in a fiery speech delivered by Tom's Columbia co-strategist J.J. Jacobs at an August conference in Detroit. The struggle, Jacobs said, was not to be likened to a pendulum that swings back and forth. The struggle was a pendulum swinging with implacable force in one direction, hitting a brick wall,

crashing through it and even then continuing on at full speed, ever forward. The illogical savagery of that metaphor shocked Tom, whose experiences of the previous year had tempered and broadened his worldview.
The Tom of the '68 occupation thought it was action, and action only, that
would shake people out of their complacent torpor. He now realized that
the occupation's success had resulted from the painstaking education and
organization that SDS had carried out for years before the actual event. It
was the speeches, the petitions, the one-on-one conversations and conver-
sions in dorm room after dorm room—the very behavior that Tom had
formerly derided as toothless and ineffective—that had given the occupation its ideological heft and validity.

The Weathermen had concluded that their charisma—their macho
willingness to charge head-on into a situation—was what had made
people follow them. But Tom's experience in jail had given him proof that
education and organization—while not as sexy or immediately gratifying
as spontaneous actions—*did* work. Long hair and social alienation was
not enough to build a movement around, Tom concluded. To prove it, he
and his colleagues crafted an initiative that incorporated some of Progressive Labor's tactics if not its hard Communist Party line, called the Citywide Movement. The idea was to encourage students to continue to fight
inequities at their high schools and universities, but also to become involved in the struggles of constituencies. In the resulting position paper,
"Building a Citywide Movement," Tom wrote that the goal was to turn college students "away from campus-oriented provincialism," to tie separate
struggles together to create a "multi-issue movement, not an alliance of
high school and college students, or students and GIs, or youth and workers, or students and the black community. The way to do this is to build
organic regional or sub-regional and citywide movements, by regularly
bringing people in one institution or area to fights going on other fronts."
But the plan was perceived as weak tea by the Weathermen, who constituted, in effect, a new New Left.

The revised Weatherman manifesto, distributed that fall, contained a
chapter about the Citywide Movement. But it was at odds with the rest of
the document, which posited a People's War already in progress that was

being fought worldwide and, on the home front, by American blacks. It was the task of white revolutionaries (as all the drafters of the Weatherman manifesto were) to expunge their white privilege to earn the right to fight in that war. "A revolutionary mass movement is different from the traditional revisionist mass base of 'sympathizers,'" the document read. "Rather it is akin to the Red Guard in China, based on the full participation and involvement of masses of people in the practice of making revolution; a movement with a full willingness to participate in the violent and illegal struggle. . . . The strategy of the [revolutionary youth movement] for developing an active mass base, tying the citywide fights to community and citywide anti-pig movement, and for building a party eventually out of this motion, fits with the world strategy for winning the revolution, builds a movement oriented toward power, and will become one division of the International Liberation Army, while its battlefields are added to the many Vietnams which will dismember and dispose of US imperialism. . . . Long Live the Victory of People's War!"

"Completely screwy," Tom thought. Ruefully, he realized that he was no longer on the cutting edge of the revolution. With their sexy, edgy, outlaw vibe and their willingness to stop at nothing to achieve their goals, the Weathermen had become the new movement cowboys. Anyone who was not willing to sign on to the program was a sellout—yesterday's news. Worse still, Tom had relinquished his much-prized independent status only to be betrayed yet again by an organization to which he had committed his body and soul. Tom watched as his Columbia comrades J.J. Jacobs and even Mark Rudd bought into this new way of thinking. Of SDS, the organization he once led, Rudd proclaimed, "I hate this weird liberal mass of nothingness."

Tom's Little Red schoolmate Kathy Boudin had also become a true believer. After graduating Elisabeth Irwin in 1961, Kathy attended Bryn Mawr, spending her senior year abroad in Leningrad. Back in the states, she became a militant revolutionary. During the 1968 Democratic convention in Chicago, Kathy was jailed after she set off a stink bomb in a hotel. A year later, she was in the core group that formed the Weathermen at the SDS convention. EI classmate Dave Sarlin remembers encountering her on a Greenwich Village Street during those years. After they exchanged pleasantries, Kathy demanded: "What are your politics?" Decades later, Sarlin and other members of the class of '61 began the weekend-long celebration of their thirty-fifth reunion by taking a train to Bedford Hills prison in upstate New York to visit Kathy who was serving a twenty-five-year sentence for her part in the part in the 1981 Brinks robbery. On the train to Bedford Hills, Sarlin thought of another classmate, Angela Davis, who had also served time in prison on charges of murder. "There aren't many classes that can boast that six percent of their number made the FBI's Most Wanted list," he reflected.

Now, Tom was relieved to be on the sidelines. "Maybe I was happy with the intellectual distance rather than being a wholehearted chanter of slogans," Tom said. And thinking about the charges of arrogance that had been leveled at him, he could only smile. The Weathermen had cornered the market on it.

That summer of 1969, the Weathermen launched guerilla actions, raiding high schools to incite working-class students to revolution.

"They organized squads to barge into blue-collar high schools in Pittsburgh, Milwaukee, Boston, and other cities, pushing teachers around, binding and gagging them, delivering revolutionary homilies, yelling 'Jailbreak!' wrote Todd Gitlin in his book *The Sixties*. "The kids were bewildered. . . . Some two hundred Weatherman organizers spent the summer trying to convince tough white teenagers in Detroit, Columbus, Pittsburgh, Boston, and elsewhere that they were tougher, hence deserved to be followed into battle against 'the pigs'—as if all that was holding the young multitudes back from an uprising was the fear of losing. They carried National Liberation Front flags through July Fourth celebrations, planted them in the sand at lakeside beaches, barged into hamburger joints and schoolyards, talked about 'kicking ass' and 'getting us a few pigs,' and dared the local kids to fight."

Gitlin continued: "The point was 'not primarily to make specific demands, but to totally destroy this imperialist and racist society.' Fighting in the streets would train the fighters, would take 'the first step toward building a new Communist Party and a Red Army,' would 'do material damage so as to help the Viet Cong.'"

To Tom, it was a tragic waste of a historic opportunity. "If SDS had been around to explain what was happening, we would have had a really large movement in America," he said many years later. "But that summer SDS tore itself to shreds."

On June 28, 1969, the gay rights movement was born at the Stonewall Inn down the street from Tom's Greenwich Village apartment building. Days later, Tom and Susan packed their bags and set out for the Bay Area. There was so much more work to do to end the war—and the East Coast was not the place to do it.

Elisabeth Irwin, educator, psychologist and iconoclast, founded Little Red School House and served as its director until her death in 1942. *Credit:* Photo courtesy Archives of LREI (Little Red School House & Elisabeth Irwin High School).

"THE SCHOOL will not always be just what it is now, but we hope it will be a place where ideas can grow, where heresy will be looked upon as possible truth and where prejudice will dwindle from lack of room to grow. We hope it will be a place where freedom will lead to judgment—where ideals year after year are outgrown like last season's coat for larger ones to take their places."

After New York City withdrew its funding for Irwin's educational experiment, Little Red School House reopened as a private school in 1932 at 196 Bleecker Street in Greenwich Village. *Credit:* Courtesy Archives of LREI.

Little Redders of the 1940s embarking on a field trip. The school was one of the first extend the educational experience from within the four walls of the classroom to the outside world. *Credit:* Courtesy Archives of LREI.

Tom's father, Leo Hurwitz, groundbreaking documentary filmmaker. *Credit:* Photo by Peg Lawson, collection of Tom Hurwitz.

Tom Hurwitz in the Sevens (second grade) building a model city. *Credit:* Photo by Leo Hurwitz, collection of Tom Hurwitz.

Jane Dudley, Tom's mother, was a choreographer and a principal in Martha Graham's dance troupe. *Credit:* Photo by Leo Hurwitz, collection of Tom Hurwitz.

Middle school students of the early 1960s rehearse a play inspired by the Civil Rights movement. *Credit:* Courtesy Archives of LREI.

Elliott (second from left) and classmates receive direction from drama teacher Mary Van Dyke as they rehearse their senior play, "Idiot's Delight." *Credit:* Courtesy Archives of LREI.

Kathy Boudin

Would you realize what Revolution is,
call it Progress; and would you realize
what Progress is, call it tomorrow.

- Victor Hugo

Angela   Davis

Do I contradict myself? Very well
then, I contradict myself.
I am large, I contain multitudes.

- Whitman

Elliott Abrams

Never look down to test the ground before
taking your next step: Only he who keeps
his eye firmly fixed on the far horizon
will find his right road.
-Dag Hammarskjold

Thomas D. Hurwitz

The game enforces smirks: but we have seen
The moon in lonely alleys make
A grail of laughter of an empty ash can,
And through all sound of gaiety and quest
Have heard a kitten in the wilderness.
-Hart Crane

Photos and self-selected quotations of Angela Davis and Kathy Boudin from "Expressions,"
the Elisabeth Irwin High School yearbook, 1961; and Elliott Abrams and Tom Hurwitz,
1965. *Credit:* Courtesy Archives of LREI.

Tom (left) in a window of Mathematics Hall during the student occupation of Columbia University. *Credit:* Photo courtesy of Paul Cronin/Sticking Place Films.

The March on the Pentagon, October 21, 1967. (l.-r.) Abbie Hoffman, Peter Gessner, Tom, Susan Steinberg, Jerry Rubin (back to camera). *Credit:* Photo by Peg Lawson, collection of Tom Hurwitz.

Harvard students demonstrate against Students for a Democratic Society in Harvard Yard, April 22, 1969. *Credit:* Associated Press.

Harvard Democrats pose for the 1972 Harvard Law School Yearbook. Elliott Abrams is in the back row, first from left. Future New York Senator Charles Schumer is back row, third from left. *Credit:* 1972 Harvard Law School Yearbook, Courtesy Historical & Special Collections, Harvard Law School Library.

CHAPTER SIX

Paper Airplanes

ELLIOTT ABRAMS, 1965–1969

In late summer 1965, Joe and Mildred Abrams drove their son Elliott to Cambridge, to begin his freshman year at Harvard University. In Greenough Hall, Elliott surveyed his new living quarters with pleasure. The three-person suite on the ground floor had a common room with a working fireplace and a bay window looking out on Harvard Yard. One of his two roommates had already arrived. The next day, Al Sida, Hispanic from the rough streets of Compton, a city outside Los Angeles, joined them. Across the hall was Dan Hastings, who came from a bedroom community outside of Detroit. He had grown up reading *The New Republic* and the writings of William F. Buckley and joined the Harvard chapter of Young Republicans.

Established in 1639, Harvard had long been a destination for the children of America's privileged class. By the time Elliott arrived, Harvard had produced five U.S. presidents and countless White House officials, members of Congress and leaders of industry—in short, the people who ran the country. Since the end of World War II, admissions policies had been expanded, making the school a realistic destination for Catholics and Jews from middle-class families like Elliott and future New York Senator Charles Schumer, class of '66. African Americans, Asians and Hispanics students were, however, still a rarity.

In Elliott's freshman year, the school still expected starchy propriety from its students as evidenced by a strict dress code at meals. But that was about to change and to Elliott, its steady decline was as good a metaphor as any for the countercultural revolution in action. "Forever, for centuries, men at Harvard wore a coat and tie to breakfast, lunch and dinner," said Elliott. "Sophomore year they eliminated it for breakfast so you could go to breakfast looking like a bum. Junior year they eliminated it for lunch and senior year they eliminated it for dinner. When I was a freshman the dining hall looked like a gentleman's club and by the time I graduated it looked like *Animal House*."

In 1965, exclusive societies called "finals clubs," like the Porcellian, still excluded Jews and blacks. But such clubs seemed passé to many students who were instead drawn to campus chapters of liberal organizations like Young Democrats of America, Americans for Democratic Action (ADA) and the Young People's Socialist League (YPSL). In his first semester, Elliott joined the Young Democrats of America. In the spring, he switched to ADA, a reform-minded group co-founded by Eleanor Roosevelt in 1947. Significantly to the left of these organizations, and quickly gaining in popularity on campus, was Students for a Democratic Society. Elliott's initial dislike of SDS quickly turned into active loathing; the blinkered arrogance of its leaders was all too reminiscent of the attitudes he had hoped to leave behind at Elisabeth Irwin.

In Elliott's sophomore year, he, Sida and Hastings moved to Adams Hall, a dorm known for its artsy and intellectual inhabitants. Here, Elliott expanded a circle of friends. One was Arthur Waldron, class of '70, who did his part to keep up dress standards at mealtime—and then some—coming to dinner wearing a three-piece suit and a watch fob. Daniel Pipes, class of '70, was the son of noted Russian historian Richard Pipes. Steve Kelman, class of '70, who came from the same Long Island/Queens milieu as Elliott, was 'culturally and politically to the left of his friends, growing his hair and founding a chapter of YPSL on campus. All, however, considered themselves anti-communist liberals. "There was a community, a kind of solidarity" among everyone who was not a revolutionary," said Kelman. Pipes agreed: "Not to be extreme was nowhere. The U.S. was good or terrible. Capitalism was good or bad."

The friends' favorite Cambridge hangouts were Joe's Pizza, where the Mamas and the Papas hit "California Dreamin'" seemed to play on a continual loop on the juke box, and Hazen's delicatessen, which was famous for a waitress named Theresa who served a generation of Harvard kids taking orders in the strongest Boston accent Elliott had ever heard. "If you ordered a knockwurst on a roll she would call into the kitchen: 'I got a nahkwost woikin.' And the knockwurst, by the way, was a quarter." In a weeknight ritual, the friends would watch the beginning of the 11 p.m. news in the dorm, run down to Hazen's, pick up an order and get back in time for Johnny Carson's monologue on *The Tonight Show*. "That was life," said Elliott.

It was a life that didn't include much dating—a state of affairs the gang blamed in part on their unfashionably moderate worldviews. "Not being radicals hampered sex lives. It was hard to get girls," said Hastings. They, along with other Harvard men, however, would travel to the nearby women's colleges to meet blind dates. Wellesley was a particularly desirable locale for Elliott before he bought a car, as it was accessible via public transportation. "At Wellesley you'd sit in the lobby and the girls would come down the stairs. You'd have seven or fourteen guys from all these different colleges to pick up their blind dates. There'd be some gorgeous girl coming down and everyone would sort of go 'me, me, me!' Or there would be a girl who was not quite so attractive and you'd think: 'Oh no, I don't want that date, don't let that be my date.'"

When not at Joe's or Hazen's, the chums hung out in their suites drinking beer (if any controlled substances were partaken of, no one will admit it), listening to the Beatles, Bob Dylan and Jimi Hendrix on the stereo and talking politics. "Elliott was the best informed man I ever met," said Hastings. "I was astounded by his range of references, and his mastery of current events was unexcelled." As a mainstream Democrat, Elliott was more liberal than Hastings—a difference they aired in spirited, good-natured arguments. "He was a skillful debater," Hastings said, "but a nice guy; too nice a guy to intimidate you." Pipes, who would one day serve with Elliott in the Reagan administration, found him "dapper, confident, calm and whimsical. He took political antics with a grain of salt."

In late-night bull sessions, Elliott regaled his friends with tales about the radical high school he had attended, one so far to the left that it counted Angela Davis (who was then gaining national prominence) among its alumni. Griping about SDS, which they viewed as violent, arrogant and out-of-control, was always a favorite theme. To Elliott's mind, it combined the worst of two worlds, EI's Old Left politics and a new and bitter brand of anti-Americanism. Elliott and Kelman ceded grudging respect to "hereditary radicals"—red diaper babies like Tom Hurwitz, for example—to whom they had both been exposed in their high school years. At least they came by their politics honestly, the young men agreed, unlike the dilettante scions of monied and prestigious families whose attraction to SDS represented little more than a hunger for novelty, a desire to be among the in-crowd, a rebellion against their parents and sexual frustration.

"I remember [journalist] Eric Sevareid in one of his broadcasts quoting [a student] who said 'You don't know what hell is if you haven't been raised in Scarsdale,'" recalled Elliott, "It was so completely stupid that it was offensive too. And it was phony. On that issue, Kelman and I saw completely eye to eye. These are people who, in their ideological nonsense, claimed to be for the 'working classes.' But of course the only working class people they ever saw besides the people who dished out their food in the Harvard dining rooms were the Cambridge police for whom they had contempt."

Elliott's position on the most important issue of the day, the United States' involvement in the Vietnam War, was a bit harder to pin down. "We were so worried about the idea of a Vietcong victory and the spread of Communism in Asia we probably understood where [President] Johnson and [Vice President] Humphrey were coming from," said Kelman. But, he added, that view was so outré that it needed to be softened for public consumption.

"If you wanted a ticket of entry into campus political debate, there were certain things you had to say," he says. "Our public positions were critical of American policy for being too military and allying ourselves with military right-wing elements rather than more center-left elements.

We were opposed to the escalation of Vietnam. We supported negotiations and free elections."

Pipes, however, recalls that Elliott was less reticent about defending U.S. involvement in Southeast Asia. "I remember one fine fall day, coming from an anti-war demo," Pipes said. "We agreed that Vietnam was a just war that had to be fought. Communism was evil. War would prevent it from spreading. It was a long-term threat to the U.S.," he said. By sophomore year, according to Hastings, Elliott's perspective had changed—not on the evils of communism but about whether the United Sates could win the war and such a victory was vital to U.S. interests. Elliott also wondered whether the United States was propping up a corrupt dictatorship in South Vietnam.

In February 1968, the first of several articles by Elliott appeared in the liberal biweekly magazine *The New Leader*. In "The Sky Is Falling," Elliott used the collective "we" of his generation. Clearly critical of the war, he posed the question: "How will we convince young people in the rest of the world, now watching films of the bombing of North Vietnam, that America still deserves the love their parents gave it in 1945?"

In the Adams dining hall, as in the EI lunchroom, Elliott did battle with his leftwing foes. But this time he didn't fight alone: Pipes and Waldron were at his side. "They were very good debates as I recall them. Not slanging matches. These were actually arguments."

In fall 1966, Elliot's sophomore year, SDS organized one of its first major actions against the war when it learned that Secretary of State Robert McNamara—Harvard School of Business class of '39 and a former Harvard professor—had been invited to speak to a select group of students. SDS went into high gear, planning a demonstration and demanding a debate with the man widely considered to be a chief architect of the war.

On November 7, the morning McNamara was to arrive, Elliott saw bed sheets hanging from the windows of the dorms painted with peace signs and slogans inveighing against the war and McNamara. Even Quincy House, the traditionally conservative dorm in which McNamara was speaking, had sheets fluttering from the windows that read: "Napalm

SDS," "Kill the Cong!" Another, much to Elliott's amusement, read "Bad day for Gordon Linen." (Gordon Linen supplied Harvard's bed sheets.)

Quincy quickly became the focus of a chaotic scene with protestors, counter-protestors, press and faculty surrounding the building. McNamara had declined to hold a Q&A about the war with SDS, and the group was hoping to waylay him for an impromptu debate as he exited the building. Finally, Mike Ansara, an SDS leader, announced through a loud speaker that McNamara would be ushered out of a back entrance.

"When McNamara comes out, everyone lock arms so he can't leave!" Ansara cried, according to Kelman. Rushing to the back of Quincy, the protestors spied the limousine—with McNamara in it. They circled the vehicle, with some of the students sitting in front of it—making it impossible for it to move.

At that point McNamara stoically exited the car and, to the crowd's astonishment, climbed onto its roof. Taking the microphone from Ansara, he agreed to engage with the protestors. The students, acclimating themselves to the sight, began to pepper him with questions, their rage growing rapidly. All at once, McNamara's composed veneer shattered. "Look," he yelled, "I went to school at Berkeley and spent four years there doing a lot of the same things you here are doing."

The shouting grew louder. "[The difference is]," he roared over the din, "I was tougher and I was more courteous." Now there was total pandemonium. Above the din, McNamara added: "And I'm still tougher." At that point Ansara asked the crowd to disperse, which they did with some alacrity. In the next two days, 2,700 students signed a petition apologizing to McNamara.

A year later, on the morning of October 26, 1967, some three hundred students from Harvard and its sister school, Radcliffe, staged a sit-down protest in Mallinckrodt Hall, holding captive a recruiter from Dow Chemical Corporation. As at Columbia, Dow Chemical's involvement in the Vietnam War—Dow was the military's leading supplier of napalm—was a touchstone of outrage. This time around the action was short-lived. At about 6 p.m., the protestors voted to free the Dow representative. That evening, Kelman recalled, "A group of friends were sitting on the sofas in Elliott Abrams' room downstairs in Adams House, drinking beer and whining to each other about how the Dow thing showed that the New Left had now become the same old totalitarian Left, daring openly to attack civil liberties."

In his sophomore year, Elliott was elected head of national campus ADA. At the time, the organization was in the midst of a struggle regarding what position to take about the war and which Democrat to back in the hotly contested presidential primary. Lyndon Johnson had decided not to seek another term, leaving the field to Vice President Hubert Humphrey, who had fallen out of favor with many liberals for his refusal to criticize Johnson's escalation of the war, and Eugene McCarthy with his more emphatic stance against the war. Elliott supported Humphrey. It was against this background, in the spring of 1967, that Elliott attended ADA's national convention in Washington D.C. At the Shoreham Hotel, 400 delegates passed a formal resolution expressing their "disenchantment and dismay over many aspects of administration policy in Vietnam."

While at the convention, Elliott was summoned to meet Allard Lowenstein, an activist and standard-bearer for a number of progressive causes who had served on Senator Humphrey's staff in 1959. Now, Lowenstein was spearheading the "Dump Humphrey" movement.

Elliott recalled: "I show up and [Allard's associate] Curtis Gans says 'Alan wants to talk to you,'" Elliott said. "So he brings me to see him and said 'Al, this is Elliott Abrams.' And Al said one thing to me: 'Resign!' One word—no pleasantries, no how do you do—nothing. Resign! I have no memory of my response except shock at someone who doesn't shake your hand but says 'resign.'" Although he did not step down, Elliott was voted out in the next election.

In August 1968, Elliott attended the Democratic National Convention in Chicago under the aegis of Bayard Rustin, a key strategist and organizer for the Civil Rights movement. In the few months between the ADA national conference and the convention, with the assassinations of Martin Luther King Jr. and Senator Robert Kennedy, the country became more bitterly set against itself than at any time in its history except the Civil War. Now, in Chicago, rioters and policeman clashed on the streets and brawls broke out in the convention hall. Elliott saw little of it as he shuttled between his lodgings at a dorm at the University of Chicago and Rustin's suite at the Conrad Hilton Hotel, where he manned phones and ran errands. "The only time I got a whiff—literally—of it was walking through the lobby of the Conrad Hilton when some stink bombs had been set off," he said.

When Elliott returned to Cambridge to begin his senior year, he found Harvard students inflamed by the Columbia occupation of the previous spring. The year before, said Kelman, "those of us against the war had the feeling of being part of a large but somewhat suspect minority." This shift was in large part attributable to a change in the draft policy made over the summer. Formerly, students could remain exempt through graduate school. Now, they would be eligible once they completed their undergraduate work. This had little effect on Elliott, who, after getting his physical at the Cambridge City Hall draft board was assigned a 1-Y classification, due to a bad back, that made him eligible for service only in case of war—the U.S. had never formally declared war on North Vietnam—or in the event of a national emergency.

Through the winter of 1969, as insurrections occurred on campuses across the country, it remained an open question as to whether or not Harvard would follow suit. Elliott thought not. Life at Harvard was just too confortable for its students. In addition, perhaps learning from the example of the Columbia occupation the year before, Harvard had responded to demands to establish a Black Studies department and had done away with academic credit for ROTC courses. Still, the administration was preparing for the worst. Harvard law professor Archibald Cox, who had served on a commission studying the Columbia uprising, recommended that in the event of a building occupation there should be a "fast bust or no bust."

Just before dawn on April 9, five hundred students surrounded the ivy-covered mansion of Dean Nathan Pusey just off Harvard Yard, chanting "Smash ROTC" and "ROTC must go." It was a far cry from Harvard tradition of freshmen stopping in front of the dean's home while caroling on Christmas Eve and of the dean's coming outside to shake their hands. This time, when students received no response from inside the darkened house, the demonstrators stuck their list of demands to the door with a knife.

Later that morning, Elliott walked to Memorial Church where an SDS rally was scheduled to begin at noon on the church's steps. The night before, SDS had voted to postpone a proposal to occupy a building the next day. Elliott was curious as to what would happen next. At noon, SDS leaders appeared not in front of Memorial Church but across Harvard Yard at University Hall. Dozens of students entered the building; the deans and administrators were told to leave the building and some were forcibly ejected. Elliott and other students remained in the yard all afternoon as rumors of a police bust circulated. But by the time it got dark and Elliott and his friends returned to Adams for dinner, It was generally agreed there would be no bust that night.

By 6 p.m., at least two hundred students occupying Memorial Church had settled in for the night. The campus had been locked down. From the building, students leaned out windows calling to each other. A red and black SDS banner hung from a window on the second floor. Above it a student leaned halfway out of the building, making announcements through a bullhorn. "Revolution" by the Beatles blared from the speakers perched on the window sill. "Mainly the atmosphere was fun," Michael Kazin, a co-chair of SDS, said years later. "But it was more than an adolescent uprising. We did not aim simply to desecrate the temple. We were fighting a war to stop the war."

At 4:30 a.m. Thursday, April 10, Elliott was awakened by SDS members outside Adams shouting: "The bust is on!" Soon after, fire alarms went off in all the dorms. Elliott and his friends ran to Harvard Yard and, in what Elliott described as an "an uncharacteristic fit of bravery," climbed over a gate. In front of University Hall he saw hundreds of policeman in full riot gear wielding long clubs. "The effect they created that misty morning was not merely terrifying but grotesque," Elliott wrote weeks later in *The New Leader*. "One thought of Dada paintings, with the ridiculous juxtaposition of unrelated objects: The State Police uniforms, for example, were baby blue. The sight of Harvard Yard filled with hundreds of police took a while to grasp as real." After loading two hundred of the occupiers onto busses, the police began to randomly attack spectators.

Elliott initially observed the unfolding events with a mixture of scorn, incredulity and a sense of perverse satisfaction. This, after all, was the logical outcome of SDS's outrageously wrongheaded strategy. But he was also deeply shaken by the events he had witnessed. Later that morning, Kelman returned to his room to find Elliott at his desk, his face buried in his arms. "Steve!" he exclaimed, clearly shaken. "Those police were brutal! A lot of kids got hurt. You can't just ignore that."

At 10:30 a.m. on the morning of the bust, 2,500 students gathered in Memorial Hall and voted to strike until Monday. Whatever sympathies Elliott had for the protesting students did not extend as far as endorsing the closing of the school. Mounting their own protest, he, Waldron and Pipes formed the Ad Hoc Committee to Keep Harvard Open. Granted, it was extremely ad hoc, consisting of making and wearing buttons to that effect, attending classes themselves and urging others to do the same. In a 1986 interview, Elliott called the formation of the group one of his proudest moments at Harvard.

That Monday, thousands of students attended a mass meeting at Harvard Stadium to decide whether or not to extend the strike. Forty years later, Elliott retains two precise memories of that occasion. The first was a speech by Professor Juan Marichal, a Spanish expatriate who had spent years in exile after General Francisco took power following the Spanish Civil War.

"He gave an impassioned plea for why universities should never close—ever—and should not allow themselves to become involved in politics. But what was striking about this day—on which, theoretically hung the future of the university and the world and Vietnam—was what the students were doing during, say, this two hours of speeches. Paper airplanes. Lots of different political groups were handing out lots of pieces of paper telling you what you should think about this or that or why the university must be closed or why it was complicit and why the war was Fascism and blah, blah, blah. And what the students were doing was turning those into paper airplanes. So as you looked at Harvard Stadium that day hundreds, *hundreds* of paper airplanes were being thrown back and forth. That was in a certain sense the real Harvard."

But in an article by Elliott printed in the *New Leader* just weeks later, there is no mention of paper airplanes but instead a real sense of respect for how the moderate students and faculty worked together to wrest the agenda of reform—some if it, he granted, much needed—away from the extremists. At the meeting in Harvard Stadium, students voted to adopt a list of demands similar to, but separate from, those of SDS. They declined to pass a motion to strike until those demands were met but did extend the strike for three days. The next day, the administration declined to press criminal charges against those arrested and to recommend changes in governance.

"Harvard seems headed back to normality," Elliott wrote. "The sense of community that was apparently lacking at Columbia and Berkeley appears to prevail here....the crisis has brought about some reform. Harvard has proved itself to be a pretty fair place after all."

PART THREE

CHAPTER SEVEN

The Belly of the Beast

ANGELA DAVIS, 1969–1970

> Tall, evil, graceful, bright-eyed man-child—Jonathan Peter
> Jackson—who died on August 7, 1970, courage in one
> hand, assault rifle in the other [and] to Angela Y. Davis, my
> tender experience, I dedicate this collection of letters; to
> the destruction of their enemies I dedicate my life.
>
> —*Soledad Brother:*
> *The Prison Letters of George Jackson*

Before Angela embarked on her academic career at UCLA, she and
Kendra joined an American Communist delegation traveling to Cuba. The
group arrived in Havana just before the country's signal national holiday:
the Day of National Rebellion. Sixteen years earlier, Fidel Castro had led an
assault on the Moncada Garrison, a stronghold of dictator Fulgencio
Batista. The rebel forces were decimated by Fulgencio Batista's troops—
most were killed, and those who survived, like Castro, were imprisoned.
But July 26, 1953, was considered the starting point that led to the pre-
dawn hours of New Year's Day 1959, when Fidel Castro came to power,
turning the country into a one-party socialist state.

Angela looked forward to taking part the mass rally usually held on
that day. But when she arrived she found it had been cancelled in lieu of

the "Campaign of the Ten Millions"—a drive to enlist every man, woman and child in an effort to produce 10 million tons of sugar and coffee beans, the country's staple crops. Angela's disappointment was quickly forgotten. On the way to the hotel, the bus carrying the group drove through the grounds of Havana University. She reflected on how the school had been "reserved for the sons and daughters of the wealthy. Now the students were the children of workers and peasants—Black and Brown alike." The delegation was taken to their hotel: the Havana Libre, formerly the Havana Hilton. It was, she wrote in her 1974 autobiography, "now freed from the veined fingers of decadent old capitalists." This revolution had led to a socialist utopia.

On July 26, Angela joined workers as they were bussed to the fields to harvest sugar cane. "Buses, vans, trucks and automobiles were packed with young and old, proudly dressed in work clothes, singing as they made their way to the country[side]. It seemed as if every able-bodied resident of Havana was rushing to the fields as though to a joyous carnival. . . . They were finished with the politics of class and race, done with the acid bile of outdoing one's neighbor for the sake of materially rising above them."

Angela's idealization of the new society was absolute, as was her regard for its leader. "A widely accepted falsehood about Cuba had to do with the role of Fidel Castro," she wrote. "According to the propaganda, he was not only a 'tyrannical dictator,' imposing an iron will upon his people; he was projected as an infallible charismatic figure, whom the people were expected to worship. . . . I looked hard for pictures and posters of Fidel . . . but there were no portraits of the Prime Minister anywhere to be seen. When I asked some of the companeros why . . . they told me that he himself had prohibited people from mounting pictures of him in their offices or work centers. This upset people sometimes, I learned, for they thought he was more self-effacing than was necessary."

Angela returned to Los Angeles in early September, eager to take up a two-year contract teaching at UCLA as an assistant professor of philosophy. She soon learned about an article that had appeared in the UCLA paper, the *Daily Bruin*, soon after she had left for Cuba. It stated that an unnamed member of the Communist Party had been engaged to teach in

UCLA's philosophy department (the author, William Divale, was later revealed to be a paid informant for the FBI). A week later, the *San Francisco Examiner* identified Angela as the mystery professor and further alleged that she was a gunrunner for the Black Panther Party.

Initially bemused, Angela became alarmed when she received a letter from the chancellor of UCLA demanding to know if she was a member of the Communist Party USA. The chancellors were under the leadership of Governor Ronald Reagan. A contract player for Warner Bros., Reagan was elected president of the Screen Actors Guild in 1947 and testified in that capacity as a friendly witness before HUAC. Reagan harbored a visceral hatred of communism and had scant sympathy for the counterculture movement that was arguably most active in his state. The first significant rebellion at a university, after all, had taken place at UC Berkeley in 1964, when students demanded the right to advocate for political causes on campus and also protested a loyalty oath for faculty that was still in effect from the Blacklist days. Angela's childhood friend Bettina Aptheker and her future husband, Jack Weinberg, were leaders of the Free Speech Movement that culminated in a mass protest and campus occupation in December 1964.

After careful consideration, Angela drafted a letter to the regents asserting that inquiring into the political beliefs of a professor was impermissible on constitutional grounds and as a matter of academic freedom. That said, Angela freely acknowledged her membership in the Communist Party. "While I think this membership requires no justification, I want you to know that as a black woman, I feel an urgent need to find radical solutions to the problems of racial and national minorities in the white capitalist United States. . . . The problems to which I refer have lasted too long and wreaked devastation too appalling to permit complacency or half measures in their resolution." On September 19, the regents adopted a resolution calling on the president of the university to terminate Angela's appointment. She had not yet taught a class and had not even been slotted to teach in the fall semester. Signaling his support, the head of the philosophy department, Donald Kalish, asked if she would like to teach "Recurring Philosophical Themes in Black Literature."

The regents' action reignited the student body of UCLA. Black and white students protested on campus carrying picket signs reading: "Stop political repression!" and "No political tests!" The faculty, too, backed Angela, issuing a statement that read in part: "We are witnessing the beginning of a political purge in the University of California: an attempt to remove or at least silence the university faculty and students who hold liberal views on such problems as the Vietnam War, the militarization of the American government, racism in America, student participation in the university and so on. Who will be next? Someone who opposes atomic testing? Someone in the fight against offshore oil companies who have polluted the Santa Barbara coast? Such purges are the instruments of totalitarian governments. They cannot be tolerated in our free society."

Unexpectedly and suddenly, Angela was transformed from an obscure doctoral candidate to a nationally known figure. With that fame came thousands of expressions of rage and physical threats delivered by letter and phone. Angela's friends at the Che-Lumumba Club procured a bodyguard to stay with her day and night. In addition to fears for her own safety, Angela worried about possible repercussions for her parents in Birmingham and for her sister, Fania, and her husband, Sam Jordan, who lived in San Diego; her brother Ben, now a football player with the Cleveland Browns; and her youngest brother, Reginald, attending college in Ohio. Soon after, Sam was shot in the shoulder in a scuffle with police. Both he and Fania were arrested. Herbert Marcuse put up much of the bail money to get them released. Furious, Angela went public, charging the San Diego Sheriff's Department with "Carrying Ronald Reagan's racist, anti-Communist policies to the extremes of pre-meditated murder."

On October 1, the regents, trying to find middle ground in the face of critical media coverage, decreed that Angela could teach, but denied credit to any student who enrolled in her class. The philosophy and law departments of UCLA immediately filed a lawsuit against the regents, beginning a battle that would take years to wind through the courts.

Days later, Angela, looking composed and even relaxed, strolled toward Royce Hall surrounded by a crush of students and cameramen. Wearing a floral V-neck dress, her hair in the tall Afro, a hairstyle that was already being associated with her, Angela entered a 2,000-seat lecture hall to deliver her first lecture to a standing-room-only crowd. Afterward, Angela spoke to the press in front of the hall.

"Before I proceeded to lecture today I asked the students whether or not they wanted me to teach, they indicated that they did and therefore I lectured and they indicated that they wanted me to continue to lecture," she said, before taking questions.

Indeed the students responded well to Angela. Kalish remarked upon the strong rapport Angela established with her students who made free use of her office hours at which she could be found at her desk amid piles of books in English, German and French, stacks of thesis notes, class lists, memos from lawyers, coffee cups, half-eaten sandwiches, candy wrappers and stubbed-out cigarettes. The walls of her office were adorned with posters of Eldridge Cleaver and Bobby Seale. "For students she was a model of what a teacher should be: young, involved, willing to fight, and highly intelligent. She was altogether extraordinary," said Kalish.

By 1970, George Jackson, who had spent his entire adult life in a California prison, had become an international cause célèbre. Bob Dylan wrote a song about him; playwright Jean Genet wrote the forward to Jackson's bestselling book of collected letters from prison; his name became synonymous with the rallying cry for prison reform and triggered prison rebellions across the country, including the most famous one of all: Attica. To the liberal and radical left he was a tragic hero, representing to them, as Mumia Abu-Jamal does today, a generation of African American men in latter-day bondage in a brutal U.S. prison system that was the U.S. government writ small.

George Jackson was born September 21, 1941, to working-class African American parents in Chicago, the second of five children. George was lightly complected, with wide-set eyes topped by thick brows and a brooding expression that could break unexpectedly into a delighted smile. He had a sharp mind. He was also possessed by a rebellious spirit that put him at odds with the law at a young age, and he became involved in progressively more serious crimes. When George was fifteen, his parents, Lester and Georgia, moved their family to Los Angeles in hopes that a change of scene would have a positive effect on their wild son. But the move only made things worse. South Central L.A.—Watts—was a rough neighborhood that only exacerbated Jackson's illegal activities. Jackson's first arrest came in 1957 for stealing a motorcycle. Released, he was apprehended again only two weeks later for burglary. Found guilty, Jackson was sent to the California Youth Authority in Paso Robles, 100 miles north of Los Angeles. It was there that he met and became fast friends with James Carr, another young man with a rebellious streak. Jackson escaped from the Youth Authority and hightailed it back to Chicago, where he was captured and taken back to Los Angeles in chains.

Four years later, on February 1, 1961, he was involved in an armed robbery of a gas station in which $70 was stolen. Jackson claimed he had been an unwitting passenger in the car, but, guided by his court-appointed lawyer, he agreed to plead guilty in exchange for a short jail term. Instead, the judge sentenced Jackson to one year to life under California's indeterminate sentencing policy, a common practice at the time.

At age nineteen, George began his odyssey though the California prison system, doing most of his time in San Quentin and Soledad—two of the state's most infamous penitentiaries.

Reunited with his friend Carr in Soledad, the two co-founded a gang called the Wolf Pack, a group of black prisoners who, in the racially polarized prison—a state of affairs actively fostered by the guards, according to the prisoners—fought the Mexican Mafia and the white Aryan Brotherhood. Self-defense was not the Wolf Pack's only goal. George excelled in all the prison hustles, coordinating a thriving and extremely profitable black market that sold cigarettes, dope, rotgut moonshine and sex.

In prison, George turned from a thief into a murderer who killed without compunction and even seemed to get a charge out of it. "George was too casual about killing people," Carr later wrote. Describing George's murder of a black-market rival, Carr recalled: "I had this big twenty-inch file ground down to a knife. It weighed two pounds and would go right through Jack Fox. But George was a romantic—he had read too many pirate stories and the Arabian Nights and Shakespeare. He had a romantic idea of killing someone right. He wants to take [a] little knife and cut Jack's throat. . . . George ran down and grabbed the dude from behind, reached around and cut his throat—but he didn't cut deep enough. Jack started to run. George grabbed him by the coat and kept on sticking him. . . . By the time George finally downed him, Jack had tumbled down the stairs and out the door, covered with blood."

George's activities continually landed him in solitary, where he would eventually spend 70 percent of his prison term. Outside prison, George had demonstrated no interest in school, but, pent up in solitary twenty-three hours a day, his self-education began. George had always been a voracious reader, obsessed with the superhero mythos he absorbed from the countless comic books he devoured and the tales of Jack London. Now, while going through four packs of cigarettes daily, he turned to philosophy, reading the works of Lenin, Trotsky, Engels, Mao and other revolutionary thinkers. "They redeemed me," he said. As Angela's discovery of *The Communist Manifesto* put the violent world she had grown up in into a logical context, so too did the discovery of Marxism give George a context for the brutal prison system in which he found himself. It also offered a new way of looking at the divisions between inmates of different races and classes as well as the divide-and-conquer strategy of the prison officials and guards.

When not deep in his studies, teaching himself martial arts and learning several languages, George was a prolific letter writer, penning missives in tiny print in order to fit as much text as possible on two sides of the 8½ x 11 ruled sheet of paper allotted for each letter. He wrote in the grandiose style of a highly intelligent teenager with a narrow, if intense, frame of reference.

After five years in Soledad, despite repeatedly being denied parole, George harbored high hopes of being freed. "I should be out of here this year," he wrote to his mother in February 1965. "I have complied with all of their demands: group counseling, school, clean conduct record. I go to [the parole review] board next time they meet. You could start writing letters to the Adult Authority now, the more the better." In 1966, George was still hoping for parole, urging his father to line up work for him to increase his chances of release. But by the beginning of 1967, now at San Quentin, George had begun to lose hope. "I have at least another fourteen or eighteen months to do," he wrote his father. "Of course I could do the rest of my life here."

In December 1968, George was denied parole for the eighth time, but the parole board promised that his release petition would be granted at the parole board's next meeting. Three days later, George was told there had been a mistake—he was being transferred back to Soledad. Still, the officials said, if George kept his record clean, he would receive a definite release date in June. But when June arrived, the parole board at Soledad professed to know nothing of that arrangement and denied George parole once again.

After a period of near despair, George emerged a revolutionary. "He was a tough, sometimes brutal prison gangster," said author Eric Cummins, "and this made him the best proselytizer for revolution on the yard." George began to conduct clandestine study groups on Marxist theory and the works of Franz Fanon, a black French philosopher and revolutionary whose works, particularly *The Wretched of the Earth,* had a huge impact on U.S. radicals of the day. The book advocated the international uprising of oppressed peoples against their colonizers. The work gave George and his followers a sense of connection to the revolution going on in the outside world both in the United States and around the globe, particularly in Vietnam and Cuba. "The project he took on was to [transform] those who were behind bars, moving away from a criminal mentality to a revolutionary mentality," said Angela years later. The study group evolved into a revolutionary brotherhood called the Black Guerilla Family. George the rebel had finally found his cause.

On January 13, 1970, a brawl between black and white inmates erupted in Soledad. Without warning, a guard in the watchtower took aim and fired, killing three black inmates. Three days later, a Monterey, California, grand jury ruled the killings justifiable homicide. That evening, in an apparent act of retaliation, a group of Soledad prisoners killed a white guard, John Mills, by throwing him off the third tier of the prison. George, along with two other prisoners, Fleeta Drumgo and John Cluchette, were indicted for the murder.

Publicly, George claimed that he and the other "Soledad Brothers," as they quickly came to be called, had been unjustly targeted for activist pursuits. Privately, George indicated that he may well have been involved in the murder. In a letter to one of his many female admirers, he wrote: "I don't prefer anything as mild as pen and paper. . . . In my fancies I see myself growing up to be a VC type, a Che-type cat with all four paws on the ground, a kiss for some, a claw for the malicious." Years before, such words could have been attributed to George's youthful machismo. But by 1970 the prison-hardened convict was in dead earnest.

In February 1970, Angela picked up the *Los Angeles Times* and saw a front-page story about the indictment of Jackson, Drumgo and Cluchette for the murder of the Soledad guard. Accompanying it was photograph of the men in court, their faces "serene and strong," she wrote, but with their legs and arms shackled.

Weeks later, Angela attended a meeting in which George's lawyer, Faye Stender, laid out the defense's case for the Soledad Brothers. Then George's mother, Georgia, spoke. Angela's schedule was almost comically overburdened: carrying a course load, completing her doctoral work and participating in Che-Lumumba Club's political and community-based activities. She was also speaking at events all over California about her court case,- "exposing and challenging Ronald Reagan, and seeking support for our side." But she was remarkably moved as Georgia Jackson spoke about her son, and it suddenly began to seem presumptuous to spend so much time fighting for a job when George was fighting for his life. "A determination began to swell immediately to do everything within the limits of the possible to save George from the gas chamber. Angela began to organize and speak at rallies all over California.

In May 1970, Angela and George met for the first time, in a court hearing. The analytical, detached persona that Angela had long used as a shield was pierced. She attributed almost godlike characteristics to George. "George looked more vibrant than I had imagined. I had thought the scars of the last decade would be immediately apparent, but there was not a trace of resignation, not the least stamp of bondage in which he had spent all the years of his adult life. He walked tall, with more confidence than I had seen before. His shoulders were broad and muscular, his tremendous arms sculptures of an ancient strength, and his face revealed the depth of understanding of our collective condition and his own refusal to be over-whelmed by this oppression. I could hardly believe the refreshing beauty of his smile."

To Angela—who had long harbored feelings of guilt that she had been sheltered from what she saw as the genuine black experience—George was the real thing: a true revolutionary who had kept the faith despite the pitiless environment in which he found himself. And although George did not lack for female devotees while in prison—he fathered a child with one of them—the fact that a stunning academic and radical would take an interest in him was intensely flattering. In some ways, each was living the kind of life to which the other aspired. The fact that neither had any real idea of what the other's world was like made aspiring to it all the easier. It was unsurprising that they fell in love before they even met. Now, the two began an intense correspondence in which politics and passion were inextricably intertwined. Angela's letters to George alternate between hard-eyed political analysis and achingly florid prose that only a young woman in love for the first time can conjure. She signed most of these let-ters "your wife."

"Dearest Angela," George wrote in kind, "I hope you have discovered that I love you deeply and would touch you tenderly, warmly, fiercely if I could if my enemies were not at present, stronger."

With George's encouragement, Angela befriended his seventeen-year-old brother, Jonathan. Only seven years old when George was imprisoned, Jonathan had been visiting and corresponding with his older brother for virtually his entire life and idolized him. The rage he felt at his brother's imprisonment had grown by the year, and he had become obsessed with the idea of freeing him from jail. After the killing of the prison guard,

Jonathan wrote in his high school newspaper: "They couldn't get George one way so they are now trying to crucify him for a murder that he did not commit. If he's bound up tight, I'll hold back the night and there won't be no light for days."

Angela immediately took to the young man, and George supported the big sister-little brother bond that grew between them. "Jon is a young brother and he is just a little withdrawn but he is intelligent and loyal," George wrote to her, adding, "He is at that dangerous age where confusion sets in and sends brothers either to the undertaker or to prison."

To give Jonathan a constructive channel through which to express his frustration, Angela invited him to join the Committee to Free the Soledad Brothers. He rarely missed a meeting, sitting quietly while his elders strategized. Possessing writing skills that rivaled his brother's, he wrote the text for brochures and flyers espousing George's cause. When George urged Jon to look after Angela and keep her safe from the "racists and re-actionaries who might try and make [Angela] a martyr," the young man became Angela's bodyguard.

On the morning of June 19, 1970, Angela spoke at a rally for the Soledad Brothers as part of a roster that included Jane Fonda. An hour into the rally, a reporter informed Angela that at a meeting of the regents, blocks away, the Board of Regents, including Governor Reagan, had once again voted to dismiss her. This time, it was not for her membership in the CPUSA but for her supposedly unprofessional activism in support of the Soledad Brothers. Governor Reagan announced the decision after the meeting, saying. "Academic freedom does not include attacks on faculty members or on the administration of the university or speaking to incite trouble on other campuses."

Angela's speeches were inflammatory. She referred to the police—as al-most all black and white militants did at the time—as "pigs." She accused California officials, including Reagan, of working in concert to suppress radical political activists, especially those involved in prison and justice system reform, and characterized the case against the Soledad Brothers as one in a "long series of repressive and genocidal measures taken by the prisons in the state."

After Reagan's press conference concluded, the press quickly shifted ground to get Angela's reaction. With Jonathan beside her, Angela shifted the focus away from herself: "I'm going to keep on struggling to free the Soledad Brothers and all political prisoners because I think that what has happened to me is only a tiny, minute example of what is happening to them," she told the reporters.

The shy young woman who first walked through the doors of Elisabeth Irwin in 1959 had emerged as a forceful and charismatic presence. This was the persona of the Angela Davis the world came to recognize in print and on television as the face of the Black Power movement. Cultural commentator Allistair Cooke called her "the newest star on the Left to replace Abbie Hoffman."

But the admiration Angela commanded in liberal and radical circles was more than matched by the hatred and fear she inspired among conservatives. The political climate was becoming increasingly dangerous for Angela and other black radicals. FBI Director J. Edgar Hoover called the Black Panther Party "the greatest threat to the internal security of the country." Although Angela was not a member of the Black Panther Party, she was a vocal supporter of the group.

The regents' decision had relieved Angela of her teaching duties, pending further legal action, but Angela continued to straddle the academic and radical worlds. She had not yet completed her dissertation and was determined to do so by the end of the summer of 1970. To that end, Angela took a flat in Los Angeles to concentrate on her writing. But as always, the pull of the movement proved irresistible. Angela had been recognized as a legal investigator for George, making her a part of the Soledad Brothers legal team. The defense had successfully argued for a change of venue from Salinas to the Bay Area. Accordingly, George and his fellow defendants had been transferred from Soledad to San Quentin. The statewide Soledad Brothers Defense Committee asked Angela to spend time in San Francisco to help strengthen the coalition and she agreed. At the beginning of August, Angela drove up to San Francisco.

On the morning of August 7, 1970, a trial was in session at the Superior Courthouse in the Marin County Civic Center. The defendant, James Mc-

Clain, who had resided in the infamous B Block in Soledad with George, was accused of stabbing a guard. This was the second time McClain had been tried for this murder, the first trial having ended in a hung jury. Judge Harold Haley presided. Prosecuting the case was Assistant District Attorney Gary Thomas. Thomas had rested the state's case the day before, and McClain, acting as his own lawyer, began the day by calling his first witness, Ruchell Magee, another inmate from B Block. William Christmas, another of McClain's witnesses, waited in a holding area.

At 10:45 a.m. Jonathan quietly entered the courtroom wearing a trench coat and carrying a briefcase and a paper sack. He took a seat in the second row of the nearly empty spectators' section. Minutes later, Jonathan stood up and, holding a Browning .380 pistol, announced calmly: "All right gentlemen. This is it. I'm taking over now." From his briefcase he pulled out weapons and passed them out to McClain, Magee and Christmas.

"Did you bring the tape?" McClain asked Jonathan. In response, Jonathan tossed him a roll of white adhesive that McClain used to attach a shotgun to Haley's neck so that the barrel of the weapon was aimed at the judge's head. The men then selected three female jurors as hostages, as well as the judge and the assistant district attorney. According to those who survived the ordeal, McClain was the most levelheaded of the escapees, tempering Jonathan's adrenaline-hyped rage. He treated the hostages courteously, even gently, talking Jonathan out of choosing an infant and an elderly woman as hostages.

The men now moved the terrified hostages into the wide court hallway. There they lingered long enough for a photographer who heard about the escape attempt over his police radio to rush over to the courthouse and take posed pictures of the would-be escapees and their hostages. In one photograph, McClain is pointing his pistol at Haley's head with his right hand and propping up the butt-end of the rifle aimed at the judge's head with his left. The judge, looking grim but composed, helps McClain support the rifle.

The men stayed in the hall for about a half hour. Finally, Jonathan, McClain, Magee and Christmas herded the hostages into an elevator. At the main floor they exited the courthouse, led by McClain, who, still propping up the rifle attached to Haley's neck, was pointing his pistol at the police who had gathered at the scene. Behind them were the rest of the hostages, surrounded by Magee, Christmas and Jonathan, all armed.

Once outside the civic center they made their way to the parking lot and loaded the hostages into a yellow Ford Econoline van that Jonathan had rented the day before. With Jonathan driving, the van made its way out of the parking lot and to the service road that led to the highway. On that road, police and San Quentin prison guards, crouched and hidden, were waiting. One of them opened fire. As a full-blown shootout ensued, Thomas stood in the van and yelled out the window "Stop firing! Please stop firing!" before taking a bullet to the spine that left him paralyzed. Judge Haley, Christmas and Jonathan were shot dead.

It is unknown what exactly Jonathan hoped to accomplish with his rash plan. Witnesses later reported overhearing various statements by the escapees about calls for the release of George and all political prisoners. According to Bettina Aptheker, one of Jonathan's objectives was to reveal to the world the dimensions of George's ordeal." In his book, *The Road to Hell*, Paul Liberatore cites FBI sources who described an elaborate plot in which Black Panther commandos planned to give Jonathan and his comrades cover as they drove away with the hostages. According to those sources, another team would give them cover as they secured a plane at the San Francisco Airport, at which point the hostages would be released in exchange for George. The plane would be flown either to Cuba or to Algeria. According to Liberatore, a communiqué by the Black Guerrilla Family that was released to radical groups after the melee stated, "Jonathan Jackson was deserted [by the Panthers]. Huey Newton ordered his functionaries to stay out of the Marin affair. Jonathan was to have had the assistance of the Black Panther Party."

In retrospect, the idea that such a far-fetched plan could be carried out with any expectation of success strains credulity. The question is how much Jonathan, who was seen huddled in intense conversation with his brother in the prison visiting room the day before the event, believed in its reality at the time.

That evening, Angela was watching the evening news when the images of the aftermath of the attempted escape flashed on the TV screen. She saw Jonathan's corpse dragged from the blood-soaked van by a rope tied around his waist.

"During the few months of our friendship," Angela wrote, "I don't think I realized how wracked he must have been by that decade of cumulative frustrations, by that terrible sense of impotence before the walls, the bars, the guns, and those tidy courtrooms presided over by fastidious white judges."

Angela, who had armed herself since her run-in with the irate Black Panther, had ramped up her arsenal in the weeks leading to August 7, legally buying hundreds of rounds of ammunition and more guns. Days before in fact, she had signed an autograph for the admiring proprietor of a pawnshop at which she purchased a shotgun and a box of shells. But it is hard to conceive of Angela involving herself and a young man she had come to love as a brother in a scheme with virtually no chance of success; one that would almost certainly result in Jonathan's death or capture.

On the night of August 7, witnessing the events of the morning play out in grainy black and white, Angela knew two things for certain: The guns Jonathan had smuggled into the courtroom were registered in her name, and the police would be coming for her.

CHAPTER EIGHT

Tommy Takes Charge

TOM HURWITZ, 1969–1971

Tom and Susan's first place in San Francisco when they moved there in the summer of 1969 was a house owned by Jerry Rubin in the neighborhood of Haight-Ashbury, the epicenter of the counterculture movement. Tom's goal was to help establish a Bay Area SDS regional office. His work as a full-time activist and organizer was subsidized by a monthly $50 stipend from Leo and a small inheritance from his grandmother. Tom and Susan soon moved into a spacious, gaily painted house on Bateman Street, living with another activist couple and female friend. The three women of the house were vegetarians and, accordingly, were dubbed "Rat," "Tat" and "Touie" while the meat-eating men were called "Pork" and "Chop."

Although very much in love with Susan, Tom was still not ready to settle into a monogamous relationship. The couple established ground rules in which each was free to conduct casual sexual dalliances within agreed-upon parameters: outside the house and/or when one of the partners was out of town. Susan was not an enthusiastic participant in the "arrangement," but, overwhelmed by Tom's domineering personality and the prevailing cultural ethos, said nothing. She did, however, see her situation mirrored in the lives of other movement women. On paper, revolutionaries were working to create a classless society, but women clearly wielded less clout. On one occasion, Susan and a group of women were sitting in a living room waiting for a meeting to begin. A local movement man walked in, looked around and asked, "Isn't anybody here?"

"There was an absolute devaluing of women," said Susan. "A lot of us felt really tired of that and really resentful." They were not alone. Women across America were beginning to chafe at the double standard between the sexes. As the Women's Liberation movement began to flower in San Francisco, Susan joined one of the many consciousness-raising groups being formed during that time. It changed her life. "It was mind-boggling to be with other women who had the same kind of experiences. It was extraordinarily moving and exciting and hopeful." Gaining self-confidence, Susan began to carve out a role in SDS as she found her voice in political meetings and at rallies. Tom, oblivious to the cultural sea change, sensed that Susan was drifting away from him but didn't know why or how to stop it.

Shortly after Tom moved to Berkeley he received a letter from the local draft board ordering him to report to the Oakland Induction Center for a pre-induction evaluation and a physical. Tom had feared this would happen because he had lost his student deferment status when he withdrew from Columbia and was now classified 1-A—available for military service. On the day, Tom smuggled leaflets into the waiting area advising his fellow conscripts of their rights. When the officer in charge entered the room most of the young men hurled the crumpled fliers at him. Tom planned another surprise. In the examination room, he took off his shirt to reveal a Vietcong flag that he had painted—inadvertently upside down— on his chest.

But the doctor's reaction surprised Tom. Instead of being shocked or enraged by the stunt, he quietly commented that the flag had been responsible for the deaths of several of his friends. Back in the waiting room, Tom scribbled anti-war slogans in the margins of his questionnaire and was told to leave the center. He returned home, the paint staining his chest for several days. While the draft board deliberated on Tom's case, Tom was assigned a high number in the draft lottery, making it unlikely that he would be called. Tom was relieved, but the doctor's sober response to his stunt had made an impression. He never again displayed the flag in a demonstration and he eliminated the protest chant "Ho Ho Ho Chi Minh" from his repertoire.

Over the summer, Weathermen horror stories from the East Coast had made their way to the Bay Area as the group's increasingly bizarre and violent and "Custerific" (Black Panther Fred Hampton's caustic epithet) actions escalated. Despite SDS's bitter break with the Weathermen at its Chicago convention in June, SDS chapters across the country worked to support the faction's first major action: "Four Days of Rage," to be held in Chicago in October, built around the rallying cry, "Bring the War Home." The Weathermen hoped to deploy thousands of anti–Vietnam War protestors throughout the streets of Chicago.

Locally, Tom was coordinating a September protest to greet the International Industrial Conference, a gathering of five hundred corporate leaders from sixty countries. "The leading imperialists of the world plan to meet . . . to formulate plans to tighten their stranglehold on the throats of the people. The people have other ideas," read an article for the action, under the headline, "Kick the Ass of the Ruling Class." Thousands of protestors were expected, but on the day itself, it seemed to Tom that there were more police in gas masks than demonstrators. The weak response didn't bode well for the Chicago action and sure enough, on October 8, hundreds, not thousands, of protestors, armed with makeshift weapons, ran aimlessly through the Chicago streets, breaking shop windows and setting fires. The inevitable confrontation with the police resulted in severe injuries on both sides and 250 arrests. Kathy Boudin was one of those arrested. Contrary to the Weathermen's hopes, the action did nothing to encourage uprising among the American people; instead, the television coverage of the event confirmed the worst fears of many about the counterculture movement: These were not principled young people fighting for change—they were thugs, pure and simple.

The failure of the "Kick the Ass of the Ruling Class" rally and the self-destructive anarchy in Chicago left Tom feeling rudderless. The election of Richard M. Nixon' as president in November amplified his frustration. His personal life was coming apart as well. On December 6, the Bateman

Street communards piled into Tom's van to make the fifty-mile drive west to the Altamont Speedway to see the Rolling Stones in concert. They were so far away from the stage that it took a while for word to reach them that a young man in the audience had been stabbed by the Hell's Angels. As hysteria overcame concertgoers, the friends, high on acid, managed to make their way back to the van and return safely home. Something clicked for Susan during that experience. Days later she broke up with Tom, returned East and joined a group traveling to Cuba. Upon her return, she settled in New York and began to build a new life for herself.

In late fall 1969, Tom connected with a friend from his days as an SDS functionary, Donna Mickleson. Two years earlier, she and Fred Gardner— Little Red and Elisabeth Irwin class of '59—opened a storefront in Columbia, South Carolina, near Fort Jackson, offering coffee and sandwiches to soldiers who gathered to share their combat experiences and voice their opposition to the war. The coffee house was immediately popular, attracting over six hundred GIs a week. It marked the start of the GI movement as other coffee houses opened up near military bases around the country and became centers around which to organize anti-war activities. The GI movement gained steam in 1968, after the Tet Offensive, and into 1969 as news spread throughout the United States of the My Lai massacre, in which hundreds of unarmed civilians had been killed by U.S. soldiers in the South Vietnamese town the year before. On October 15, 1969, protests under the banner of the Moratorium to End the War in Vietnam took place across the country. A month later, a half a million demonstrators converged on Washington for a second Moratorium march.

It was at this juncture that Tom met Kent Hudson. Several years Tom's senior, he had been a civil rights organizer, risking his life for the cause during the Freedom Summer of 1964. Along, with his wife, Soumi, he had established the Green Machine, one of the roughly one hundred existing GI coffee houses, in Vista, California, outside of Oceanside, which was home to Camp Pendleton, a huge Marine base. Now they wanted to expand their activities, and hold their own Moratorium march and demonstration scheduled for December 14, 1969. But they were in need of a seasoned organizer to put the event together. Attracted to the cause and eager to get away from the Bay Area, Tom signed on to the project.

In early December, Tom made the 500-mile journey down the California coast in his green Dodge van, into the arid, mountainous landscape to the drowsy city of Oceanside, a half hour north of San Diego and just 20 miles from President Nixon's San Clemente retreat. He reached Camp Pendleton by early evening. Under the palm trees ringing the base, anti-war organizers and protestors handed out leaflets as cars entered and exited the heavily guarded facility. As darkness fell, Tom drove seven miles though Vista, a small, formerly industrial town, past dusty bungalows and into the hilly countryside dotted with fruit trees, pulling up to a house with an adjoining four-car garage topped by a sheet-metal roof. This structure served as the coffee house, the Green Machine, a makeshift space furnished with mismatched tables and chairs and a stereo system. Within a few months of its opening, the Green Machine was attracting a good number of both black and white marines from Pendleton who came knowing it was a safe place to vent their frustration, fear and anti-war sentiment. The Pendleton brass was predictably displeased by this state of affairs and sent infiltrators to spy on the proceedings. The local police force also kept the site under surveillance but found nothing to fault. "We were vigorously non-violent," Hudson recalled. "No dope, we did everything we could to be just as clean as possible. It was not a hippie project. We were not into youth culture at all."

Adding to the Green Machine's cachet were the occasional visits by celebrities, notably Jane Fonda, who had devoted herself to the GI movement, going on tour with a USO-like revue called "FTA," which stood for "Fuck—or Free—the Army," a play on the acronym's usual meaning as shorthand for the Army's motto, "Fun, Travel and Adventure."

Hudson was pleased to welcome the young organizer into his home. "So Tommy walks in and takes over—in almost a military fashion—the organization of the demonstration and it's a good thing he did because it's something he did well."

Since the Moratorium march was only two weeks away, Tom set eagerly to work. One of his first acts was to establish a cordial relationship with the Oceanside police force, which, although it had to particular affinity for Hudson and his colleagues, was not openly hostile to them. In particular, Tom forged a solid working relationship with a middle-aged police officer, Sergeant Robinson. The two men, though very different in age, background and political outlook, developed a mutual respect for one another.

At 2 p.m. on December 14, a thousand soldiers—many of them African American—and their supporters marched down the main street of Oceanside. Afterward, the jubilant Marines stayed in town, shooting the breeze on street corners and outside bars and nightclubs. As dusk began to fall, some white Marines—deliberately planted by the military, according to Tom—began shouting racial epithets and other insults at the black soldiers. The bright mood of the day quickly soured. Name-calling escalated into bottle throwing and fistfights. Tom immediately saw that a ginned-up race riot was in the offing, one that would nullify the good will generated by the march. He flagged down Sgt. Robinson's squad car, and together they patrolled the street. Spying a group of black soldiers becoming increasingly enraged by the taunts of the white soldiers, Tom jumped out of the car and walked straight into the group of black soldiers. "Brothers, we can't do this now. We're going to destroy what we've built here. If we do this we're going to shoot ourselves in the foot. Let's just calm down." The situation defused, Tom got back into the car and, recruiting a black Marine named Ernest, they continued to patrol the town, talking to the blacks and whites.

Tom had signed on to organize only this one march in Oceanside, but now he was hooked. After months in a movement bubble, here was a place in which he could really make a difference in people's lives. "We were the object lesson that organizing worked," he said. "Weathermen were running around saying 'you can't organize white people,' 'black people are involved in a People's War,' 'the whole world is rebelling, you have to make a choice—white skin privilege,' all that bullshit, and here [it] was . . . working."

Tom returned to the Bay Area, packed up his things, turned around and drove back to Hudson's after the New Year to start the 1970s as a GI

organizer. He returned to Vista just in time for an exciting event at the
Green Machine: His old schoolmate from Elisabeth Irwin, Angela Davis,
had agreed to take time out from her teaching duties at UCLA (and her
ongoing legal battles with the regents) to come talk to the GIs. Because she
had also just become involved with the Soledad Brothers' cause, there were
fears for her safety.

"When Angela came we decided that we were getting her and ourselves
into trouble because we heard rumors from the GIs that there were gangs
of non-governmental organizations that were going to shoot her. So at
that point I went and saw Angela's sister, Fania, who was living with Herbert Marcuse in San Diego," Hudson recalled. "She sent some guns up."

Although Hudson was aware of the potential danger, he also was dead
set against the group taking up arms. "I was convinced that once we went
down that road we were going to lose, because we were against the war and
if you think about it, using guns was no way to win." But Hudson was out-
voted by the rest of the group. In preparation for Angela's arrival, they went
into high-security mode. Assuming the role he'd played during the Columbia occupation, Tom took command of security preparations: stringing
barbed wire around the site and digging trenches, appointing look-outs
and establishing a network of communications via walkie-talkies. The goal
was simple: to get the Marines into the Green Machine to hear Angela and
then get them all out again, without anyone getting killed.

On the night, the Green Machine was packed with 150 Marines, most
of them African American, eager to hear the stunning movement super-
star. Tom greeted Angela warmly, reminding her that he had been her "little brother" at Elisabeth Irwin. But there was little time for reminiscing. As
Angela spoke to the GIs, Tom took up his post in the attic, armed with a
shotgun, with Hudson, unarmed, both the lookout for intruders. At the
end of the evening, which passed without incident, Angela and her people
were immediately whisked away.

On March 6, shortly before noon, a tremendous explosion leveled a red
brick townhouse on West 11th Street in Greenwich Village, blocks away
from Little Red School House. Ted Gold, Terry Robbins, Diana Oughton,

Cathlyn Wilkerson and Kathy Boudin, members of the Weather Underground, as the Weathermen were now called, had been building a bomb in
the basement when it detonated. The intended recipients of the bomb are
in dispute: Some say it was for Fort Dix, New Jersey; others are convinced
it was going to be planted in Columbia's Low Library. It's quite possible
that the amateur bomb makers were undecided about the issue at the moment they annihilated themselves. Gold, Robbins and Oughton died immediately. Wilkerson and Boudin—her clothes blown off her body—fled
the house, somehow unharmed, and took refuge with a neighbor.

Tom was organizing outside Camp Pendleton when he heard the news.
He had known them all through SDS; had worked with them before the
Weathermen split and had been lovers with Oughton. "I really felt as if I
was at the end of the world. Even though I rejected what they stood for,
they were my friends. I loved them."

In the spring of 1970, the Green Machine, which operated under the
auspices of the national organization Movement for a Democratic Military, expanded their operations, opening an office in Oceanside and planning another huge march and demonstration for May 16.

Putting aside his grief, Tom redoubled his efforts with the GIs; there was
plenty to do. Earlier in the year, Hudson and his wife had split after many
years of marriage. Hudson, dejected, left the Green Machine to teach in a
university in San Diego. Tom and five others now took up residence in a
house on the main street of Oceanside, which contained offices and the new
iteration of the Green Machine. Angela's visit had been an effective recruit-
ment tool, especially for the African American Marines, and other movement celebrities, including Fonda and folk singer Phil Ochs, visited the new
headquarters to speak to the Marines who were embracing the group's anti-
war ethos in greater numbers. The Green Machine's newsletter, *Attitude
Check*, which rolled off the office mimeograph, tripled in circulation. A
huge rally and march was scheduled for May 16, Armed Forces Day, at
which Fonda and Hayden were scheduled to speak.

On May 4, the Ohio National Guard gunned down four students during a peaceful protest at Kent State University. Ten days later, two students

were shot and killed by the National Guard during protests in Mississippi's Jackson State College. These events had a profound effect on Tom and his comrades, but fevered preparations continued for the march. Tom tried to cover every contingency that might prevent a violent eruption at the event. When a young man appeared out of the blue offering to set up walkie-talkies for the march, Tom gave him the green light despite strong suspicions that he was a police plant. Tom wanted full transparency between his group and the police. The more they knew, he reasoned, the less chance of a potential misunderstanding.

The day of the event, a Saturday, was sunny and warm. Tom and his comrades led ten thousand people—four thousand of them GIs—down Oceanside's main street and into the Beach Bowl, an open-air amphitheater by the ocean, filling it to capacity. From the band shell, looking out on the mass of people sitting shoulder-to-shoulder on the concrete steps, Tom welcomed the crowd. Then the program began, with speakers and rock bands entertaining the enthusiastic crowd. An hour into the program, Sgt. Robinson approached Tom, who was watching the show from the wings.

"We've had a bomb threat," the sergeant said tersely. "Someone called in saying there's a bomb hidden in the amphitheater. We need to clear the place so we can search for it."

"Gimme a second," Tom said, buying time as he tried to assemble an alternate plan on the fly. After a moment, he said, "Let me propose an alternative," and detailed his idea. The sergeant needed some convincing but he had worked closely with Tom over the last six months and had come to respect the young man's judgment.

"OK," he said finally.

Now, Tom took the stage, interrupting a speech in progress. Leland Lubinsky, a young man who had just been introduced to Tom that morning was sitting in the audience. "All of a sudden there was Tommy at the microphone talking to the crowd as if we were all sitting around in his living room."

Tom began in a deliberate tone of voice. "Once again, welcome to People's Armed Forces Day. Just for the next few minutes, I want you to think of yourselves as a People's Army because we have a very important task to do." He paused to take a breath. "A bomb threat has been called in." The crowd went silent. Tom plowed on: "The police want us to clear the amphitheater and if we do this, it's the end of the rally. I have another idea: With as much discipline as we can, I want you to look around, look at your brothers and sisters, look at your feet. If you see a bag that you didn't bring in, gently open it. If you see anything suspicious, raise your hand."

Slowly, the people in the packed amphitheater began to follow his instructions.

"He almost hypnotized the audience into his state of calmness and made it seem like [it was] the most natural thing in the world for people to look under their feet for bombs," Lubinsky said.

After a minute, Tom asked: "Does anyone see anything suspicious?" he asked.

No hands went up.

"Congratulations," Tom said. "You're a People's Army." And the program concluded without further incident.

———

The exhilaration that followed the triumphant Armed Forces Day rally quickly dissipated. Despite growing opposition, the war seemed to be nowhere close to ending—if anything, it seemed to be escalating. Soldiers were returning from duty with stories about civilian slaughters and incidents of fragging—soldiers in open mutiny, in many cases murdering—superior officers. Tom and his friends had been too busy before the march to truly consider the ramifications of the Kent State and Jackson State shootings. Now that they did, it seemed a real indication that a government crackdown on dissent could be imminent—especially in Ronald Reagan's California. The government had been assassinating Black Panthers for years, Tom thought. Now, it seemed, the lives of white revolutionaries might be in danger as well. Short of that, Tom thought a mass roundup and detention of West Coast activists was a real possibility.

In June, he traveled to the East Coast to procure forged papers for his friends in case they had to go underground. Day by day on this journey, however, Tom's mission began to seem unnecessary, perhaps even a bit foolish. After all, the land war in Vietnam had started to wind down and Nixon's approval ratings were bottoming out in the low 20s. More importantly, Tom had started to view the Kent State killings in a new light. "If it wasn't a trial balloon by design, then it was a trial balloon in fact," Tom said. "Because I think what the government was doing was allowing each situation to get more and more violently repressive so they could see what they could get away with in the country."

Tom became more convinced that his fears about a West Coast crackdown by the authorities had been exaggerated as he talked to activists on the East Coast. "It seemed to me that the situation was getting looser and looser." He returned to Oceanside weeks later.

A few weeks later, as two-dozen organizers and Marines were concluding a meeting at the Green Machine headquarters on a late-summer night, machine gun fire sprayed without warning into the living room windows. "I'm hit!" yelled Corporal Jesse Woodard, a black Marine, as he fell to the ground. Tom crawled to the back of the house, grabbed a shotgun and went outside. Several cars parked in front of the house had been riddled with bullets but otherwise all was quiet. Inside the house people were tending to Woodard, who was bleeding profusely from a wound in his chest. (Woodard survived the shooting.)

After an ambulance took Woodard away, the police and the media arrived. The group was terrified. The attack revived their fears of martial law and internment camps. There was little doubt in Tom's mind that one if not more of his friends would be murdered in the coming weeks. In siege mode, the housemates surrounded their headquarters with sandbags, fenced off the back yard, put concertina wire on the roof, built a lookout post in the attic and took regular target practice. Still heartsick about losing Susan, Tom was often preoccupied by the thought that he would die without ever seeing her again.

Now Tom considered his options. When he'd returned from the East Coast he'd found the Green Machine under new leadership. Two women—

former Black Panthers—had stepped into the vacuum left by Hudson's departure. Feeling out-of-place and his usefulness at an end, Tom moved back to the Bay Area.

Once there, however, belonging to no organization, with no immediate task at hand and no significant other, Tom spent the early fall months of 1970 indulging in sexual liaisons with a number of movement women. "At that point, I was free of the movement. I was on vacation and I was free of steady relationships so I was at my loosest. I just really wanted to sleep with anybody I could. The movement at this time in California just had extraordinary women, and I had a lot of beautiful friends." One of those women was a cousin's ex-girlfriend. Another fling involved a good friend of hers; both members of the same women's liberation collective. One of the women fell deeply in love with Tom, a situation he was at a loss to know how to deal with.

In October, Tom accompanied friends on a three-week hike in the Sierras. In his absence, Tom's two bedmates compared notes. Then they reached out to friends in the tight-knit Bay Area activist community and quickly ascertained the extent of Tom's womanizing.

Tom returned, relaxed and recharged from his hike. He let himself into his apartment to find a full-blown tribunal of enraged ex-lovers and female friends awaiting him. "I walk into the alcove of the house and [one of the women] is swearing at me—'How could you do this? How could you humiliate me? How could you come between me and my best friend?'"

At the best of times, Tom could be clueless about the effects of his behavior on others. Now he stood, stunned, as the women vented their collective rage at him. After giving Tom an earful about his transgressions, the ad hoc trial unceremoniously kicked him out of his own apartment. Tom toted his backpack to another movement house, seeking refuge. But word had spread, and his reception there was only marginally less hostile and he was told to leave. As he turned to do so, he was blindsided by a powerful punch to the jaw delivered by one of the female residents. Tom pushed her away and fled.

The next few days were a blur. News of Tom's disgrace and summary condemnation spread throughout Berkeley and San Francisco. He was informed that he would have to face two more tribunals to answer for his behavior: one composed of men and one of women. The men's group went pretty easy on him, with the exception of his one male housemate from Tom's collective on Bateman Street who was displeased with the way Tom had treated Susan. The second women's tribunal was another matter. In the intervening days, they had become even enraged. In the course of a five-hour meeting, Tom struggled to defend himself. "What have I done with you that you haven't done with me?" he asked plaintively. But even if he didn't fully comprehend his compatriots' wrath—"I hadn't done anything that was particularly oppressive except sleep with people," Tom later said—he was still devastated.

"I felt all these people had discovered the evil inside of me," Tom said. "They were my movement colleagues and they were calling me no better than an imperialist." Utterly demoralized, Tom caught a ride back East, vowing never again to return to the Bay Area.

———————

Tom got back to New York in December 1970. It was a relief to be on the familiar streets of the city, to see his mother, Leo and Peggy and to feel the chill of winter. Staying in the apartment of a friend, he encountered another houseguest, Barbara Zahm. Tom had known Barbara, albeit intermittently, for a few years. They first met in the spring of 1966 when he and Debbie had traveled west to meet her parents in Los Angeles. One night they attended a party thrown by the Zahm's, close friends of Debbie's family. The Zahms were like a West Coast version of the Hurwitz clan, active in the Los Angeles left-wing artistic community of writers, actors and producers, many of whom had been blacklisted. The father, Nathan, was a constitutional lawyer and the mother, Beatrice, an educator and psychologist who had founded an experimental high school for troubled teens. At that time, Tom had never been to L.A., but this seemed a reasonable microcosm of its bohemian life. High school and college students and their parents mingled in the house and outside by the pool, blithely passing joints back and forth. The fete was in honor of the Zahm's only daughter, Barbara, who was about to take leave from UC Berkeley, where she had been involved in the Free Speech movement, to travel the world.

Feeling awkward in the unfamiliar environment, Tom made his way through the big house, coming upon Barbara holding court in her bedroom, sitting cross-legged on her bed in form-fitting toreador pants and a midriff top. She wasn't one of the angelic-faced, straight-haired beauties Tom was usually attracted to, but he was struck by her intense face, which was dominated by large dark eyes and full lips and topped by unruly curly black hair. Even more than her looks, Tom was fascinated by her fierce intelligence and her natural command of the room. For her part, Barbara noticed Tom only in passing. He seemed like a nice-enough guy.

In 1967, Tom was hitchhiking in San Francisco when Barbara, by complete chance, picked him up. They did a simultaneous double take. "Aren't you Barbara?" "Aren't you Tommy?" Now, three years later, Tom sat with Barbara on her bed as they talked for hours and then made love. By the morning, they were a couple.

Barbara's last few years had been as tumultuous as Tom's. After her going-away party, she left for Europe with no plan other than to explore the world. She made her way to Greece, arriving shortly before the junta in April 1967. In Athens, Barbara fell in love with an older man named Jurgo, a pharmacist well respected in the city's political and artistic circles. After a few months, Jurgo proposed marriage. Barbara was torn, weighing her love for him against the prospect of continuing her travels and leaving her beloved California behind. With Jurgo's support, Barbara decided to continue her travels. He saw her off as she boarded a plane for Israel.

That night, tanks rolled into Athens. For five days after the coup by right-wing army generals, Barbara unsuccessfully tried to contact Jurgo, having no idea whether he had been arrested or killed. Finally, she got him on the phone. He was perfectly safe, he assured her. Barbara continued her travels, keeping in touch with him as best she could. Finally, he asked her to return to Athens, which she did. Now Jurgo presented Barbara with a choice. Although he was carrying on his day-to-day life, Jurgo told her that he was an active member of the resistance fighting against the junta. "You shouldn't stay," he said. "It's dangerous work. But if you want to stay there's a lot of work we can do."

Barbara stayed. For the next five months the couple hid fugitives, helped them escape and smuggled updates about the progress of the resistance to the outside world. Although Barbara lived in a state of constant fear, she took pride in the knowledge that as an American she was particularly useful to the cause. At one point a CBS reporter approached Jurgo, offering to smuggle out a taped message from the resistance. Jurgo took the offer to the resistance leaders and returned home that evening with a script, telling Barbara they had to record it and get it to the reporter by 6 a.m.

She read it, eagerly at first but then with growing dismay. "It was lies and propaganda," Barbara said. "And I said, 'I can't do this, this is bullshit. We have to rewrite this and tell the truth. I'm risking my life doing this and I don't mind doing it—but I won't risk it for a lie.'" The couple argued until 2 a.m. Finally, they rewrote the script, this time giving a realistic assessment of the state of the resistance, recorded it and got it to the reporter just in time for him to make his plane to New York. Weeks later, Barbara's parents, who had not heard from their daughter in weeks, were eating dinner while watching Walter Cronkite on the evening news. They rejoiced when they heard Barbara's voice coming from the television.

By the spring of 1968, the couple's position was becoming untenable. Several members of their resistance cell had been arrested and were being tortured, it had to be assumed, to obtain the names of their comrades. "We have to leave now!" said Barbara. But Jurgo argued for holding out a bit longer. Barbara, convinced they had run out of time, bought a ticket for Los Angeles on a flight leaving that evening and extracted a promise from Jurgo to follow her within the week. But with the eerie timing that seemed to punctuate Barbara and Jurgo's love affair, she got word upon returning home that Jurgo had been arrested the night after she had left. Over the next year, Barbara received intermittent letters from Jurgo smuggled out of prison.

Jurgo spent a year in jail before, but with the help of Barbara's father, he was eventually released. Barbara was hopeful that Jurgo would find a way out of the country and join her in California but he was still unwilling to abandon the struggle, and Barbara, now persona non grata in Greece, could not get to him. The next two years were hellish ones for Barbara as she endured a sexual assault and then a car accident that put her in a wheelchair and necessitated multiple operations on her ankle. In 1970, with the repression in Greece starting to ease, Barbara made plans to reunite with Jurgo, who by now had become an influential figure in Greek politics. In December, she flew to New York, having booked a flight to Athens. But as the time for her flight approached, Barbara began to agonize over the wisdom of the trip. "In my gut, I didn't think we'd be able to make it. We were different people now," she said. A day before she was to leave, Barbara came to a decision. She called Jurgo and told him she would stay in America. In 1980, Barbara received word that Jurgo, his health broken from his year in prison, had died.

The night Barbara reconnected with Tom he told her about the GI movement, and together they decided to put their respective personal dramas aside and dedicate themselves to doing their part to ending the obscenity that was the Vietnam War.

Within weeks, Tom and Barbara were on their way back to California.

CHAPTER NINE

The Family

ELLIOTT ABRAMS, 1969–1972

After graduating from Harvard in the spring of 1969 with a B.A. in political science, Elliott, who had lived all his life on the East Coast, wanted to take a year off to tour Europe before starting Harvard Law School. His parents, however, were eager for him to continue his education without a hiatus. A compromise was struck: Elliott would take the year off but would enroll in the London School of Economics.

Elliott spent the summer of 1969 in his parents' Upper East Side apartment (the family had moved to Queens several years earlier) before flying to London. When he returned to the States in the fall of 1970 to begin law school, it seemed as if the worst excesses of the New Left might be finally winding down. Its flagship organization, SDS, had lost any hope of winning over mainstream America the previous summer when the Weathermen had staged a coup at the SDS national convention in Chicago. After the 11th Street explosion, its leaders had disappeared. The group, now called the Weather Underground, continued intermittent "guerilla actions" but was disavowed by all but the most intransigent left-wing revolutionaries. The Vietnam War, the one issue around which Americans of all political persuasions had rallied, dragged on, but the draft was starting to ease up, defusing, for many, a focal point of outrage.

But if the New Left was losing the political battle, it seemed on track to win a larger and more enduring one. The transformation of cultural and sexual mores that began with the youth rebellion of the 1960s had branched out into women's rights and gay rights initiatives. Those, and other identity-group-based organizations were making strides for their constituencies, often with assists from the Supreme Court. To conservatives, the Court, presided over by Chief Justice Earl Warren until 1969, seemed bent on memorializing the counterculture's inroads into American society. Elliott, who had grown up idealizing Earl Warren as one of greatest legal minds in American history, came to scorn him for what he perceived as intellectual dishonesty, a sentiment encouraged by his law professors.

"We would read these decisions from the Warren court and many of them were crap. William O. Douglas—a great liberal hero—his opinions were frequently garbage—intellectually third-rate. Thurgood Marshall made third-rate knee-jerk decisions of a liberal variety. From a liberal point of view they got to the right place—it's a shame that the opinions were not at [a high] intellectual level," Elliott said.

> Roe v. Wade [decided in 1973, Elliott's last year of law school] is an indefensible decision intellectually. This was a great shock to me. When I was in law school one of the things the faculty prided itself on was this kind of wake-up call. There's a famous phrase literally carved in stone in one of the buildings, something like: "In the world of intellectual combat they lived by the sword and died by the sword." The idea was—put your politics aside here—Is this a good decision? Is this craftsmanlike? Is this persuasive? Because the great judges, from this point of view, are not liberals or conservatives, they're the great judges.

In law school, Elliott kept the conservative friends he had made in his undergraduate years and made new ones. A group was beginning to coalesce into what would become the vanguard of the neoconservative movement in the 1980s—a movement that, in many cases, sprung from the same lineage as that of his Elisabeth Irwin classmates on the New Left.

In the 1930s, striving Jewish sons of Eastern European immigrants flocked to the City College of New York which offered free education at its campus in West Harlem. Irving Howe, Irving Kristol, Daniel Bell and, a few years later, Nathan Glazer, bonded over their love of socialism, literature.

As member of the Trotskyite school of thought, they waged verbal battle with the Stalinist students in the school cafeteria., They went on to gain prominence in the then-small circle of New York intellectuals that Kristol called "The Family." But as the anti-communist liberals made their way in the world, becoming editors, writers and academicians, they became disillusioned by the blind acceptance by the Old Left of communist dogma in the face of atrocities and aggressions by the U.S.S.R. In the 1960s, they were deeply disturbed by the nihilism and lack of discipline on the part of the New Left as its members rebelled against the country's universities. By then, all but Bell had renounced their liberal beliefs, in many cases leading to rifts with friends and colleagues who remained committed to the cause.

By the 1970s, two generations of conservative Democrats, or "paleoconservatives" as they sometimes called themselves, had established themselves in New York and Washington, D.C. They were a tightly knit group—a new family that was, in fact, connected by blood and marriage in many cases. Kristol married historian Gertrude Himmelfarb for example, and their son is pundit William Kristol. Second-generation members of The Family of disaffected liberals included Elliott's friends Paul Wolfowitz, Douglas Feith, Richard Perle and Robert Kagan.

The members of the younger generation were as committed to their beliefs as their New Left counterparts, but one signal difference between them was the way they related to the older generation. "One of the most remarkable features of the neoconservative movement is the filial piety that pervades it," writes Jacob Heilbrun in his book *They Knew They Were Right*. "The sons and daughters . . . soaked up not only their parents' teachings but also their animosities." As a result, there was no generation gap as there was between hereditary radicals like Tom and their parents. They were ready to be midwives to a worldwide socialist revolution, but in doing so they turned away from their template for that revolution—the Soviet Union—and looked to Cuba and China for inspiration.

The young neocons in the making had been raised in prosperous households and had no firsthand experience of the Depression-era poverty their parents had endured, nor had they encountered the raw and socially acceptable anti-Semitism with which their parents had been forced to contend. But like their parents—and unlike their New Left counterparts—they well knew what it was like to be the outsider; to be marginalized because of their unpopular views. They would bear the scars of that ostracism into adulthood, proudly defining themselves by the enemies they made.

As much as he fit in with this group, Elliott was also somewhat of an outsider in the sense that his parents had never been affiliated with the New York intelligentsia to which many of his friends' parents belonged. Nor were his parents part of the Old Left guard; if that had been the case, he could have achieved distinction by rebelling against them. Joe and Mildred were middle-class professionals. Elliott was proud of his father's work on behalf of penniless immigrants, helping them to get a foothold in their adopted homeland. But he had no desire to join Abrams and Abrams (Elliott's older brother Franklin had joined the practice after graduating from Yale Law School). "The Wall Street firms had always sneered at this kind of law," he wrote. "You never made a big fortune, mostly because your clients were usually poor, or at best middle class."

In his second year of law school, Elliott and Dan Hastings took up residence in the converted attic in the home of their undergraduate sociology professor, Nathan Glazer. Forty-eight-year-old Glazer had been a junior member of the CUNY clique, was now politically right-of-center, though, unlike many of his colleagues, he never relinquished his ties to the Democratic Party. Glazer's road-to-Damascus moment came in 1963 when, as a professor at UC Berkeley, he recoiled from the extreme behavior of students in the Free Speech movement. As a young man, he had served as editor of *Commentary*, a magazine founded in 1945 as a forum for social, cultural and Jewish issues as seen through the lens of the anti-Stalinist Left. Now, his experiences at Berkeley provoked him into joining forces with his old CCNY buddies Daniel Bell and Irving Kristol to launch a magazine called *The Public Interest*. Irving Howe famously wrote: "When intellectuals cannot do anything else they start a magazine." Such magazines proliferated in the 1920s through the 1960s. When Glazer came on board in 1945, *Commentary* was the most influential of these publications. In 1960, Norman Podhoretz became its editor and, over the next two decades, oversaw its transition from a publication friendly to progressives of all stripes to the flagship of what would become the neoconservative movement.

In 1972, Elliott was noticed by the tight knot of New York intellectuals when Glazer, impressed by an article Elliott had written for *Perspectives* magazine titled "Black Capitalism and Black Banks," brought him to meet Podhoretz in the Upper West Side apartment he shared with his wife, Midge Decter, also a prominent writer.

Born in 1930 to Jewish Eastern European immigrants, Podhoretz attended Columbia University, where he became the protégé of Lionel Trilling, a literary and intellectual lodestar of New York intellectual circles and editor of the influential *Partisan Review*. Like Kristol, Podhoretz started adulthood as a fervent liberal only to be transformed, with the attendant zeal of a convert, to the conservative cause—a cause that he did much to promote when he assumed the editorship of *Commentary* in 1960.

In addition to his disgust with the New Left's anti-American stance, Podhoretz was also repelled by what he perceived to be its anti-Semitism, as illustrated by its anti-Israel reaction to the Six Day War. "After the Jewish state's lightning victory in 1967, . . . Israel suddenly became suspect in the eyes of the left. Formerly looked upon as a shining socialist experiment, it was now impolite to defend the [so-called] oppressor and occupier of the Palestinian Arabs. . . . It was a pivotal moment in the emergence of the neoconservative movement," wrote Heilbrun.

By the time Elliott met Podhoretz, the forty-two-year-old intellectual, his wife and three adult children constituted the first family in New York's conservative Democratic hierarchy (Irving Kristol being the reigning power in Washington, D.C.). Elliott was dazzled. "He was a very impressive figure," he recalled. "A leading intellectual in New York."

Impressed with the young man, Podhoretz invited Elliott to write an article for *Commentary* and worked closely with him to edit the piece, "The Quota Commission," about affirmative action in U.S. universities. As flattered as Elliott was by the attention of the eminent man, he was amused by Podhoretz's decided editing style. "I remember the last line of the article [said] something like . . . 'As Congress has legislated and the

Supreme Court has confirmed.' And I remember saying to Norman, 'you know the term affirmed is a legal term—you affirm a lower court decision. Confirmed is not a legal term. I guess I'm not sure in that sentence that confirmed is the right verb.' To which he replied: 'I am.' And that was the end of that argument. He was a very firm editor. But that was a start of a friendship."

It would prove to be the most significant relationship of Elliott's life. The two men were clearly ideologically in sync, but more importantly, their temperaments were remarkably similar given the differences in their upbringings. Growing up in Crown Heights, one of the toughest sections of Brooklyn, Podhoretz burned to make a name for himself in the literary salons of Manhattan. At Columbia, he toggled between his desire to fit in with the cultural establishment—to become a "facsimile WASP"—and to rebel against that establishment by flaunting his streetwise Brooklyn style.

As a second-generation Jew growing up in Queens, Elliott had experienced none of Podhoretz's childhood privation, yet from the day he entered Elisabeth Irwin, his ambition and drive had also made him a target of ridicule. Elliott and Podhoretz also shared, as Heilbrun put it, "an instinct for the jugular and, more important, a knack for self promotion by going against the grain of tribal opinion." In Podhoretz, Elliott had found a mentor who had succeeded not in spite of but because of his "bad" qualities. It was okay to be nakedly ambitious in the social, cultural and political spheres; it was not a problem to dissemble, even to lie, and to fight dirty in pursuit of a worthy goal. Ultimately, it was fine not to apologize for the supercilious sneer he had been accused of wearing since he was a child. Perhaps, in fact, most people merited such scorn. In his memoir, Making It, Podhoretz wrote: "Most of the books I read about America assured me—and continue to do so to this day—that success was the supreme, even the only, American value, and yet at Columbia College the word 'successful' glided automatically into the judgment 'corrupt.'

On an autumn morning in 1972, Elliott stood in a traffic island in the center of Harvard Square in front of a newsstand gazing at the October issue of Commentary that contained his article. Oblivious to the throngs of people eddying around him to get to the Metro, Elliott slowly circled the kiosk several times, looking for the magazine in the display case at the end of each lap. Elliott's father was thrilled at his son's accomplishment. "My son writes for *Commentary*," he *kvelled* to anyone who would listen.

In December of 1972, emboldened by Nixon's crushing victory over Sen. George McGovern, Podhoretz and Decter, Kristol and Jeanne Kirkpatrick, a hawkish history professor at Georgetown University and other members of the family, formed the Coalition for a Democratic Majority. In a full-page ad in the *New York Times*, under the banner "Come Home Democrats," they pronounced McGovern's defeat a "clear signal to the Democratic Party to return to the great tradition through which it had come to represent the wishes and hopes of a majority of the American people—the tradition of Franklin D. Roosevelt, Harry S. Truman, Adlai Stevenson, John F. Kennedy, Lyndon B. Johnson and Hubert H. Humphrey." Although no one was using the term at the time, the "neoconservatives" had announced their arrival.

PART FOUR

CHAPTER TEN

"Angela Is Welcome in Our House"

ANGELA DAVIS, 1970–1971

A week after the Marin courthouse kidnapping and shootout that left a judge, Jonathan Jackson and two of his fellow conspirators dead, a warrant was issued for Angela Y. Davis, charging her with first-degree murder in the death of Judge Haley, kidnapping and conspiracy. Angela, however, was nowhere to be found.

The day after the shootout, Angela stood in a gas station rest room in Los Angeles. Under the greenish glare of the phosphorescent light, she pushed her hair into a tight elastic cap and pulled on a wig. After gazing warily at the all but unrecognizable image in the mirror, Angela exited the rest room and ducked into a waiting car, which carried her to the house of a sympathetic family. There she watched the FBI's nationwide manhunt for her unfold on network news.

Through an underground grapevine, Angela got word that police and FBI agents were besieging her comrades in the Che-Lumumba Club and the Soledad Defense Committee family as well as her friends—anyone who had any connection to her. Her sister, Fania, was arrested and then released. Clearly, it was too dangerous to remain in California. With the help of friends, Angela was spirited away to Chicago where she came under the protection of David Poindexter, a thirty-six-year-old African American, reputedly with a large inheritance at his disposal, who was willing, whether out of dedication to the cause or a desire for adventure, to become a fellow fugitive.

Together, they boarded a train to Miami, where they rented an apartment. Angela, confined to the space and having little to do all day but watch television, learned that she had achieved the dubious distinction of being the third woman to make the FBI's Ten Most Wanted list. "Angela sightings" were being reported from Los Angeles to Paris to Montreal, resulting in the detention of hundreds of tall, light-skinned black women. From Miami, the fugitives drove to New York City. Knowing that she could be apprehended at any moment, Angela considered fleeing the country. After much thought, she decided that if worse came to worst, jail was a better option than exile. At least in the United States, Angela reasoned, she would have the support of her family, friends and the movement. How many times had she been far from the action—whether it was at Elisabeth Irwin when the Civil Rights movement was peaking in the South or in Germany during the Watts riots—when her comrades were fighting, suffering and dying for the cause. This time, Angela resolved to stand her ground.

That did not mean, however, surrendering herself to the enemy. To buy time, Angela drafted a statement to the press affirming her innocence but indicating that she had fled the country and would return to clear her name when the climate of hysteria surrounding her case had cooled.

In October, she and Poindexter registered as a married couple at the Howard Johnson Motor Lodge in the Hell's Kitchen section of Manhattan. On October 13, two months and four days after she had taken flight, Angela left the motel to kill a few hours at a movie. Her hair was straight, parted in the middle and severely pulled back from her face, on which she wore oversized, round, black-framed glasses. She was conservatively dressed in a dark cotton shirt tucked into a simple black miniskirt.

Re-entering the motel in the late afternoon, Angela noted impassive, dark-suited men milling about the lobby. She tamped down the now-familiar feeling of panic that spread through her. She was probably imagining things, Angela told herself. The stress of life as a fugitive had taken its toll: At this point, every white man in a suit seemed to her like an FBI agent ready to pounce. Resolutely, Angela made her way across the lobby and into the elevator. Exiting on the seventh floor, she spied a man peering out of one of the doors in the hallway. Another man, who had entered the elevator with her, followed her out. Suddenly, agents burst out of every room on the floor and converged upon her shouting "Are you Angela Davis?" "Are you Angela Davis?" One of them pulled a gun.

Moments before, when Angela realized that her capture was imminent, an unexpected sense of calm had possessed her. Now there was a sickening moment of terror as she pictured her corpse sprawled and bleeding on the cheap hallway carpeting.

The agents cuffed Angela's hands painfully behind her back, escorted her downstairs and bundled her into the back seat of a black sedan, one of several that drove away from the motel.

Once the car was safely in motion, the agent in the passenger seat turned to Angela. "Would you like a cigarette Ms. Davis?" he asked.

"Not from you," she replied.

They brought her to the sterile FBI headquarters on East 69th Street, where she was kept for several hours before being driven downtown to the Women's House of Detention on Sixth Avenue and Greenwich Avenue, a massive ten-story brick building that loomed over the townhouses and tenements of Greenwich Village. Disoriented as she was, Angela still recognized it; she had walked by it countless times on her way to Elisabeth Irwin as a teenager and vividly recalled the din made by the female inmates as they rained down curses and pleas from the many-windowed jail.

Still handcuffed, Angela was placed on a bench in a grimy waiting area. As Angela's eyes adjusted to the dim light, she saw her image on a paper flyer under the words "Wanted by the FBI." If that weren't surreal enough, directly next to it was a poster picturing her former classmate, Kathy Boudin.

Hours went by. Angela was left alone except for an African American prison matron who approached her at one point and whispered, "A lot of officers here—the black officers—have been pulling for you." At 1 a.m., Angela's paperwork was processed and she was escorted to the jail's mental ward, where she had been temporarily assigned to a holding cell with three other women. Though the hour was late, Angela could hear muffled voices rising up from the street. One of the women informed Angela that over two hundred protestors—black, white and of all ages—had gathered around the building. Sure enough, if she listened closely, Angela could hear the well-wishers yelling their support.

Unable to sleep, Angela thought of her family. She took some comfort in knowing that after all these weeks on the run they would at least know she was alive. She thought of George, in a prison 3,000 miles away. Despite her wretched surroundings and the fact that the charges levied against her carried the death penalty, for the first time in many weeks Angela did not feel alone. The chanting of the crowd continued. Straining her ears, she could just make out the words: "Free Angela Davis!" "Free all political prisoners!"

The capture of Angela Davis made front-page news in papers across the country. President Richard M. Nixon publicly congratulated the FBI on the capture of the "terrorist." *Newsweek* put Angela on its cover and devoted six pages to her story.

Although the Communist Party was divided on what official stand to take on Angela's case—some feared that the extreme nature of the accusations against her would reawaken the Red Scare atmosphere that had died down in the last decade—it nevertheless rallied to her aid and supplied her with an experienced attorney, John Abt, who had previously defended Paul Robeson and other high-profile members of the Communist Party. Abt's first act was to fight Angela's extradition to California, where she would face capital charges. The party also formed the National United Committee to Free Angela Davis and All Political Prisoners (NUCFAD), which was chaired by Henry Winston, an African American party leader who had lost most of his sight due to a misdiagnosed brain tumor during his decade in prison, served for running afoul of the Smith Act of 1940. (Several prominent CPUSA leaders had been convicted and sent to prison in the 1950s under this law, which prohibited advocating the violent overthrow of the government.) Franklin and Fania were elected national coordinators of NUCFAD.

Days into her stay at the House of Detention, Angela had joyful reunions with Bettina Aptheker and Margaret Burnham, childhood friends from her days in Advance, the Communist youth club held in Aptheker's parent's Brooklyn brownstone. Aptheker, on the national committee of the CPUSA, was living in San Jose, California, with her husband and son when she heard the news that Angela had become a fugitive. Like almost all of Angela's friends, Aptheker was questioned about Angela's whereabouts by the FBI. At Jonathan's funeral, she approached Franklin and Kendra, asked after Angela and offered her services should they be needed. When she heard Angela had been captured, she resigned her job as West Coast editor of the CPUSA newspaper, *People's World*, and went to work full-time to free Angela. It was wonderful to reunite with her old friend, even under such dreadful circumstances, communicating via phone in the jail visiting room through plexiglass smudged with fingerprints from countless previous visits.

Another friend from Advance, Margaret Burnham, was fresh out of law school and, having just passed the bar, also readily agreed to serve as one of Angela's lawyers. A core group—Aptheker, Franklin and Kendra, Fania (who was pregnant with her first child), and Charlene Mitchell—obtained the status of legal investigators and thus became an integral part of Angela's defense team.

Angela, Abt and Burnham crafted a legal strategy on the premise that Angela was a political prisoner. Still in the mental ward, she had been consigned to solitary confinement, under guard twenty-four hours a day. To Angela's team this represented a clear attempt to keep her from talking to her fellow prisoners about communism, racism and other incendiary matters, and they filed a federal lawsuit charging that Angela was the victim of undue discrimination. To emphasize the point, Angela went on a hunger strike—no huge sacrifice, she wryly noted, given the wretched food served in the "House of D." On the tenth day of her fast, Angela scored her first legal victory: A Federal Court ruled that holding her in maximum security was in violation of her rights. She was moved in with the general population, where her spirits were raised by the camaraderie of the other prisoners, who were protective of the celebrity in their midst, warning Angela to be on the lookout for "Mickey"—the mice that infested the dilapidated building—and offering her other survival tips. At lights out the women would call "Good night" to each other, their voices ringing up and down the corridors. Then, in unison, they would shout, "Good night, Angela!"

While Angela was on the run, signs reading "Angela is welcome in our house" could be seen in the windows of black households across the country. Now, support for Angela among the African American community increased. "Free Angela" committees formed in black churches around the country, and progressives of all races in Europe, Africa, Asia and Latin America took up her cause. According to Aptheker, five months after Angela's arrest there were two hundred NUCFAD committees in the United States and sixty-seven abroad. Within weeks of her arrest, virtually every black newspaper in the United States had demanded her unconditional release or, saving that, at least her release on bail. The National Conference of Black Lawyers formed a committee of black law school professors to consult with the defense team. The country's premier black writers, artists, thinkers and politicians, including Nikki Giovanni, Maya Angelou, Nina Simone, Julian Bond, Rev. Ralph Abernathy and Coretta Scott King made pilgrimages to visit Angela and were vocal in their support. In his "Open Letter to My Sister Angela Y. Davis," which appeared in the *New Statesman* in London and the *New York Review of Books*, African American writer James Baldwin wrote, "We must fight for your life as though it was our own, which it is—and render impassable with our bodies the corridor to the gas chamber." Soul singer Aretha Franklin publicly offered to post bail, should it be granted, putting $250,000 in an escrow account to that end. "I have the money," Franklin said. "I got it from black people and I want to use it in ways that will help our people."

Due to the public scrutiny, Angela's circumstances at the House of D had improved, and she was now able to receive visitors in her cell. It was a rare evening when Angela did not entertain family, friends and supporters in her cell. At first Angela would not let Sallye visit for fear of the distress it would cause her. But beneath Sallye's ladylike manner was a bedrock of resolve, unsurprisingly given the years she had lived on "Dynamite Hill" in Birmingham. The petite matron, she proved to be an effective advocate on her daughter's behalf, giving speeches around the country despite receiving several bomb threats and often concluding her comments with a raised clenched fist in a black power salute.

As they had since the first night of Angela's imprisonment, supporters held vigil in front of the House of Detention. At a large rally in December, they developed a call and response with the inmates above, chanting: "1, 2, 3, 4, House of D has got to go!" "Free our sisters, free ourselves!" "Free the Soledad Brothers!" "Long Live Jonathan Jackson!" From her window, Angela called out the names of her prison mates: "Free Vernell . . . Free Helen . . . Ann . . . Joan . . . Laura . . . Minnie . . ." until she was too hoarse to continue.

Hours later, at 3 a.m., a guard woke her to escort her downstairs, where, he said, her lawyers wanted to talk to her. Disoriented—what lawyer would want to meet with her at such an hour?—Angela accompanied the guard and descended to the first floor. There, she was greeted not by a lawyer but by the deputy and assistant wardens and plain-clothes officers. Angela was told that the U.S. Supreme Court had denied her appeal to block extradition to California and that she was being flown to the state immediately.

"This was the first time I had seen male guards in the House of D," Angela recalled. "Realizing why they were there, I jumped up, took a battle stance and prepared to defend myself. One of them grabbed my arm. I kicked him. When the other man came to his aid, they both knocked me to the floor. By the time I could get up, the deputy warden and some of her female helpers were in on the action. . . . At this moment, the two officers standing on the sidelines . . . both threw themselves into the fight. Their entrance into the battle was a shock. . . . But it was even more of a shock to discover that they were not trying to subdue me but rather were beating up the men who, by now, were really roughing me up." When the scuffle subsided, Angela was handcuffed and, still dressed in her thin cotton sleeping shift, she was loaded into a van, and driven to McGuire Air Force Base in New Jersey. A plane, surrounded by men with shotguns, rifles and machine guns, waited to take her to California. She was now in fear for her life. She was being moved in the middle of night with no press or public in attendance and was convinced that any involuntary sudden movement on her part—a twitch or a stumble—would be interpreted as an attempt to escape and a pretext for her murder.

When the plane landed, Angela was taken to the jail in the Marin County Civic Center. In front of the complex where, four months earlier, the scene of the shootout for which Angela was now on trial had taken place, support- ers now chanted "Free Angela Davis." Her hands cuffed in front of her, Angela managed to raise her arms in a double-fisted gesture of defiance.

In contrast to the House of Detention, the Marin County Jail was mod- ern, antiseptic and brightly lit, though that made it all the more frighten- ing to Angela. But she was comforted by the fact that she was closer to her political brothers in San Quentin—especially George.

On January 5, 1971, Angela was taken into court. Standing next to Ruchell Magee—the one surviving prisoner of the Marin shootout—she was formally charged by the State of California with murder, kidnapping and conspiracy—capital charges that carried with them the threat of the death penalty.

By the beginning of summer 1971, Angela had been in the Marin jail for six months and had been a prisoner for eight months. The confinement had compromised Angela's health—she had developed a rash that now covered most of her body—but her spirits were reasonably high. Howard Moore, a skilled, savvy African American lawyer and a veteran of numer- ous civil rights cases, had recently joined the legal team. Angela spent her days writing and planning her legal defense and had even been assigned an extra cell that functioned as an ad hoc office.

On August 21, 1971, Angela and Aptheker were in the visitors section of the jail working to finish the manuscript of *If They Come in the Morn- ing*, an anthology of essays about the prison system by political prisoners and their advocates, when Moore joined them. Shortly after he arrived, a deputy entered the room and tersely instructed Aptheker and Moore to leave. Assuming it was a bomb threat, Angela's visitors left assuring her they'd be back after the situation was resolved. Angela was returned to her cell. Hours later, a female deputy escorted Angela to her work cell, where Moore and Burnham were waiting. One look at them signaled that something was desperately wrong and Angela feared she knew what it was. There was a long silence. Neither Moore nor Burnham, whose eyes were swollen and red, could seem to bring themselves to speak. "Don't let it be something about George," Angela thought. But the longer the silence continued, the more certain she became that the worst had occurred.

"George?" she managed to get out.

Moore nodded. Angela fell into Burnham's arms. "The pigs killed him, Angela," Moore said. "They murdered him."

George had been shot in the back by a San Quentin guard, a fact his supporters stressed as they portrayed him as a slain freedom fighter. But, as with the police reaction to insurrection the year before, the attack was not unprovoked. George had all but assured his death in the execution of a plan that in some ways echoed Jonathan's suicidal bid to free his brother.

By the time George made his break for freedom, a little more than a year after the Marin shootout, a significant number of Black Panthers had been set free by the judiciary system—Erica Huggins, Bobby Seale, Huey Newton and the Panther 21, for example—through acquittal or because their cases had been dismissed due to improper police conduct in making their arrest. It's possible, even likely, that George, too, might have been freed. But by then, his sense of fatalism was matched only by his rage. The self-taught scholar, writer and political leader, for whom even the prison's Aryan supremacist group professed a grudging respect, was convinced that "Fascist Amerika" was going to keep him in chains for the rest of his life. Having nothing to lose, George decided to try for freedom.

Earlier that summer, George had been transferred from Soledad to San Quentin to await the start of the Soledad Brothers' trial, slated to begin August 23. There, in an area called the "Adjustment Center," he worked on his second book, *Blood in My Eye*. Unlike *Soledad Brother*, the collection of letters that had made him an international celebrity, this was a collection of essays that reflected his full embrace of armed revolution. "The objective of ALL our activity is, in the end, a creation of a people's army—not an acquittal here and there" that would communally administer "a blade in the throat of Fascism."

In San Quentin as in Soledad, George was in constant contact with his "female army," as he described the devoted band of women who came to see him. Also paying frequent visits were members of the Black Panthers, especially his old friend Jimmy Carr, who had recently been released from prison. With them, George planned his escape. A letter later discovered in the pocket of Carr's pants—with both Jackson and Carr's handwriting on it—outlined a plot in which Carr, backed by a Panther guerilla unit, would first break George out of San Quentin, then effect Angela's escape and lay low in the Sierra Nevada Mountains while building an army large enough to take on the American government. In one scenario, George would then become the leader of the People's Army while Huey Newton headed up the political arm, the Black Panthers.

George named the plot the "August 7 Movement" in honor of Jonathan, who, in a role reversal, he had come to idolize. His baby brother had died for him. Now it was George's turn to step up. But like Jonathan, George had misplaced his trust in Huey Newton. According to Paul Liberatore's book, *The Road to Hell*, Newton had become increasingly unstable since assuming leadership of the Black Panthers. Liberatore alleges that he was involved in pornography and prostitution. Newton had convinced George to sign over most of the royalties of his book, *Blood in My Eye*, and was pitching a movie based on the book to his contacts in Los Angeles.

In the meantime, George was amassing a stash of weapon parts smuggled into prison by his lawyers and female admirers, and eluding detection with elaborate ruses. According to Liberatore, George once concealed a short length of pipe and a .22 caliber bullet in a block of cheese and his friend Johnny Spain reportedly smuggled shotgun shells and cartridges by the guards in hollowed-out bars of soap. Jackson wrote to another prisoner, "I've been bringing weapons in with every visit, and in two weeks exactly there will be a violent confrontation with weapons against the pig."

On August 6, George appeared in court with his lawyer, asking to be moved from San Quentin to the San Francisco County Jail, which was under the courtroom, in anticipation of the Soledad Brothers' trial. When the judge denied the request, Jackson, by some accounts, jumped on a table yelling "Power to the People!" and "Death to the Pigs!"—chants that were picked up by his supporters in the spectator section of the courtroom. When guards then tried to restrain George, he lit into them, sparking an all-out brawl. Carr, who was in attendance, was re-arrested, reducing the chances of the escape plan's success from slim to virtually nil.

As August wore on, the mood in the Adjustment Center became increasingly fraught. On August 8, fifty enraged prisoners surrounded a guard in the chapel plaza outside the building. Tower guards fired warning shots, but not in time to prevent the guard from being stabbed. When the man suspected of the assault was put into solitary, the inmates reacted by throwing excrement at the guards through the bars of their cells. On August 21, two days before the start of the trial, George was being escorted back to his cell on the second tier of the center when he pulled a small pistol and a bullet clip from his full Afro. Echoing the words of his slain brother, he announced, "All right gentlemen, this is it, I'm taking over."

With that, George ordered four of the guards present to flatten themselves on the hallway floor and a fifth to pull the lever that opened the cells on his tier, out of which emerged Johnny Spain and another prisoner carrying electrical cord with which they hog-tied the guards. "The black dragon has come to free you!" George reportedly proclaimed to the prisoners. "Our plans have changed. It's now or never. We've got to stick together, comrades. If you're with me, go to the doors of your cell. If you're not, don't come out." Twenty-seven inmates accepted the offer.

As the white prisoners desperately tried to lash themselves into their cells using bed sheets, the newly freed prisoners covered the guards' faces with pillowcases, used razors and makeshift knives to slit their throats and then threw them onto the floor of George's cell. According to one guard, George then entered the cell and shot another guard point-blank in the head while he was in the act of pleading for his life. Two white inmates, unaware of the revolt, appeared at the entrance to the wing carrying a lunch tray for George. They were immediately hustled into George's cell and also murdered with the now-blunted weapons.

Those outside the tier still had no idea what was going on. A face appeared in the glass pane of the door to the Adjustment Center—a guard coming to see what was delaying his colleagues. "Open this door or I'll

blow your motherfucking head off!" screamed George. The guard dived
for the ground as Jackson shot through the glass. Escaping back into the
yard, the guard alerted the rest of the prison about the uprising. According
to the testimony of the surviving guard on the tier, George went back into
his cell and shot another dying guard in the head.

By now alarm sirens were sounding all over the prison and the guards
had mobilized. Sharpshooters armed with machine guns moved into position around the parapet surrounded the Adjustment Center. George,
knowing that his escape attempt had become a suicide run, paused behind
the door that led into the yard. "It's me they want," Jackson told Spain,
who was following him. Pistol in hand, he kicked open the door and
darted out into the sun-flooded yard, shooting as he ran, heading for the
20-foot-high north wall. He made it about 75 feet before a sharpshooter
hit him in the ankle. George faltered but kept moving. Moments later, a
guard in the south tower shot George through the neck, killing him instantly. It was just before 3 p.m. The entire event had taken place in under
an hour.

To those willing to ignore the part George played in his own destruction and the savagery he had inflicted on others, he was a martyr. Bob
Dylan expressed that view in a song he wrote after George was killed,
lauding the man who "Wouldn't bow down or kneel" and whom the authorities hated "Because he was just too real." A month later, on September
9, more than a thousand prisoners gained control of Attica State Prison in
western New York State and took forty-three hostages. They produced a
list of demands to improve conditions in the prison. The standoff, which
lasted five days, captured the world's attention and engendered much
sympathy for the prisoners' plight and what many saw as their reasonable
demands, which ranged from better living conditions to religious freedom
to enriching the educational programs at the facility. But Governor Nel-
son Rockefeller remained intransigent. On September 13, tear gas was
dropped into the yard containing the prisoners and hostages; state troop-
ers opened fire. When it was over, twenty-nine inmates and ten hostages
had been killed.

In the days after George's death, an alternately heartbroken and enraged Angela focused on bringing what she saw as the cold-blooded murder of Jackson into the public eye, casting him as a symbol for all political prisoners. She issued a statement asserting that both George and Jonathan had been murdered by fascist bullets, referring to George's death as a "summary execution." She then eulogized him.

"For me, George's death has meant the loss of a comrade and revolutionary leader, but also the loss of an irretrievable love. . . . I can only say that in continuing to love him, I will try to express his love in the way he would have wanted—by reaffirming my determination to fight for the cause George died defending. With his example before me, my tears and grief are rage at the system responsible for his murder."

CHAPTER ELEVEN

Politics of the Purge

TOM HURWITZ, 1971–1972

In the spring of 1971, twenty-five-year-old Tom Hurwitz and twenty-six-year-old Barbara Zahm arrived at Leland Lubinsky's home in Loma Linda, California, with two dogs, Monk and Moca, a banjo and a considerable number of copies of Mao's *Little Red Book* in tow. Loma Linda was a bucolic area dotted with fragrant orange groves and apple orchards, remnants of the once-thriving agricultural region, surrounded on three sides by mountains visible only periodically, when the ubiquitous fog lifted.

Lubinsky was short and rail thin, with long red hair and a curly red full beard. His parents had been progressive FDR Democrats of Jewish Eastern European extraction who, before they moved west, had been active in the trade-union movement in New York. After graduating from high school, Lubinsky, entranced by his relatives' World War II stories, enlisted in the army, serving a tour of duty in Vietnam with the 101st Airborne. The year he served, 1968, marked the height of U.S. ground troop involvement and saw the greatest number of fatalities of the war: 16,589 killed in action. Lubinsky quickly became disenchanted with America's presence in the country: "My unit was stationed in Wei, and as we marched through the city somebody had made sure that the Vietnamese had lined the streets to welcome us. But I had been raised on those Walter Cronkite documentaries on the liberation of Paris and these people sure didn't look like they were being liberated."

Lubinsky came back injured and heartsick—only fourteen of his two-hundred-strong company had made it home alive—and determined to do his part to end the war. He enrolled in the junior college in nearby San Bernadino, a town, sixty miles west of Los Angeles, whose mix of farmers, hippies, soldiers and students gave it a funky frontier-town vibe. Finding the junior college full of soldiers living on the three air force bases in the area base but who were permitted to attend school, Lubinsky started to organize on his own. At an SDS meeting in Stanford, California, he connected with full-time GI Movement organizers. Lubinsky had met Tom in Oceanside during the run-up to the People's Armed Forces Day demonstration in May 1970. Initially impressed with the transplanted New Yorker's cosmopolitan style, Lubinsky's admiration grew as he witnessed Tom's handling of the bomb scare in the Beach Bowl. Before he left Oceanside, Leland made Tom a standing offer to join his chapter of Vietnam Veterans Against the War. Tom and Barbara moved into Leland's house, a ramshackle structure built by his grandfather that stood in back of the family's hardware store, and assumed a small room with drab green walls, a large window and a raised bed built into the wall.

Another mainstay of the collective was Barry Romo. After graduating from high school in San Bernadino, he had enlisted as second lieutenant and received a Bronze Star. Tom and Barbara arrived in Loma Linda, he had participated in a veterans' march on Washington, D.C., in which he, along with hundreds of other soldiers, threw their medals on the capitol steps. There was also Richie, a surfer boy and jack of all trades, and Mark, a veteran attending the junior college on the GI bill, and his wife and baby. Another married couple, San and Chi Mei, lived in a small house on Leland's property. San's father had been a highly placed general in Chiang Kei-Shek's army in China and had escaped with his family to America after the Communist revolution in 1949. Rebelling against his upbringing, San was now a committed Maoist, dogmatic and zealous as only the converted son of the ruling class can be. Maoism was the group's guiding philosophy, and they took care to guard against anti-revolutionary thought patterns through continual self- and group-criticism, a practice that melded Catholic confessional with the informant culture spawned in Stalin's Soviet

Union and Mao's China. "We were sort of sucked into the Red Guard mentality," said Lubinsky. "The collective had strings of self- and other criticism sessions. They could last all weekend. It was a very unpleasant experience in retrospect."

A parade of friends, movement people and squatters constantly moved in and out of the Lubinsky house, and the group rented a movement house on San Bernardino's main drag. The Loma Linda collective's attempts to organize the airmen stationed at the nearby Norton Air Force Base, the March Air Reserve Base and George Air Force Base were not as effective as the Green Machine's efforts in raising the consciousness of Camp Pendleton Marines. The airmen dropped bombs from thousands of feet, making them more physically and emotionally removed from the deaths they caused. But there was still much else to do. The collective saw themselves as the nucleus of a broader movement forming ties with student radicals, the remnants of the once-active Communist Party in the area and local unions, specifically the carpenters' union, whose members labored at factories constructing La-Z-Boy chairs and mobile homes. Lubinsky's collective also organized demonstrations and peace marches, leafleted the community college, published a newspaper—the *March Beacon*—and ran a food and babysitting co-op out of a movement house they rented on E Street, the main drag of San Bernardino. It was Tom's SDS Citywide Movement in action. The community was receptive to their efforts. "You could give out five hundred leaflets [at any given time] and get fifteen hundred to your demonstration," said Lubinsky. "That was the zeitgeist."

For the first time in years, Tom, now in a committed, if often turbulent, relationship with Barbara, began to feel that he was living something approaching a normal life. "It had been four years of non-stop action," he said. "Lots of hookups and fevered, quick relationships, going from there to there. I was tired of being just a movement person." Tom got a job at the mobile home factory and developed a love of the California car culture, even becoming a decent mechanic. Tom took pride in the fact that, with the help of Richie and a book, he could take apart a Volkswagen piece by piece and reassemble it.

Barbara had also found a measure of peace in Loma Linda. Although still nursing the psychic wounds from her ill-fated romance with Jurgo, she found something close to contentment in Lubinsky's collective. "Tommy and I were very attached and work very well together. We were good strategists; we respected each other's ideas. As a rebound situation for me it worked because I was very motivated to accomplish whatever I could in this world," she said.

Mornings, after a scramble to use the one bathroom in the ramshackle house, the collective would eat breakfast together as Barbara played Otis Redding's cover of the Rolling Stones hit "I Can't Get No Satisfaction" on the phonograph, after which they started their day, which often consisted of "meeting after meeting after meeting," according to Lubinsky. In the evening, after dinner, they would sit on the porch, drink tequila and sing Old Left anthems. Particularly in demand was Tom's performance of *The Internationale*, rendered with a country-western twang to the accompaniment of his banjo. On Sunday nights they would gather around the radio to listen to the "Dr. Demento Show."

In September 1971, San, who had assumed an unofficial leadership role in the collective, proposed that a delegation travel to Los Angeles to lodge a complaint with the Chinese embassy regarding a dissident who had been jailed in Taipei. San himself could not make the trip because it would jeopardize his student visa, but he selected a small group to go in his place and appointed Tom its leader. "Brook no excuses," were San's parting instructions "Don't let them off the hook." Leaving San, Chi Mei, Lubinsky and Barbara behind in Loma Linda, Tom and his group drove down to Los Angeles. Gaining an audience with the embassy counsel, Tom forcefully but politely delivered the group's message, which the counsel received in a diplomatic but non-committal fashion. Tom, knowing he had been ignored but not seeing the usefulness of pressing the point further, withdrew with his delegation.

On their return, San immediately called Tom aside to debrief him. When Tom explained what had happened, San grew cold. "Did you demand that this man be freed."

"Yes."

"But did you refuse to leave until they had agreed to free him?"

"No, I didn't," Tom replied, describing the situation and defending his rationale.

San was implacable. "You failed at your task—the collective sent you to go and demand his freedom and you just asked questions."

"Well, San," Tom retorted, "I don't see it that way. I did everything I could do in the most effective way possible. If you feel like we should go back we can."

"No, there's no going back," San replied somewhat cryptically.

"I'm sorry you feel that way," said Tom. He was disconcerted by the encounter but assumed it would blow over. Still, it was a relief to take off with Barbara the next day for a planned vacation to San Diego to visit Green Machine founder Kent Hudson who was teaching at UC San Diego. After five days of socializing and lounging in the sun, the couple returned. It was immediately clear that something was very wrong as the collective greeted Tom with cold stares. Befuddled, Tom approached Lubinsky, who could barely look him in the eye. "Thing's around here have changed, Tommy," he said.

Alarmed, Tom approached the other housemates. Those who weren't actively hostile seemed acutely uncomfortable but none would give him a reasonable explanation for the dramatic change in atmosphere. This awkward situation stretched on for several days until a sheepish Lubinsky pulled Tom aside. "It's not going to work out with you staying here," he said, barely able to look Tom in the eye. When Tom pushed for an explanation, he could get nothing but variations on that phrase.

Enlightenment came later that day, when San convened a meeting of the collective around the kitchen table. By now, Tom was feeling thoroughly gaslighted. Barbara, however was livid. "What the hell is going on here?" she demanded. "You've got to tell us what we did," Tom implored.

As San looked on, silent, each member of the collective took their turn pointing out Tom's failings as a revolutionary and as a person. They cited his bourgeois leanings and insufficient revolutionary fervor. But mainly they indicted Tom's "commandist" tendencies, in other words, the arrogance that had been brought to his attention by friends, lovers and colleagues on both coasts over the last three years. Tom struggled to defend himself, torn, as always, between sincere remorse and indignation of one who thinks himself truly ill used. "Yeah, I'm arrogant, if being arrogant means I think I have the right to make suggestions that are more weighty than the next person's suggestion," Tom said. "I'm a good organizer. I know I've made waves but I've also tried to improve."

Now San spoke up for the first time. "All the people feel that you've been insufficiently revolutionary and so we will cast you out and Barbara too." He decreed that Tom and Barbara be purged from the collective and from Lubinsky's house.

Tom was devastated but defiant. "We became the people on whom everyone could project their feelings of inadequacy and frustration. We had come in from the outside with no real friends in the area, it was so easy to throw us out without alienating anyone else." Barbara, knowing that Tom had endured a similar purge at the hands of the women's collective in Berkeley a year earlier, was incensed. "It was the same shtick, and as far as I could see wasn't really true," she said. "When we were at Leland's we were studying Chairman Mao's Red book. There was a lot of "self-crit" and a real misunderstanding of what the Cultural Revolution was about and it wasn't until later, when we were in China, that we understood how devastating it was to the Chinese people. You could see it was silly at the time. What did they want from Tom? It was about him being a white male and dominant but his intentions were always good. He so believed in the movement that he would do self criticisms and . . . try to find out about what his failings were." Tom and Barbara packed up their belongings and left Lubinsky's "glorified shack," as Barbara affectionately called it, and a life they had come to love.

CHAPTER TWELVE

The State of California vs. Angela Y. Davis

ANGELA DAVIS, 1972

At dawn on February 18, 1972, Angela, entering her thirteenth month of imprisonment, was getting dressed in her cell, absentmindedly listening to the transistor radio. Angela's legal team continued to grow. Veteran civil rights lawyer Leo Branton was now attorney of record, backed up by Moore and Doris Brin Walker, a longtime CPUSA member who had represented defendants before the House Un-American Activities Committee. Additionally, Angela herself had won the right to act as an attorney on her own behalf.

By this time, the defense team had successfully convinced presiding judge James Arnason to change the trial venue from Marin—where the well-respected judge Harold Haley had been killed and where Assistant District Attorney Gary Thomas, now permanently paralyzed still lived—to San Jose. Much of the Davis family, including Fania, her newborn daughter, Eisa, Sallye and Frank, when he could find time to leave the garage he ran in Birmingham, would spend the duration of the trial there as guests of Aptheker, her husband, Jack, and young son, Josh. The National United Committee to Free Angela Davis and All Political Prisoners (NUCFAD) had rented headquarters nearby.

Now, as Angela waited for the matron to take her to the van that would transport her to the courthouse, she heard a news report came over the radio: The California Supreme Court had abolished the death penalty. Minutes later, Margaret Burnham entered the cell, giddy with joy. "This is the one day I wouldn't mind being on San Quentin's Death Row," Angela exclaimed as the two friends embraced. "There must be a carnival going on over there."

The ramifications of the California Supreme Court's decision for Angela's case were monumental: Whatever the outcome of the trial, she would not die in a California gas chamber. Neither would the two surviving Soledad Brothers, Ruchell Magee and John Cluchette, and those who had participated in the August 7 shootout. Angela was so relieved for herself and for her comrades that it took a while for her to comprehend that Burnham was now saying something about a bail hearing.

"What kind of a bail hearing?" Angela asked.

Burnham looked at her friend with amazement.

"Angela, the death penalty has been abolished. Don't you realize that this undercuts the whole legal basis for Judge Arnason's denial of bail? He has nowhere to turn now. He has to let you out!"

Taking it all in, Angela laughed freely for what felt like the first time since she had heard the news of Jonathan's death.

On the evening of February 23, after fevered efforts to raise the $102,500 bail over a holiday weekend (Aretha Franklin, who had offered to post bail when Angela was first arrested, was out of the country and could not be reached) and overcome a host of objections from District Attorney Albert Harris, Angela walked out of the Marin jail wearing slacks and a black sweater, her hands uncuffed. At the sight of her, a jubilant cry rose from the throng of supporters that had gathered in front of the courthouse, among them Fania, Franklin and Kendra.

At Bettina Aptheker's home, Angela was greeted by local and national staffers from NUCFAD. Immediately, she met with the Chicano Defense Organization. Santa Clara County, where the trial would be held, had a large Hispanic population and its support would be crucial during the trial. Before returning to meet the supporters who had crowded into the house to greet her, Angela called her parents in Birmingham.

"Knowing the deep personal pain they had suffered and their complete devotion to the fight, I felt happier for their sake than I did for my own," she later wrote. Sallye left Birmingham immediately to be with her daughter.

Angela picked her mother up at the airport the next day and the two attended a small dinner hosted by General Secretary of CPUSA, Gus Hall. "After dinner, when I had finished one glass of champagne—all I dared to drink—I toasted practically everyone who was present." Spontaneously, the group began to sing *The Internationale,* the anthem of communists and socialists the world over, followed by "Lift Ev'ry Voice and Sing," the unofficial anthem of African Americans. As they sang, the black waiters serving the group joined in.

On February 28, jury selection for *The People of the State of California vs. Angela Y. Davis* began in a snug courtroom of the Superior Court of Santa Clara County in San Jose. Along with her lawyers and legal investigators, Angela's team included two psychologists observing the voir dire to evaluate prospective jurors. The group had grown so large that they required an L-shaped table to accommodate them. The defense team began the trial on an auspicious note: The day before, the two surviving Soledad Brothers, Fleeta Drumgo and John Cluchette, were found not guilty on all charges relating to the killing of guard John Mills, the murder had set in motion the chain of events that brought Angela to trial.

Despite the best efforts of the defense team, an all-white jury was sworn in on March 14. But before the trial could begin, an event took place that would set the dramatic—at times almost melodramatic—tone of the proceedings. The court received a call from an eighteen-year-old girl whose mother had been seated as a juror. Brought into the chambers, the somewhat hysterical young woman insisted that her mother harbored an intense bias against black people and had deliberately misrepresented her views on racial matters in order to secure a place on the jury. "God help Angela Davis if my mother is on that jury!" the girl cried. Although the juror in question vehemently denied the charges, she was reluctantly convinced to recuse herself.

On March 27, Assistant Attorney General Albert Harris, delivered the prosecution's opening statement. Since Angela had not been at the Marin courthouse at the time of the escape attempt, Harris' case would, of necessity, be circumstantial. It was therefore essential that the prosecution ascribe reason for Angela to have involved herself in the conspiracy. "[Angela's] basic motive was not to free political prisoners but to free the one prisoner that she loved," Harris said. "The basic motive for the crime was the same motive underlying hundreds of criminal cases across the United States every day. That motive was not abstract. It was not founded on any need, real or imagined, for prison reform. It was not founded on a desire for social justice. It was founded simply on the passion that she felt for George Jackson."

Harris had an earnest manner but no gift for oratory. His statement took a full day. The defense's opening statement was scheduled for the next, to be delivered by Angela. But arriving at the Santa Clara Civic Center the next morning, Angela and her team learned that, in an eerie echo of the Marin County shootout, three prisoners in the men's jail located in the complex had taken guards hostages in an escape bid. The episode ended with a San Quentin guard shooting and killing one of the prisoners. Court was cancelled for the day, leaving the defense to ponder whether or not to request a mistrial in light of the escape attempt. But after much discussion, it was decided that any contamination of the jury pool was preferable to a mistrial that would mean starting the entire process from scratch.

The next morning, Angela approached the podium located by the prosecutor's table. After arranging her notes and stealing a glance at Harris, Angela began her address to the jury in the pleasant academic manner with which she had delivered scores of lectures to her students at UCLA, speaking in measured cadences and smiling often at the jury.

After flatly denying any complicity in the conspiracy, Angela listed in detail her political activities and associations in order to establish her bona fides as an activist whose goal was to help establish, by legal means, "the creation of a movement encompassing millions of people, indeed the majority of the people in the United States today, a movement which will ultimately usher in a more humane, socialist society." Angela then addressed

Harris' theory that she had participated in the plot spurred by an obsession with George. Far from denying her attachment to him, Angela affirmed her "love and affection" for George and mocked Harris' portrait of her as an "evil, sinister creature pushed to the brink of disaster by ungovernable emotions and passions." "Members of the jury," Angela said, "this is utterly fantastic, this is utterly absurd. Yet it is understandable that Mr. Harris would like to take advantage of the fact that I am a woman—and women in this society are supposed to act only with the dictates of their emotions and passions. This is a symptom of the male chauvinism which prevails in our society."

At this point, Harris was perhaps starting to perceive the tactical error he'd made in presenting Angela as a woman with a fatal attraction for George Jackson. Apart from the fact that her demeanor seemed to refute any such notion, the introduction of the theme of feminism—then still widely referred to as "women's liberation"—could not have been more timely. Weeks before the case had started, *Ms. Magazine* had debuted on newsstands and had made an impression on at least one juror, forewoman Mary Timothy, a housewife with a liberal bent. The magazine, founded by Gloria Steinem, was seen by many as a novelty item that, in the words of television news anchor Harry Reasoner, would "run out of things to say" within six months. But those who counted out the magazine underestimated the power of the movement, which had been gaining legitimacy since the late '60s, when black and white chafed against being relegated to the roles of secretaries and sexual playthings in the supposedly radical organizations to which they had devoted themselves. That movement had since made significant headway in raising consciousness among women across America, including many who were considerably more mainstream. Angela's firsthand experiences with the Black Power movement and of being incarcerated had sensitized her to the issue. And tactically, invoking it was an effective way to establish a link with the eight white women jurors with whom she otherwise had virtually nothing in common.

Continuing her statement, Angela stoutly denied any knowledge of Jonathan's possession of her guns. She defended her ownership of such weapons as a necessary means of self-defense not only for herself but also for all black Americans. Angela told the court of her experiences growing up in Birmingham and about the hundreds of death threats. "I was convinced with good reason that I needed some sort of protection if I intended to live out my years," Angela said.

She then addressed why she had fled instead of turning herself in after she had been indicted. "The evidence will show that I had good reason to make myself unavailable at that time," Angela said. "The evidence will show that I had good reason to fear police violence should I voluntarily submit to the authorities at that time. The evidence will show that at many times in the past black and Chicano people—particularly political activists—have been victims of police violence. The evidence will show that I had ample evidence to fear unjust treatment by the courts of California, that I had reason to fear the prospect of many months of incarceration without bail, an eventual trial before an all-white jury, therefore not composed of my peers."

After speaking for two hours, Angela allowed herself to close with a dramatic flourish. "Members of the jury, . . . [w]hen you have sat patiently, almost to the point of exhaustion and will have heard all sides of the heated contest which will unfold in this courtroom—when you have sat in calm deliberation—we know—we have the utmost confidence—that your verdict will be the only verdict that the evidence and justice demand in this case. We are confident that this case will terminate with the pronouncement of two words—Not guilty!"

Six weeks later, Harris concluded the state's case after calling 104 witnesses and presenting 200 exhibits. That evening the defense team met to discuss the day's events. These nightly sessions often became heated free-for-alls that lasted into the early hours of the morning as the team argued strategy. But even by those standards, this evening's discussion was particularly intense.

As promised, Harris had presented his case in exhaustive detail. He called witnesses who placed Angela and Jonathan together in a motel, visiting George in prison and renting the yellow van used in the getaway attempt days before the incident. (The defense vigorously contested the accuracy of these identifications.) Harris especially stressed that on the day of the shootout, Angela had arrived at the San Francisco airport appearing to be in a great hurry, buying a last-minute ticket to Los Angeles. Further, Harris presented a scrap of paper found on Jonathan's body that contained a phone number corresponding to a pay phone at the airport. But the heart of Harris' case was the cache of letters between Angela and Jackson. Prevailing over vociferous objections from the defense, Harris concluded his case by reading lengthy passages from the letters, which contained a potent mix of the political and the personal. "The night after I saw you in court for the first time in months, I dreamt . . . we were together fighting the pigs, winning. We were learning to know each other," Harris read to the jury in an incongruous monotone.

In another letter, Angela continued an ongoing exchange between the two about the place of black women in the movement. She gently rebutted George's contention that women, by seeking to protect their husbands and sons from harm by urging them to be submissive, only played into the divide-and-conquer strategy of the "barbarous capitalist society." The solution to this dilemma, Angela wrote, "is not to persuade the Black woman to relax her reins on the Black male but to translate the 'be a good boy' syndrome into a 'take the sword in hand' attitude. . . . [Women] too must pick up the sword" and alongside their men fight "this war which has been declared on us." The letter continued in that analytical vein—a treatise more than a love letter, its gist being that "Women's liberation in the revolution is inseparable from the liberation of the male." Toward the end of the letter, Angela wrote: "Jonathan and I have made a truce. As long as I try to combat my tendencies to remind him of his youth, he will try to combat his male chauvinism." Although that letter contained none of the amorous heat Harris had promised in his opening statement, in others, militant rhetoric was interspersed with passages clearly written by a woman who had "instantly and unexpectedly fallen in love" for the first time and who was experiencing "high tides of unanticipated joy."

Writing to George from her prison cell, Angela confided: "Something inside you has managed to smash through the fortress I long ago erected around my soul. . . . If you knew what a hard time I'm having tapping out these few words—my mind wanders into other worlds full of you . . . Today, today, though time seemed short, eight hours but a moment, it was a moment containing a happy, living eternity. Temporarily, I'll say goodby [*sic*], goodnight. I'm going over to the other cell, to rejoin you. Love you, love you with love even more unbounded, even more unconquerable. Your life-long wife."

But many passages Harris read out loud did not suggest a woman planning a desperate jailbreak, a fact he seemed to realize he was in the process of reading them. "We have learned from our revolutionary ancestors that no individual act or response can seize the scepter of the enemy." Also, from a letter Angela wrote to George after learning that a comrade had been found dead on the side of a road with two bullets in his head: "Accepting the murder of a comrade in struggle is not easy. Our first instinct is rage—to return the attack even if it be blind. We must learn to plan the attack, gear it towards the total annihilation of the monster and not just stick pins in the sole of his feet."

But Harris gained confidence as he read another selection, emphasizing every word to make sure the jury realized its full import: "Frustrations, aggressions cannot be repressed indefinitely. Eventual explosion must be expected. . . . For the Black female the solution is not to become less aggressive, not to lay down the gun, but learn to set the sights correctly, aim accurately, squeeze rather than jerk and not be spoiled by the damage. We have to learn how to rejoice when the pig's blood is spilled."

Shortly after this reading, Harris rested his case.

Now, Angela's team had to decide how to present its defense—or whether to present one at all. Throughout the trial, their strategy had been to stipulate that the prosecution was correct on several of the most potentially damaging points of evidence in order to increase their legitimacy in the eyes of the jury. They freely admitted that Angela had purchased the weapons that were used on August 7. Angela had, in fact, signed an autograph for the admiring proprietor of a pawnshop where she purchased a shotgun and a box of shells just days before the escape attempt. The team also conceded that Angela had an emotionally intense relationship with George Jackson.

Concluding that the prosecution's case was weak at best, the defense team decided to present a "pin-point" defense. Accordingly, they called only twelve witnesses, who were meant to establish that Angela was in Los Angeles on August 5, thus refuting the prosecution's eyewitness who had placed her with Jonathan at a garage with the "getaway" van. Cumulatively, the witnesses presented a coherent narrative detailing Angela's movements in the hours before and after the shootout.

Ellen Broms, a friend of Angela, Franklin and Kendra's, testified that on the evening of August 7, Franklin and Angela paid her a visit in her Los Angeles house. After dinner, the three spent the evening listening to records and playing Scrabble. At 10:30 p.m., Broms testified, Kendra called, urgently telling them to turn on the news. At 11 p.m. the shootout at the Marin County Civic Center led the news. This, Broms said, was how Angela learned of Jonathan's death. Angela became so distraught that Broms gave her a sedative, and both Angela and Franklin spent the night in her house.

The next morning, Angela and Franklin read a more detailed report in the newspaper and there saw the photographs of Jonathan in the courtroom hallway posing for the camera and holding a shotgun. The carbine looked similar to one Angela owned, both agreed. The newspaper article also mentioned a shotgun used in the shootout. In Broms' account, Angela told Franklin that she had given a shotgun to Jonathan days before, instructing him to take it to the headquarters of the Soledad Brothers Defense Committee for security reasons. Now, fearing the worst, Angela and Franklin left Broms' house.

Angela's ex-roommate and member of the Che-Lumumba Club, Valerie Mitchell, then took the stand. Mitchell testified that on August 1, Jonathan visited her house, which served as headquarters for the Soledad Brothers Defense Committee, asking to use the mimeograph machine. In the hallway closet of the house, Angela, who had lived with Mitchell for a time, had stored some of her weapons. While Jonathan printed leaflets, Mitchell left to run some errands. When she returned, Mitchell said, Jonathan was gone.

On the morning of August 8, according to Mitchell, Angela and Franklin showed up at her house in evident distress. Were the weapons still in the closet? they asked. When Mitchell said she had no idea, the two looked for themselves. Two carbines and a Browning automatic, along with ammunition and clips corresponding to the munitions used in the escape attempt, were missing.

"Oh shit!" said Franklin.

"Oh no," said Angela.

The two then left. The next time Mitchell saw Angela, she testified, she was a prisoner in the Marin County Jail.

Fleeta Drumgo, one of the two remaining Soledad Brothers, was the last witness for the defense. Drumgo testified that although he had occupied a cell adjacent to James McClain in San Quentin and had frequent contact with Jackson, he had heard of no plan to take hostages in the Marin courthouse.

On Friday, June 2, 1972, Judge Arnason charged the jury and they retired to deliberate. Leaving the courthouse and stepping into the sunlight, Angela saw that a large crowd of family, friends and supporters, their children and pets in tow, had gathered to await the verdict. The atmosphere was festive, as picnic blankets were spread and impromptu games of football were organized. Angela and her team drove to a restaurant for lunch but no sooner had they entered the bistro than a call came in for Angela. It was Fania, calling from Arnason's chambers. The judge wanted to speak with her immediately. Angela was shocked; was it possible that a verdict had been reached so quickly? At the courthouse, Fania passed the phone to Arnason. "Don't leave," he said tersely. "Stay there until I contact you again," and abruptly hung up.

Before Angela and her party could even begin to speculate on the reason for the call, plain-clothed policemen entered the restaurant and took up positions around the room. Angela's group was then ushered into the back dining room and the door was locked behind them. Minutes later, Howard Moore arrived, out of breath and clearly alarmed. The public relations man for the sheriff's department accompanied him. "There's been a hijacking," said Moore, "and they think the hijackers want you to come with them."

In the courthouse, the judge asked Angela to stay put until the problem was resolved. As she waited, Branton and Walker managed to obtain details from an FBI agent. Apparently, four African American men armed with explosives had commandeered a plane in Seattle. They then delivered their demands over the cockpit radio: When the plane landed in San Francisco, Angela was to be waiting on the runway wearing a white dress with a half million dollars and five parachutes in her possession.

Angela breathed a sigh of relief: She was wearing a red dress.

The press pounced on the story "Hijackers Demand Angela," screamed the front page of the *San Jose News*. It wasn't until early evening that the real story unfolded. There had, indeed, been a hijacking, but the men, who had been apprehended without injuries to anyone involved, were stymied when questioned about Angela. She had apparently not factored into the hijacker's plot; her name had not, in fact, been mentioned at all. Someone, somewhere, had dished up a final dollop of drama for the proceedings.

That episode put to rest, Angela and her family resumed what, other circumstances, would have been a carefree family reunion. As Saturday deliberations concluded without a verdict, a friend threw a barbecue to which the entire neighborhood came, turning it into a full-on block party. As Ben, who played defensive back for the Cleveland Browns, started a game of touch football, Angela, Burnham and Aptheker began to jump rope double-dutch style as they had as children in Brooklyn. The sight was so infectious that Angela's father, Moore and Branton, throwing off their usual dignified personas, joined in. As the children realized there was a celebrity in their midst, they crowded around Angela, clamoring for her autograph.

As they adjourned Saturday evening, the jury took the unusual step of asking to carry on deliberations on Sunday, raising hopes—along with fears—that a verdict was at hand.

On Sunday morning, Angela was chatting with Branton when Moore burst through the door. He had made his way from his apartment to Angela's at a dead run. A verdict had been reached. Dressing quickly, Angela sped to the court. After the elation of the previous night, her mood plummeted. It was hard to grasp that almost two years after Jonathan had been gunned down outside the Marin courthouse, after eighteen months of imprisonment and a three-month trial that a conclusion to her ordeal was at hand. The optimism that Angela had felt evaporated and was replaced by terror and the prospect of a guilty verdict.

Outside the courtroom, Branton, trying to ease the tension, remarked that they would know the verdict immediately once they entered the courtroom by the expressions on the jury's faces, particularly that of the forewoman, Mary Timothy. By this time, Angela was trembling. Sallye, even more petrified than her daughter, refused to even enter the courtroom. With great difficulty, the family convinced her to join them in the spectator seats, already packed with reporters.

Angela and her lawyers hung back until the proceedings were about to begin. Then they made their way to the defense table for the last time. When the jury filed in, Angela scanned their faces. They were all expressionless. Burnham began to cry quietly.

Judge Arnason took his place in front of the court and turned to the jury.

"Ms. Timothy, has the jury reached a verdict?"

"Yes, your honor. We have," responded Timothy, handing a packet of papers to the clerk, who delivered them to the judge. Arnason then handed the papers back to the clerk, who read the verdict.

On the first count of murder: "Not guilty."

Angela heard sobs and realized they were coming from Franklin.

On the second count of kidnapping: "Not guilty." Franklin began to cry even harder.

Preparing to hear the verdict on the last count, conspiracy, Angela grabbed the hands of Kendra and Burnham. At the clerk's third "not guilty," Angela and her friends screamed with joy as they embraced. She was free.

CHAPTER THIRTEEN

The Fact Book

TOM HURWITZ, 1972–1973

After being expelled from the Loma Linda collective in the fall of 1971, Tom and Barbara, exiles from the movement, took temporary refuge with a friend, Judy Briscoe, and her young daughter in Redlands. One morning at breakfast, Briscoe reading the paper, asked, "Have you been following the Gary Lawton case?"

Six months before, on April 2, two white police officers, Paul Teel and Larry Christianson, responded to a burglary call from a Riverside house. When they emerged from the patrol car, shotgun fire from the bushes killed them both. Days later, police arrested Gary Lawton, a black ex-Marine who had become a high-profile community activist in Riverside after the murder of Martin Luther King Jr. Two other African Americans were also arrested: Nehemiah Jackson, a divinity student at a nearby college, and Larrie Gardner, a street kid from the East Side. There had been several police shootings of African Americans in the weeks leading up to the murders, and it was widely suspected in the racially polarized town that these cops had been killed in retribution. To the black and activist communities, however, it was clear that the three men had been arrested in a rush to justice and that Lawton, in particular, had been targeted because of his status as a troublemaker.

Tom had heard about the case and had participated in a demonstration supporting Lawton. But he had no interest in getting more deeply involved. There were, he thought, plenty of movement lawyers and para-legals to work with political prisoners.

After spending a few months as guests of Briscoe, the couple moved to an apartment in Riverside. Tom joined the carpenters union, a "good little local," as he described it, controlled by young lefties, Chicano organizers and the remnants of the Communist Party. Instead of fighting for the working class, Tom and Barbara joined their number. Tom learned a craft, taking great pride in becoming a master carpenter, and brought in extra money working as an artist's model. Barbara got a job as a teacher's aide for the local school district. In weathering the shock of the Loma Linda expulsion, they became closer than ever.

In March of 1972, Peggy, with whom Leo had been living since 1963, died from thyroid cancer. Leo, devastated, began filming a tribute to her titled *Dialogue with a Woman Departed*. He called Tom, urging him to return to New York to help him with the project.

Tom, was ready to go. He couldn't see being a carpenter in a backwater California town for the rest of his life. Nor, he had come to realize, did he want to make political organizing his life's work. "I was sick and tired of relying on the movement for my identity," Tom said. "Having a place in the world meant something to me. It was putting too much on the movement to give meaning to my life. If an organization was in trouble and I couldn't solve it I still was dependent upon it because it provided me with legitimacy. Hitting my mid-twenties, I needed a profession." That profession, he realized, was cinematography.

Tom now had a choice to make: He could head to L.A. and use his connections there to break into feature films or he could move back East and apprentice with his father to build a career shooting documentaries. Barbara, a California girl, favored returning to Los Angeles but she could see that Tom was leaning toward New York. The day she'd reconnected with Tom, Barbara had a premonition that she was going to make a family with this man. If Tom was willing to start that family with her, she was willing to move to New York. Accordingly, they quit their jobs, gave notice to their landlord, and began a round of farewell parties. One night, they found themselves at a fundraising benefit for the Committee to Defend Gary Lawton. Lawton's wife, Chukia, an intense, petite woman with a tall Afro, gave an eloquent speech on her husband's behalf. Afterward, she pulled aside Tom and Barbara, whom she had met briefly at other functions. "We're in real trouble," Chukia told them urgently. Lawton's lawyer, Johnny Cochran, whom she described in scathing terms, had been devoting little or no attention to the case. Worse, the defense coffers were bare.

"Wait a minute—haven't the Angela Davis people been supporting you?" Tom asked.

"Not really," Chukia replied, explaining that the CPUSA had diverted the funds raised for Lawton's cause to Davis' high-profile murder case, which was also approaching its trial date. Now, only forty days before Lawton's trial was to begin, there was no money to mount a defense.

Moved by Chukia's dedication, the couple quickly conferred. Tom knew some lawyers from his GI work, and Barbara's father, an ACLU attorney, could certainly provide some leads. How hard could it be to set Lawton up with pro bono counsel? At the end of the party, Tom told Chukia, "We're leaving in a week but I know some lawyers in L.A. and at least I can put you in touch with them."

But securing a lawyer willing to take on such a mammoth project without compensation proved more difficult than Tom and Barbara had anticipated. After two weeks of an intensive search, they found David Epstein, a lawyer in his early thirties with an intense commitment to progressive causes. Epstein said he'd be willing to take on the case, but only if they could find another lawyer to work with him. They embarked on another search and found John Mitchell, a very green but game recent graduate from UC Santa Cruz Law School.

Epstein's first move was to get a three-month continuance. "I think we can do this," he told Tom and Barbara. "But it isn't the sort of thing you do alone. I need a real defense committee that will work on the case. I need a commitment from people to help and to work with us." Again, the two conferred. That evening, Tom placed a long-distance call to Leo in New York. "We'll be home in six months," he said.

Tom and Barbara set to work. At the top of their list was cutting ties with the dead weight that was the CPUSA defense team. At a meeting with the Communist functionaries, Tom laid it out. "Look, we're weeks from trial. This woman's husband is going to go to jail for the rest of his life and we're not going to be able to support him because all the money is supporting Angela Davis. We're all for Sister Angela, but we joined to support Gary Lawton; it's not happening. I move that we vote out the steering committee and vote in a new group of people who are going to do the job."

Be careful what you wish for, Tom mused days later. Early on, Epstein had filed a discovery motion. The documents named in the motion arrived within the week—in a truck containing ten thousand pages of police reports and over one thousand hours of taped interviews amassed by Riverside police and prosecutors. The only thing to do, Tom decided, was to start from scratch. Tom and Barbara were now running the show, and their collaborative powers came to the fore. Renting an office on Riverside's Main Street, Tom headed up the research team tasked with the daunting job of creating a timeline of the evening in question. Volunteers worked round the clock, wading through reports and transcribing tapes. As months passed, the team, composed of students, activists and paralegals, grew in number. Many of them crashed in Tom and Barbara's small yellow clapboard house in which they now lived.

Barbara accompanied Chukia as she spoke at cocktail parties thrown by moneyed progressives up and down the West Coast. Barbara also arranged for Chukia to lecture in union halls, church basements and other venues where Chukia's talks often moved listeners to tears. "She was one of our greatest assets," said Barbara. "She was so charismatic. If you loved her you couldn't believe her husband was guilty." Barbara also spearheaded the fundraising effort that enabled the operation to continue, organizing rummage sales, garage sales, car washes and door-to-door leafleting.

Meanwhile, Tom and Epstein were piecing together the case. "The first thing Epstein did was to visit the crime scene with Hurwitz," wrote Ben Bradlee Jr., the son of *Washington Post* editor Ben Bradlee, in his book about the case, *The Ambush Murders*. Just from the physical logistics of the crime scene, it didn't look promising for Lawton. "At the end of our walk, we looked at each other and shook in our shoes. We knew there was no way we were going to win this case. We were scared shitless. . . . They had an airtight case." OK, Tom thought. The guy is not innocent but he still deserves a fair trial.

Lawton, "blunt, intensely proud, uncompromising," according to Bradlee, did nothing to help his own case. Epstein concluded that their best shot at winning the case was to create reasonable doubt in the minds of the jurors by finding an alternate suspect. To that end, he hired a private detective who, convinced of Lawton's innocence, worked for half his usual fee.

The most damning testimony, to Epstein's mind, would come from a troubled teenager named Sally Harris. Romantically involved with one of the defendants, she was the only person who put the three accused men together on the night of the shooting. But poring over Harris' statements and her testimony before the grand jury, Barbara realized that the young girl's story just didn't add up. Sally Harris was fourteen years old at the beginning of the trial—a runaway and a drug user who attended school only sporadically. Considered unmanageable by her parents, she had served time in the city's Juvenile Hall. In 1970, she fell in love with Larrie Gardner, became pregnant and, under pressure from her parents, underwent an abortion. She had moved in with Gardner days before the murders.

Three days after the murders, amid a police roundup of anyone who could conceivably have been involved in or had knowledge of the crime, Harris was arrested and placed in the city's Juvenile Hall. Pent up in a tiny cell, the claustrophobic girl tried in vain to attract the attention of the guards, banging on the cell door and yelling at the top of her lungs. Finally, she got the ear of the matron. Harris told prosecutors that Larrie Hall bragged to her about having "blown away a couple of pigs." Under close questioning, she said that although she did not think Gardner had been involved in the shootings, he did own a double-barreled shotgun. She also picked out the other defendants from a book of mug shots, saying she had seen them in nearby Bordwell Park on the night of the killings. As the police continued to question Harris, she grew to enjoy the attention—

up until they arrested her for conspiracy to commit murder, accusing her of phoning in the bogus robbery report that had set the chain of events into action.

To Barbara, it was clear that Harris, terrified and desperate, had told the police what they wanted to hear just to get the hell out of prison. Afterward, shut up in a facility for juvenile delinquents, she had recanted her testimony at every opportunity. "If you really read the transcripts, she was saying, 'Look-it, you guys are crazy—you don't really believe this happened do you?' And they'd say: 'You're lying again. Sally, you're going to end up in prison for the rest of your life if you don't tell the truth.'"

If Harris was given the opportunity to get the real story out, Barbara knew it would hobble the prosecution's largely circumstantial case. But Epstein wasn't convinced and feared that delving further into Harris' story would only buttress the opposition's argument. Finally, Barbara prevailed upon Epstein to make the 50-mile journey to the juvenile center in which the girl was being held.

"It was amazing," Barbara said. "She said: 'Finally someone wants to hear what really happened! I've been losing my mind here for the last nine months!' So she told us the real story. She had been drugged-out that night, she had slept with someone else besides Larrie and was not there when the crime went down. So we got her an attorney, because [the prosecution's] threat was that she was going to end up in prison for the rest of her life if she didn't tell the 'truth' or that she would get charged with perjury if she changed her story. At the trial she was able to say: 'All that I testified at the grand jury was a lie. I never met Gary Lawton in my life. I know Larrie Gardner but he wasn't involved in any murder either and I certainly don't know this other guy and the whole thing was a bunch of lies that the police sort of forced me into creating!'"

On October 20, 1972, the trial began in a courthouse in Indio, California. Due to the extraordinary publicity the case had attracted on the West Coast, it took a month to select the jury of eight women and four men, all of whom were white. Each day in court, Tom sat at the defense table with his "Fact Book"—a bulging loose-leaf notebook with a paisley cover in which all the materials pertaining to the case had been painstakingly compiled and cross-referenced. Every night, the lawyers would use the book to prep the next day's witnesses. Epstein made full use of the data, trying his first felony case forcefully.

The trial lasted for three months. On February 15, 1973, the jury, deliberating for nine days, came back deadlocked. The judge dismissed the jurors and declared a mistrial. Although it fell short of an outright acquittal, the defense team saw this as a huge victory. Tom and Barbara in particular were elated. Before they came on the scene, a guilty verdict had been almost a foregone conclusion. Now, thanks to the work of scores of people who had donated months of their labor under their watch, the tide had turned. The prosecution dropped the charges against the other two defendants and Lawton was freed on bail. It would take two more trials and three more years, but he was eventually found not guilty.

Tom was giddy at the scope of their accomplishment. "Things like this just don't happen in cases. You don't defeat the prosecution on their evidence. . . . They had a key witness who tied everyone together and she turned around and said 'No, they made me say it.' We had the guy who put the weapon in the hands of our client say 'the cop bought me heroin to get me to say it.' The cop who was the key circumstantial person who put him at the scene admitted he was a racist and then admitted that he wanted to kill a [black person] that night more than he wanted to do anything else in his life. This is unheard of. We got a [hung jury] in Indio, California!"

It had been nine months since Tom and Barbara had encountered Chukia at the Riverside cocktail party. Now, handing the overstuffed paisley notebook to the team overseeing the next trial, they left California to begin a new life in New York.

CHAPTER FOURTEEN

The Prince

ELLIOTT ABRAMS, 1972–1980

Elliott met Henry "Scoop" Jackson when he volunteered to work for Bayard Rustin at the 1968 Democratic convention in Chicago. He was dazzled to meet the longtime senator from Washington and a staunchly anti-Communist, pro-Israel Democrat. "On TV he came across as uncharismatic and dull," Elliott said. But in person, "he was a wonderful man, a kind and sweet man." Elliott kept in touch with the senator, and in 1972, as a second-year law student, he joined his chums Daniel Pipes, Alan Keyes and Bill Kristol in trying to get Jackson on the ballot for the upcoming presidential election. For Elliott, that mostly entailed standing in front of supermarkets collecting signatures. Democrat Senator George McGovern, however, secured the nomination and ran against incumbent president Richard Nixon. When Jackson ended his bid, Elliott approached the senator. "If you're running for president again in '76," he said, "I want to come back and work for you."

Graduating from Harvard Law School in 1973, Elliott joined a white-shoe practice in New York. But he found the work deadly dull, and his colleagues unstimulating—especially after moving in Podhoretz's highly charged social circle. "These people don't even read *Commentary*," Elliott incredulously told a friend. In his spare time he continued to write book reviews and articles on politics and foreign affairs. No one at Breed, Abbott and Morgan seemed the slightest bit interested.

Elliott stuck it out for two years. On his twenty-seventh birthday—January 24, 1975—he could stand it no more. "I figured this was as good a day as any to say, 'The hell with it.'" He called Richard Perle, now a staffer for Senator Jackson. In February, Elliott flew down to Washington for a job interview on the senator's staff.

The contrast between the stodgy life at a law firm and life on Capitol Hill became immediately apparent. "I show up at Scoop's office and he couldn't talk to me right then because he had a meeting with the editorial board of the *New Republic*," Elliott said. "And he said 'come on, in the car.' So we go off to the *New Republic*—which was also very exciting for me. . . . And what was so funny to me was that this was not the day I started work, this was just the interview and Jackson was treating me like a member of the staff. So I figured, I am hired!" Elliott returned to New York, gave four weeks' notice to his law firm, then returned to D.C. as assistant counsel to the Permanent Subcommittee on Investigations, of which Jackson was chairman.

Elliott remembers his first day of work. "Dorothy Fosdick, who was his chief foreign policy advisor, said to me: 'There is something you can do today, cover the markup of the committee of this or that.' She gave me a room number and I said, 'Sure, great'—and then I tried to figure out what is a markup and who around here can I ask without embarrassing myself." Elliott caught on fast. Jackson plucked Elliott out of the committee after six months and assigned him to his personal staff.

In February 1975, the month Elliott started with Jackson, the senator announced his second presidential bid with the enthusiastic backing of the New York Democratic conservative set who appreciated Jackson's solid pro-Israel stance and his advocacy on behalf of Soviet Jews trying to leave the Soviet Union. Jackson's candidacy was hobbled, however, by his support of U.S. involvement in Vietnam—especially with Americans watching the images of the fall of Saigon in April 1975 on the nightly news. In May, Jackson bowed out of the race, leaving the field to Jimmy Carter.

In the fall 1976, Daniel Patrick Moynihan announced his run for Democratic Senator for New York. Raised in New York's Hell's Kitchen, Moynihan was both a scholar and a political street fighter who had served as U.S.

Ambassador to the United Nations and India and in the Kennedy and Johnson administrations. Moynihan had attracted national attention in 1965 while serving as Assistant Secretary of Labor to President Johnson when he authored *The Negro Family: The Case for National Action*. The report explored the roots of African American poverty, theorizing that it was largely the lack of two-parent families and dependence on welfare that kept blacks in poverty. That thesis drew scathing attacks from many African Americans organizations and activists (including Angela Davis) who felt that placing the blame on those suffering under poverty took the focus off the real problem: the systemic racism of American society. But Moynihan's thesis appealed to conservative Democrats like Irving Kristol and Podhoretz—who had published his work in *Commentary*. They believed that the post-war devaluation of societal norms and values was leading to a irreversible erosion of American values.

Charles Horner, Jackson's former chief of staff, now working on Moynihan's campaign, introduced Elliott to Moynihan. Impressed by the young man, Moynihan asked Elliott to serve as his campaign manager. Elliott was tempted by the offer. "I said OK—it wasn't my line of work, but Pat thought if you're a well-organized smart person you can learn to be a campaign manager, and I said, 'fine—done, but I have to talk to Scoop.'" It was an uncomfortable conversation. Jackson, still bruised from his loss in the Democratic primaries, was hurt by his protégé's defection.

Elliott joined Moynihan's team and upon Moynihan's election, became special counsel, rising to the position of chief of staff. Soon after the election, Elliott attended one of the parties that Podhoretz and Decter were famous for hosting, drawing literary luminaries like Norman Mailer, Lillian Hellman, Hannah Arndt and Lionel Trilling. This particular gathering turned out to be something of a coming out party for Elliott. At about 10 p.m., Podhoretz clapped his hands to silence the room. "Quiet everybody, we're going to hear from Charles and Elliott about Pat's initial months as a Senator."

Elliott and Horner were caught off guard—Podhoretz had said nothing to them about giving a presentation. "We're standing with our backs to the fireplace and there's this crowd waiting to hear. Charles was great because he began by saying, 'May I say what an honor it is to address the Central Committee.'"

The evening turned out to be notable for another reason. As Elliott was talking to the group, he noticed a young woman in the crowd and recognized her as Rachel Decter, Podhoretz's stepdaughter. "Wow, she's gorgeous," he thought. Since he was dating someone else at the time, that's as far as it went. Elliott also made a vivid, if fleeting, impression on Rachel. "Why don't I marry someone like Elliott Abrams," she mused.

———————

Jimmy Carter was sworn in as president of the United States in January 1977, ousting incumbent Gerald Ford, who had taken office upon Nixon's resignation in August 1974. Carter envisioned an idealistic foreign policy independent of economic or political components, one in which foreign governments would be judged almost solely on the basis of their human rights records. To Elliott and his friends, this concept was beyond unrealistic—it dwelled in Cloud Cuckoo Land and amounted to nothing short of appeasement of non-democratic regimes, which Carter's foreign policy always seemed to favor. Jeane Kirkpatrick of Georgetown University wrote an article, "Dictatorships and Double-Standards," alleging that Carter had turned a blind eye to the misdeeds of communist governments while being over-exacting when it came to American-backed regimes. The conservative Democrats were aghast at what they saw as Carter's pro-Palestinian leanings. But worst of all, Carter seemed to think that the Soviet threat had become irrelevant. To the disciples of Kristol and Podhoretz, the Soviet Union's malign influence was as strong as it had ever been. There was another reason for the their dislike of Carter: Not one significant presidential appointment had been made from their ranks—no insignificant issue to a group highly sensitive to slights. The net result was that Kristol, Podhoretz and Co.'s alienation from the Democrats was fast developing into full-blown estrangement. In 1976, the group launched—or in this case re-launched—another think tank, the Committee for the Present Danger. First formed In the 1950s, it was based in Washington and made up of conservative Democrats and Republicans brought together by their common Cold War fervor. Founding members included Podhoretz, Decter, Donald Rumsfeld, Richard Perle, William Kristol and Richard Pipes.

In the summer of 1979, Elliott resigned from Moynihan's staff to join another high-powered law office, this time in Washington. Although he found it even more unbearable than his last stint as an associate at a big firm, Elliott felt he had no choice: His father was suffering from heart disease and he needed the money and the regular hours that would allow him to return to New York every weekend to be with his family.

But the long commutes turned out to have an upside. Right before Labor Day weekend, Elliott, newly single after the breakup of a relationship, phoned of Rachel Decter. Although she and Elliott had run into each other socially off and on since they had met years earlier, they had not seen each other in many months. "We went out Labor Day weekend and we got engaged at Thanksgiving," Elliott said.

On December 24, 1979, in a move that would ultimately hasten its inevitable decline, the U.S.S.R. invaded Afghanistan. Carter, caught offguard, rapidly revised his calculus of the Soviet threat. Vice President Walter Mondale saw an opportunity to open a channel between the White House and the disaffected Democrats and arranged for a dozen or so of them to meet with Carter at the White House, among them Podhoretz, Kirkpatrick and twenty-nine-year-old Elliott.

"We thought the invasion was a wake-up call for Carter," said Elliott. "Mondale was aware that the Jackson Democrats were playing around with the idea of not supporting Carter. We were very disillusioned. And Mondale thought, let's pull these people in." Elliott, though still at the law firm, was an old hand at Capitol Hill, but joining a select group in the cabinet room to meet with the president was definitely a new and higher level.

"We had about twenty minutes with Mondale first, and he sort of warmed up the crowd cause he knew how to pull on the heartstrings of people who were Democrats," Elliott recounted. Basically he said, 'Look, whatever our differences you've got to be for the President's reelection. The Republicans are moving farther and farther right, they may nominate

Reagan. We're a family here, whatever our spats are.' It was very well done."

The delegation had decided that scholar J. Austin Ranney would lead off for their team. "We had agreed beforehand, he was going to make a nice friendly speech," Elliott said. "Austin said something to the effect of, 'You know, Mr. President, we've had disagreements with you on foreign policy. As you know, some of us have criticized you publicly. But our sense is that's passed and you have a new foreign policy and a new attitude toward the Soviet Union since the invasion of Afghanistan.'"

At that point, Elliott says, Carter broke in, indignantly saying: "'No! I don't! I have one foreign policy. My foreign policy hasn't changed. I don't have two foreign policies!'" The meeting continued, but the tone had been set. "Carter had perfect pitch for everything we *didn't* want to hear and everything that would offend us," said Elliott. Whether he meant to do it, I don't know, but he did. Within fifteen minutes about everyone in that room was voting for Reagan."

For Elliott and his friends, that meeting, for all intents and purposes, marked the end of their identification with the Democratic Party. "The feeling was, 'OK, fine, and sayonara,'" Elliott said. "The consensus was that this was a disaster and we were going to go for the Republicans." Jeane Kirkpatrick said, "We were really treated quite badly by the Democratic Party and meanwhile we [were] bombarded with friendly messages from Republicans. After a certain time it begins to seem irresistible, especially if the person [doing the wooing] seems very likely to be the next president of the United States." Ronald Reagan, another Cold War Democrat turned Republican, was a beneficiary of the disastrous meeting as his people actively wooed the contingent to his presidential campaign. By fall 1980, Elliott was working almost full-time on the Reagan campaign, handling Jewish outreach.

By then, Irving Kristol had been featured on the cover of *Esquire*, touted as "the Godfather of the most powerful new political force in America—neoconservatism." The name stuck.

In December 1980, a month after Ronald Reagan was elected president, Elliott married Rachel in a traditional Jewish ceremony in the living room of Podhoretz and Decter's Upper East Side apartment with his parents and relatives in attendance. Elliott's mentors over the last ten years—Nathan Glazer, Henry Jackson and Daniel Patrick Moynihan—witnessed the signing of the *ketubah*—the traditional wedding contract. Podhoretz opined that the union was the "closest thing to an arranged marriage that the modern world allowed." Elliott had become the crown prince of the neoconservatives.

PART FIVE

CHAPTER FIFTEEN

Family Man

TOM HURWITZ, 1973–1983

Back in New York after three years on the West Coast, Tom saw the city with new eyes. What was once the center of the universe now seemed as parochial as any other small town. He marveled at the bell jar in which he and his fellow Little Redders had been reared. He thought of Kathy Boudin, now entering her third year as a fugitive after fleeing the debris of the 11th Street townhouse. Maybe, Tom speculated, the guilt she felt growing up in such a rarified environment had been a factor in her tragic loss of perspective. After the explosion, Kathy stayed underground until 1981. Looking back, Tom could see that he had taken some ideological wrong turns too, but he was thankful that he had no blood on his hands.

Tom's life as an organizer had come to an end, and it was time to embark on a new career as a cinematographer. He was about to become a father: Barbara—soon to be his wife—had become pregnant on the journey home. The couple settled in the 93rd Street apartment Tom had grown up in. Jane, now sixty-one, had moved to London in 1970 and was teaching at the London Contemporary Dance School. Leo lived a few blocks away on West End Avenue.

In the 1970s, New York's Upper West Side, although not as politicized as it was in the 1960s, was among the city's most politically and culturally progressive neighborhoods. Many who now lived there had been radicals in their youth and were just starting families. Spacious apartments were

plentiful, and cheap to rent; the neighborhood was racially and economi-
cally diverse with children of middle class and poor families attending the
same public schools. There were food co-ops and parent-run nurseries
and day care centers. It was a rare spring, summer or fall weekend in
which there was not a block party featuring craft booths alongside tables
devoted to marshaling support for liberal and radical causes. Independent
bookstores and movie revival houses dotted Broadway. "The left was shattered but the community was cooking," said Tom.

Despite her trepidation about moving to New York, Barbara found a
comfortable niche for herself in this community, joining a food co-op and
helping to establish the Purple Circle day care co-op that became the center of her social life. This extended family assumed added importance as
Tom's cinematography career began to flourish, taking him away from
home for extended stretches of time.

Tom and Barbara's relationship continued to be marked by heated
arguments and ardent reconciliations. Tom had not experienced this dy-
namic with other women and had certainly not witnessed it growing
up. Leo and Jane's relationship had been a difficult one, but they never
argued—at least not in front of their only child. In California, the couple's
clashes had been tempered by their political work. In that sphere, there
seemed to be nothing they could not achieve when they worked in tandem. But now, with no pressing common cause to unite them, their arguments escalated. It didn't help that Barbara's relationship with Leo was
strained at best. She could see that Tom worshipped his father as, indeed,
did all the people with whom Leo surrounded himself. Barbara respected
Leo's talent and intellect but his need for devotees struck her as a bit absurd. "He needed people to sit at his feet," she said. "I already had a father
that I admired and loved and with Leo it was just—'Who is this guy?'"

Although that view was a painful one for Tom to accept, he understood. "Barbara experienced Leo's cerebral style as being cold and his narcissism as being . . . narcissism." The cause for tensions between his father
and his wife, Tom suspected, lay not in their differences but in their simi-
larities. Both were used to being the center of their respective universes—
and Tom felt constantly pulled between the two.

Leo, now sixty-four, needed Tom as he never had before. Still in deep mourning for Peggy and recently retired as chairman of the graduate school of film and television at New York University, he was morose. To fill the personal and professional vacuum in his life, he had thrown himself into crafting a film tribute to Peggy. Tom signed on to help edit the opus. Father and son spent their days in a small editing room in Leo's apartment sitting side by side. Often, Tom would stay on for dinner to keep Leo company. As the months passed the situation became unbearable.

"I couldn't hear him," Tom said. "He was just being Leo—didactic, a bit patronizing, not recognizing my contribution—all the things people have felt working with Leo." A few weeks into their collaboration, Leo decided to turn his living room into a screening room. Tom volunteered for the job, putting the carpentering skills he had acquired in California to use. As he was scraping paint off French doors, Tom broke one of the glass planes. He called Barbara, distraught, flagellating himself for his clumsiness. His own overreaction brought him up short. Just months ago, Tom had been instrumental in saving a man from life in prison; now he felt like an unworthy child terrified of his father's disapproval.

After six months of assisting Leo for a nominal salary, it dawned on Tom that that this project was not so much a movie as a never-ending exercise intended to keep Leo's grief at bay. "The film was ostensibly about Peggy, but it was really about him," Tom said. "It was self indulgent and long. The premise was wrong. The structure was wrong. It was supposed to be like sonnets, but it was endless elegies." Tom tried tactfully to point out the film's flaws, but for once, his eloquence deserted him. "My ego began to disappear. I began to lose track of who I was." The situation was also financially untenable. He and Barbara had married in August, and their child was due in December. (Mekea Hurwitz was born on December 10.) Finally, Tom mustered up the courage to tell Leo that he was going to put all his energy into becoming a freelance cinematographer. Leo took the news gracefully, but Tom's defection, in addition to the tension between Leo and Barbara, further strained the father-son relationship.

Tom set out to learn the cinematographer's craft. He joined Mass Productions, a collective of left-wing filmmakers. On his way to the first meeting

of the group in the financial district of Manhattan, Tom emerged from the
subway to see the World Trade Center, which was still under construction.
Tom looked up at the Twin Towers in wonder. "Hey," he thought. "I love this!"
Immediately following that reaction came the realization of the contempt
that Leo would have for such a crass symbol of American capitalism. Still,
Tom gave himself permission to admire the structures and to realize that not
everything new, not everything associated with capitalism, was intrinsically
bad. After months of having his ego dismantled by Leo, it was a liberating
moment.

As Tom was separating himself professionally from Leo, he met Tom
Reichman, a filmmaker who had directed a well-received documentary
about jazz musician Charles Mingus. Reichman, tall, with a mane of red
hair, took a liking to the neophyte cinematographer and offered him a job
as his assistant making industrial films. Tom's association with Reichman
launched his career. Tom was gifted with an uncanny sense of where the
camera belonged at any given moment—a crucial skill when filming cin-
ema verite, an unscripted documentary form in which the filmmaker acts
as a fly on the wall as the film subjects' lives unfold. Tom began his career
just as this genre was being forged by filmmakers like David and Albert
Maysles (*Grey Gardens*, *Gimme Shelter*) and D. A. Pennebaker (*Don't Look
Back*, *The War Room*). With a loan from Barbara's parents, Tom bought
his own camera and then began taking jobs across the country lighting
commercials, acting as a gaffer for features and doing sound on documentaries so he could watch the more seasoned cameramen at work.

In the spring of 1974, Tom got the chance to work with Barbara Kopple, a baby-faced documentarian who had decided to make a documentary
about a miners' strike in Kentucky, *Harlan County, USA*. The shoot was as
exciting as it was perilous. Even Tom, who had been in numerous riots and
more than one life-threatening situation, was taken aback. "Everyone was
carrying guns—they were everywhere you looked, on top of refrigerators
and tables," he said. "Kopple has an amazing facility that when things are
dangerous she goes toward rather than away from the danger. She disarms
the danger that way." It was a terrifying experience, but also a thrilling one
in which Tom used his developing professional skills on behalf of a docu-

mentary about the oppression of the working class, one that expressed the political vision that had inspired him as an activist.

By the time the couple's second daughter, Anya, was born in 1976, Tom was making a steady living as a cinematographer, and Barbara had completed her M.A. and then her Ph.D. in anthropology. They bought a summer home in upstate New York—a farmhouse on 70 acres of land in Rhinebeck by the Hudson River—and several of Barbara's friends from the Purple Circle bought places nearby. The Hurwitzes raised chickens and ponies on the land. Tom became a gentleman farmer. But Barbara was dissatisfied. She yearned for the professional partnership she and Tom had shared in California.

In 1979, Tom and Barbara left their daughters with Barbara's mother and traveled to China and Mongolia to make a series of documentaries for *The Big Blue Marble*, a PBS television show chronicling the day-to-day lives of children around the world. In China, they witnessed the devastation wrought by Mao's Cultural Revolution, the movement they had venerated and sought to emulate as American revolutionaries.

"In the sixties I tried to make myself believe the Cultural Revolution was a good thing," said Barbara. "I did truly believe nobody was killed. We couldn't believe how devastating the Cultural Revolution had been to people. We kept denying it. We had no idea what had happened to China and here we were hearing the reality from people. I argued with our interpreter for months—'No, no, it was important, it was transformative.' And he would say, 'You don't know what it was like to have families broken up and people being sent to prison and youth thugs taking over.'"

In the 1960s, the New Left had mocked the Old Left's unshakable loyalty to the Soviet Union. Now it was the younger generation's turn to realize that it had remained willfully blind to China's corrupt regime.

Throughout the trip, Barbara experienced increasingly painful stomach aches. As the crew prepared to cross the border from China to Mongolia, she could feel that some sort of mass was growing inside her. She decided to delay medical treatment and press on with Tom. Months later, back in the States, Tom accepted an Emmy for an episode shot in Mongolia. In his acceptance speech he thanked Barbara as one on a long list of people involved in the project. Barbara was crushed by the passing reference to their intense collaboration. "I was as much a director and a producer as he was," she said. Tom disagreed. "It would have been nice and loving to do so, but it was not how I felt at the time. It was really my show."

As they resumed their life in New York, Barbara pressed for continued collaboration. Under the banner "Zahm/Hurwitz Productions," the two made *Bombs Will Make the Rainbow Break* (1983), about children's fears about nuclear war featuring footage from a huge anti-nuke march in Central Park in 1982. In the film, Mekea and Anya can be seen frolicking in front of the Rhinebeck farmhouse. But by that time the marriage was rapidly disintegrating. Barbara couldn't understand why Tom didn't want to work with her. It was, after all, their political partnership that had brought them together; it was what they did best. But Tom wanted his own career, not a personal and professional partnership that seemed to him increasingly tense and painful.

In summer of 1983, Jane placed a call from her London flat to Tom and Barbara's Rhinebeck house. Tom was in bed with Barbara when he picked up the phone. He told his mother that the two had decided to split.

"I don't think Tom was sure that I was the love of his life," Barbara said years later. "Both of us had problems there. I knew I was going to have children with him, but I never felt like we had a stable relationship. But I was also very broken up when we split because two children later we had built a family and I had settled in—this was what life had given me. I accepted it and I was happy with it."

Tom summed up the fourteen-year partnership this way: "It was tough, painful and productive."

Angela Davis at a press conference after being dismissed from her teaching position by the University of California Board of Regents, October 7, 1969. In back of her, offering his support, is Donald Kalish, head of the philosophy department at UCLA. *Credit:* UCLA Charles E. Young Research Library Department of Special Collections, Los Angeles Times Photographic Archives.

Angela responds to the December 1969 killing in Chicago of Black Panther leader Fred Hampton by police. *Credit:* UCLA Charles E. Young Research Library Department of Special Collections, Los Angeles Times Photographic Archives.

Angela and Jonathan Jackson, George Jackson's brother (obscured, r.), leading a protest march on behalf of the Soledad Brothers. *Credit:* UCLA Charles E. Young Research Library Department of Special Collections, Los Angeles Times Photographic Archives.

Angela was one of three women
to appear on the FBI's Most
Wanted list. Her classmate,
Kathy Boudin, was another.

The FBI arrests Angela in New York City, October 13, 1970, on
charges of murder, kidnapping and conspiracy in connection with
the attempted Marin County prison break. *Credit:* Photo by Carmine
Donofrio/New York Daily News/Getty Images.

Tom (far right) at an anti-war rally in San Bernadino, California, 1972. *Credit:* Collection of Tom Hurwitz.

Susan Brown soon after the Columbia occupation. *Credit:* Photo by Peg Lawson, collection of Tom Hurwitz.

Angela, surrounded by family, awaits the verdict in her murder trial at the Santa Clara County Courthouse complex in San Jose, Calif. From left: brother, Ben Davis, with son, Ben Jr.; Ben's wife, Sylvia; brother Reggie; Angela's sister, Fania Jordan (back to camera), holding her daughter, Angela Eisa; and on far right, a leader of the San Jose chapter of the National United Committee to Free Angela Davis. *Credit:* Photo by Slava Veder/Associated Press.

Barbara Zahm in the Hurwitz' Upper West Side apartment, 1976. *Credit:* Photo by Tom Hurwitz, collection of Tom Hurwitz.

Elliott in the Reagan years.
Credit: Courtesy Archives of LREI.

Tom and Margaret Klenck on the set of "Hard Choices." *Credit:* Collection of Tom Hurwitz.

Kathy Boudin (second from left) and Angela at the fiftieth anniversary reunion of the class of 1961, in June 2011. Also pictured are classmates Kate Spindell Hays and Robert Ferrucci. *Credit:* Courtesy Archives of LREI.

Elliott in the George W. Bush White House, October 4, 2007. L.-R.: Chief of Protocol Nancy Brinker; Vice President Dick Cheney; Elliott Abrams, Deputy Assistant to the President and Deputy National Security Advisor for Global Democratic Strategy; Secretary of State Condoleezza Rice; Stephen Hadley, Assistant to the President for National Security Affairs. *Credit:* Photo by Dennis Brack-Pool/Getty Images.

Tom in 1999 shooting a documentary on the tenth anniversary of the Exxon Valdez disaster. *Credit:* Collection of Tom Hurwitz.

Angela at an Occupy Wall Street demonstration in Zuccotti Park, New York City, October 30, 2011. *Credit:* Photo by Velcrow Ripper, OccupyLove.com.

CHAPTER SIXTEEN

The King of Latin America

ELLIOTT ABRAMS, 1980–1989

At noon on November 25, 1986, Elliott sat in his State Department office watching a televised presidential press conference. It was the beginning of what he would call his "worst single day" in the Reagan administration.

On screen, a visibly drawn and irritable President Reagan made a brief statement admitting that, in spite of previous denials to the contrary, the United States had sold arms to Iran in the hope of securing the release of hostages—and that some of the money from those sales had been diverted to help the Contras, a rebel faction in Nicaragua, overthrow its government. Finishing the statement, Reagan quit the stage. Attorney General Edwin Meese stepped up to answer a barrage of questions from the press.

"Why didn't the president know [about] providing arms to Iran in return for the release of hostages?" asked an irate Sam Donaldson.

"Because somebody didn't tell him," Meese replied emphatically.

Following the press conference, Reagan accepted the resignation of his national security advisor, John Poindexter, one of the chief architects of what was being called the "Iran-Contra Affair." Poindexter's chief aide, Lt. Col. Oliver L. North, was fired.

Hours later, Abrams appeared in front of the House Intelligence Committee to deliver a bi-weekly briefing on the situation in Nicaragua. The chairman of the committee, Democrat New Jersey Senator Bill Bradley, was in a foul mood. Just weeks ago the Democrat-controlled Congress had voted to release $100 million for arms to the Contras, after years of refusing to do so. Bradley had risked political capital by breaking party ranks to vote with the Republicans.

Testifying alongside Alan Fiers, CIA chief of the Central American Task Force, Elliott denied knowing about any diversion of funds to the Contras. Further, he said he did not remember participating any discussions about fundraising for the Contras.

"We're not—you know—we're not in the fundraising business," Elliott said, with unaccustomed hesitancy.

December 8, Elliott again appeared before the committee in an attempt to walk back that assertion. Senator Thomas Eagleton laid into Elliott. "Were you then in the fundraising business?" the Senator demanded.

"I would say we were in the fundraising business. I take your point," said Elliott.

"Take my point? Under oath, my friend, that's perjury!" exclaimed Eagleton. Then, realizing that Elliott had not been sworn in for that round of testimony, he backtracked.

"Had you been under oath," Eagleton corrected himself, "that's perjury."
Elliott responded, "Well, I don't agree with that."
"That's slammer time," said Eagleton.
Elliott held firm. "Well, I don't agree with that."
Eagleton tried another approach. "Oh, Elliott, you're too damn smart not to know. You *were* in the fundraising business, you and Ollie . . . you were opening accounts, you had account cards. . . ."
"You've heard my testimony."
"I've heard it," said Eagleton, "and I want to puke."

On May 17, 1981, Elliott was sworn in as assistant secretary of state for international organization affairs under Secretary of State Alexander Haig making him, at age thirty-three, the youngest man to become an assistant secretary in a presidential administration. It was a remarkable achievement considering that, aside from his staff work for Jackson and Moynihan, the only other two items on Elliott's resume were short stints as a junior associate in New York and D.C. law firms.

Dan Hastings, Elliott's roommate from his undergraduate and law school days, attended the swearing-in with Elliott's parents. Joe's intense pride in his son overshadowed any qualms he had about Elliott joining a Republican administration. "He's so young—do you realize how young he is?" Joe repeatedly to Hastings.

"Yes, Joe, I know," Hastings replied, bemused.

By 1983, some thirty-three members of the Committee for the Present Danger, that is to say, neoconservatives, would gain berths in the new administration, many of them second-generation neocons groomed by Jackson and Moynihan: Richard V. Allen, national security advisor; Richard Perle, who had first introduced Elliott to Scoop Jackson; Paul Nitze; Paul Wolfowitz; Charles Horner; and Jeane Kirkpatrick, appointed U.S. ambassador to the United Nations.

Journalist and future aide to Bill Clinton Sidney Blumenthal called this critical mass of newly minted Republicans—the "Counter-Establishment." Although they had worked long and painstakingly to achieve significant influence on American policy, it was a dizzying ascent to power, one made all the sweeter by the continuing decline of their ideological foes on the domestic front. For although some offshoots of movements from the 1960s had thrived—particularly the feminist and gay rights movements— without the Vietnam War to rally around, the New Left was effectively a thing of the past. And with the New Left out of the way, it seemed to the neocons that the nihilistic fever dream that was the 1960s was also over and done.

Now the neocons—certainly Elliott—could concentrate on what really interested them: foreign affairs. In the mid-nineties, journalist Michael Lind, who had worked for Irving Kristol, created a tongue-in-cheek game called "Neoconservative Bingo," in which you stamped your card every time you come upon a catchphrase in a neocon-authored book or essay, for instance: "The World's Only Superpower"; "The New Class"; "The China Threat"; "Decadent Europe"; "Against the UN"; "The Adversary Culture"; "The Global Democratic Revolution"; "Down With the Appeasers!"; "Be Firm Like Churchill." "The free space in the center of the bingo card," said Lind, "would be 'The Palestinian People Do Not Exist." But there is a glaring omission on the card: the Soviet threat. With the appeasement policies of the Carter administration at an end, the newly empowered neocons could turn their energies to fighting Soviets, whose center of influence had shifted over the last few decades from Southeast Asia to Central and South America.

Several months into his appointment, Elliott saw an opportunity for advancement. Fellow neocon Ernest Lefever had been nominated for assistant secretary of human rights, a position created on Jimmy Carter's watch. But Lefever flamed out on the first day of his confirmation hearings when it became apparent that he had little or no use for the idea of making human rights a factor in U.S. foreign policy at all. For good measure, he derided the previous human rights chief, Patricia Derian. Elliott promptly presented himself to William Clark, deputy secretary of state under Alexander Haig. "You asked me to think about candidates," Elliott cheerfully told Clark. "I have figured out someone perfect for this job. Me!"

At first blush, the position seemed an unlikely stepping stone. "Compared with the International Organizations Bureau, it was smaller, less prestigious, and less influential," Elliott wrote. More to the point, many in Elliott's circle saw the office itself as a vestige of the Carter administration. Irving Kristol and Jeane Kirkpatrick were in this camp, as was Nathan Glazer. To them, the department was at best useless and at worst, it promulgated a policy that gave aid and comfort to leftist regimes—particularly in Latin America—but which seemed blithely unconcerned with oppression meted out by Communist governments.

But Elliott saw an opportunity. He would frame human rights as an organic outgrowth of democracy, one that in the long run could be protected only by democracies. Logically, therefore, the top priority for a human rights office should be to end the existence of communist states and to keep ties with authoritarian regimes—some of which, admittedly, were pretty unsavory—the better to use the influence of the United States to guide them to a democratic future. Writing in *Washington Monthly*, Eric Alterman opined, "The Abrams attempt to undercut the 'moral superiority' of the human rights community is based on the old 'teach a man to fish' homily. Get a dissident out of jail, and you'll have to get another one out tomorrow. But teach a country to become democratic, and human rights will be codified and protected forever. As long, then, as a country is moving 'in the direction of democracy,' the U.S. must do what it can to avoid antagonizing that country's military so democratic reforms are allowed to proceed. Countries that are going to or have already gone communist, however, must be pressured to make their ruling elites realize the cost of being undemocratic and refusing to respect human rights."

Elliott was sworn in on December 10, 1981—Human Rights Day. His family was again in attendance. By that time, Joe, having struggled with heart disease for several years, was in delicate health. Elliott arranged for his parents to meet President Reagan and a photograph was taken of the family, including Elliott, Rachel and their infant son, Jake. Joe died three weeks later and would never see the photograph or know that Elliott had formally changed his political party registration from Democrat to Republican.

In lobbying for the Human Rights position, Elliott had avoided Lefever's missteps, presenting himself as a centrist and drawing on the good will of his former fellow Democrats in Congress. Months later he told the *New York Times*, somewhat improbably, that his State Department colleagues viewed him as a "secret" liberal. "They thought I was a liberal mole hidden in the Reagan administration." But his policies quickly disabused anyone who might have held such a notion. "We consider anticommunism to be a human rights policy," said Abrams, encapsulating his approach. This new tack was evident in the administration's dealings with Latin American countries. In Argentina, for instance, Abrams said, "We support the government, we don't support its human rights policies." It was a somewhat muted statement given the many thousands who had "disappeared" under the brutal regime of the military junta. The administration also sought to resume military aid to Guatemala, whose newly installed dictatorship continued brutally repressive measures against its people.

But Elliott drew some of his the strongest criticism for his policy on El Salvador, a small Latin American country in the midst of a civil war between its U.S.-backed government and communist insurgents. When Reagan took office, there were reports of thousands of Salvadorans being murdered and tortured by death squads made up of El Salvador's military and government security forces. In reaction, Congress passed a law in 1981 tying foreign aid to a twice-yearly certification from the State Department that conditions were improving on the human rights front.

Elliott's first act as assistant secretary for human rights was to recertify military aid to the newly elected government of Jose Duarte. In doing so, he downplayed or denied the existence of death squads. "We don't think the situation in El Salvador is that bad," he said in 1983. He continued to certify the country despite reports of ongoing atrocities against civilians. "We think people who are friends of the United States get some points for that," Elliott said at the time. "It doesn't mean you're forgiven, but it does mean you address that government with a slightly different attitude." Patricia Derian spoke for many Democrats when she called the new human rights policy catastrophic. "They have essentially abandoned human rights and continued this incredible courtship with the sleaziest of the world leaders." Elliott also supported the deportation of thousands of Salvadorans who had come to the United States seeking political asylum.

Maintaining ties with anti-Communist governments, no matter how lamentable their human rights track record, became the way of doing business at the State Department. In addition to the hope of exerting constructive influence over those countries there was the fear that undermining those regimes could weaken them to the point where they would be vulnerable to Soviet-backed insurgents. In promulgating this theory, the administration often gave two examples: Iran and Nicaragua.

In July 1982, five months into Elliott's tenure as human rights chief, George P. Shultz replaced Alexander Haig as secretary of state. Haig's time in the Reagan cabinet had effectively come to an end in March 1981 with his infamous "I'm in charge" speech following the assassination attempt on President Reagan. With his unerring instinct for cultivating mentors, Elliott soon had a powerful patron in Shultz. Although Shultz, a pragmatic, old-style Republican, viewed the neocons "as a bit out there," he recognized that Elliott 'would make a valuable lieutenant. And the establishment of this new alliance was excellent timing for Elliott who was running short of champions on the Hill. Jackson was nearing the end of his decades-long senatorial career and Moynihan had moved away from the neocons. "The new elite disposition," he said, referring to the neocons, was falsely creating a "myth of invincible communism" in order to generate "a continuous frenzy over the threats we face in all corners of the world."

The mercurial Moynihan had soured on Elliott in particular, feeling slighted when his protégé had not stood up for him when the administration backed Moynihan's Republican opponent for the Senate in 1982—even though Moynihan's seat was secure and would stay that way until he retired in 2000. This was a somewhat unreasonable expectation given the fact that Elliott was now a Republican. "Elliott was a member of the administration, and the administration has every reason in the world . . . to want to see me lose the next election," said Moynihan. "That's called 'politics,' it ain't bean bag." In a more wistful vein, Moynihan said of his former protégé: "I don't know Elliott very well. Look, the man changed his politics and he changed his party enrollment." When Elliott learned of Moynihan's displeasure he reacted with his usual bravado. "When somebody makes what I consider to be an unfair accusation [I say] 'The hell with it. If that is what you want to think, think it!'"

Elliott and Moynihan clashed again in October 1986 when immigration officials detained a Colombian journalist, Patricia Lara, at John F. Kennedy International Airport. After spending four days in jail, Lara was sent back to Bogota with no charges filed against her. The INS gave no direct explanation for the action except to reference the Cold War–era McCarran-Walter Act that allowed the United States to expel foreign nationals likely to engage in subversive activities.

The incident attracted media attention, and Moynihan, who thought the accusations against Lara were patently false and a form of political censorship, came out swinging. On the floor of the Senate he declared the move "painfully stupid." To quell the controversy, Elliott appeared on *60 Minutes* and stated that Lara was a member of the Columbian terrorist organization M19 and a liaison with the Cuban secret police. He did not produce proof to back up the assertion. After the interview, *New York*

Times columnist Anthony Lewis excoriated Elliott in print. "There is one word for Elliott Abrams: coward. Joe McCarthy made hit-and-run attacks from the sanctuary of the U.S. Senate. To make them as a high official of the State Department is even more indefensible."

Even Elliott's brother weighed in on the matter, ruefully observing that expelling foreign undesirables without explanation had always galled their father. "It's still going on now—except that Elliott's doing it," Franklin said.

The incident clearly hit a nerve. Months later, when told by a reporter that Lara feared an assassination attempt because of Elliott's televised comments, Elliott lost his temper. "No sir!" he shouted. "The people who are doing the killing are her buddies. Patricia Lara is the best case of radical chic I have ever come across." In 1991, Lara, who denied the charges, eventually settled a lawsuit with the U.S. government and was issued a new visa.

In 1985, Elliott moved up in the State Department. That July—six months after Reagan took his second oath of office after scoring an election landslide against his Democrat opponent, Vice President Walter Mondale—Shultz handpicked Elliott to be the assistant secretary of state for inter-American affairs. In doing so, Shultz promised to "manage the emergence of Elliott Abrams as King of Latin America." As chief policy maker in South and Central America, Elliott became integrally involved with a massive extracurricular crusade by a group of top operatives in the State Department and in the CIA—a campaign they undertook with the fervent yet hazy blessing of their boss. It would destroy careers and lives and come close to bringing down the Reagan administration.

The roots of the Iran-Contra scandal began on June 17, 1979, perhaps the lowest point of President Carter's luckless administration, when Iranian extremists stormed the U.S. embassy in Tehran, taking fifty-two diplomats and staff members hostage. Four months earlier, in a country thousands of miles away, the socialist Sandinista Liberation Front prevailed over the U.S.-backed dictatorship of Anastasio Somoza in Nicaragua, and installed Daniel Ortega as its leader. The Sandinistas were backed by arms and funds from the Soviet Union. Carter banned trade with the country but did not cut off all ties. Nicaragua was one of Central

America's most industrialized nations—thanks in part to investment from major U.S. companies such as Coca-Cola and banks such as Chase Manhattan.

This, of course, was the very stance Reagan would assume with anti-communist regimes around the world. And the Sandinistas were precisely the kind of communist government, with a beachhead in the Americas, that Reagan was intent on thwarting. The Contras, the guerilla force seeking to overthrow the Sandinistas, gained an almost mythological status in the Reagan administration, seen as latter-day American colonists struggling for independence against the tyranny of England.

In 1981, Reagan suspended all aid to Nicaragua and sought funds to back the Contras. The Democratic-controlled Congress, however, balked. In 1983, it passed the first of several iterations of the Boland Amendment, which explicitly prohibited the government from providing arms to the Contras. Over the next four years, the administration and Congress would play a geopolitical tit-for-tat. Congress would block funds; the administration would find a way around the ban. Congress would then pass a more stringent version of the Boland Amendment, and the president's lieutenants would find a way to sidestep it in order to keep the Contra's' cause together, in Reagan's words, "body and soul."

The overseers of the administration's policy were Shultz; National Security Advisor Robert McFarlane; his successor, John Poindexter; and Alan Fiers, CIA chief of the Central American Task Force. But the man on the ground, the man who made things happen, was Oliver North, a zealous fabulist who had joined the National Security Council in 1981.

By the time Elliott joined the team, North had been the administration's "point man" for a year. That label hardly did justice to the scope of his efforts. North presided over and was the chief operative in a remarkably intricate and wide-ranging web of activities that included the purchase and shipment of weapons and ammunition for the Contras, air drops of equipment and arms in Nicaragua, supervising the training of the Contras and providing intelligence to them, and raising money for all of these endeavors to supplement congressional funds earmarked for humanitarian purposes only.

Elliott ran the weekly meetings of the Restricted Interagency Group (RIG) that worked on Central American issues and was attended by representatives from State, the NSA and the CIA. He quickly became the State Department's front man in its ardent support of the Contras and its chief solicitor of funds in Congress, often appearing before the House Foreign Affairs Committee to plead the administration's case.

Elliott professed ignorance of the Iran connection. Although the hostages in the Tehran U.S. embassy had been released on the day of Reagan's first inauguration, the attention-getting success of the Iranian revolutionaries' seizure of American hostages started a grotesque trend of American hostage taking throughout the Middle East, particularly in Lebanon, a country over which Iran and its new leader, the Ayatollah Khomeini, was thought to have influence. Despite the administration's emphatic declarations that they would not sell arms to Iran—arms Iran sorely needed as it became involved in a protracted war with Iraq—that is exactly what they were doing, as early as 1981. Likewise, despite the administration's vow that it would never negotiate for the release of hostages—much less provide cash, goods and service incentives—in August 1985, National Security Council head Robert McFarlane received a green light from a hospitalized Reagan for an arms-for-hostages scheme using Israel as an intermediary. North carried out this mission with relish, selling those weapons to Iran at inflated prices and using the difference to provide for the Contras. In his book *Undue Process*, Elliott states: "It was clear the others kept a good deal from me. . . . Every other senior official [in the Office of Independent Counsel] prosecuted had *known* about the diversion; I had not."

Untangling who knew what and when was made more difficult by President Reagan's trademark laissez-faire style of governance. The fervor of his firmly held big-picture beliefs in small government on the domestic front and (at least in his first term) a take-no-prisoners anti-Communist line in the foreign affairs arena was matched by his lack of appetite for the details involved in executing those policies. His unengaged style was especially pronounced in the realm of foreign affairs, as Reagan's only experience in public office had been eight years as governor of California.

However difficult it was later to determine who knew and who did what, it is clear that in the summer of 1986 Elliott played a lead role in a cloak-and-dagger escapade to procure $10 million for the Contra cause. Although the Boland Amendment prohibited the U.S. government from supplying arms and money to the Contras, it did allow the State Department—not the CIA—to approach foreign governments and ask them for humanitarian aid for the Contras. In a May 1986 meeting with Reagan and his senior advisors on how to leverage this loophole, a plan was hatched to raise money from a friendly, foreign government. Shultz approached Elliott for a suggestion as to which government would be receptive to such a request. Upon consideration, Elliott hit on the oil-rich kingdom of Brunei. Its ruler, Sultan Hassanal Bolkiah, was reckoned to be one of the world's wealthiest men, as evidenced by the 1,800-room palace he maintained. Shultz was scheduled to visit the sultan of Brunei in late June, and he agreed to sound him out on the subject. At the meeting, the sultan seemed receptive.

Now Elliott was sent to London to seal the deal. Before leaving, he consulted North on how best to arrange for the transfer of money should his mission be successful. Accordingly, North had his secretary, Fawn Hall, type the number of a Swiss account and give it to Elliott. In August, Elliott traveled to London to make contact with the sultan's envoy. Using the alias Mr. Kenilworth, Elliott called the man and, after a *Spy vs. Spy*–like coded exchange lest the phones were tapped, they agreed to meet.

"We had . . . taken a walk in Hyde Park," Elliott wrote, "and I had made the pitch. Ten million. The Contras needed it, the Sultan wouldn't miss it, so why not?" Elliott returned to Washington confident that his undercover mission had been a success; now all that was left was to wait for the money to show up. But it never did, because Hall had transposed two digits in the number she had given to Elliott.

Two other signal events in the Iran-Contra saga occurred in the summer of 1986. First, Congress finally agreed to allot funds—$100 million—for military aid to the Contras. Second, an article in the *Miami Herald* appeared with the headline "Despite Ban, U.S. Helping Contras." It was the first of a slow drip of stories exposing Iran-Contra. The event that brought the affair to public attention occurred on October 5, when the Sandinistas shot down a supply plane carrying arms provided by one of the many private networks overseen by North. Two of the three men onboard were killed outright. The third, Eugene Hasenfus, "a ne'er-do-well 'kicker,'" in Elliott's colorful phrase—a man who pushes cargo out of the plane—survived and was taken prisoner by the Sandinistas. An investigatory committee was hastily assembled. As the face of the Contra cause, Elliott was called upon to testify on behalf of the administration. On October 10, having had just five days to weave the varied strands of the story into a coherent narrative, Elliott faced what would be the first of many hostile grillings by the Senate Foreign Relations Committee. Adopting a "that's my story and I'm sticking to it" stance, Elliott, appeared in front of the panel with Fiers and CIA Deputy Director Clair George.

> SENATOR KERRY: Are you aware, any of you, of any deal by which, as part of the AWACS [Airborne Warning and Control System] transaction or subsequent to the AWACS transaction, Saudi Arabia is supplying weapons or assistance to the Contras on our behalf?
> MR. ABRAMS: No.
> MR. GEORGE: No.
> MR. FIERS: No, sir.
> MR. ABRAMS: I think I can say that while I have been Assistant Secretary, which is about 15 months, we have not received a dime from a foreign government, not a dime, from any foreign government.

Here, Elliott felt like he was on firm ground, semantically at least. Thanks to Hall's error, not one dime of the promised $10 million contribution from the sultan of Brunei had been delivered.

> SENATOR KERRY: "We" being who?
> MR. ABRAMS: The United States.

SENATOR KERRY: How about the Contras?

MR. ABRAMS: I don't know. But not that I am aware of and not through us. The thing is, I think I would know about it because if they went to a foreign government, a foreign government would want credit for helping the contras and they would come to us to say you want us to do this, do you, and I would know about that.

SENATOR EVANS: Elliott, when you said "not a dime," I did not hear the rest of what you said.

MR. ABRAMS: From any foreign government to the Contras. It would not be to us, it would be to the Contras. I suspect that we would know about it, though.

On October 14, Elliott appeared again before the committee. Driven by of a sense of duty and loyalty to his bosses, belief in the cause, and genuine ignorance, Elliott parried, obfuscated and denied.

THE CHAIRMAN (Senator Richard Lugar): Do you know if any foreign government is helping to supply the contras? There is a report in the LA paper, for example, that the Saudis are.

MR. GEORGE: No, sir, we have no intelligence of that.

MR. ABRAMS: I can only speak on that question for the last fifteen months when I have been in this job, and that story about the Saudis to my knowledge is false. I personally cannot tell you about pre-1985, but in 1985–1986, when I have been around, no.

THE CHAIRMAN: Is it also false with respect to other governments as well?

MR. ABRAMS: Yes, it is also false.

As to the "Hasenfus shoot-down," Elliott maintains that when he gave that testimony he knew there was "no U.S government involvement in that flight. None. Period." He had appeared on radio and TV and in the press saying as much. But on October 23, according to Elliott, Clair George pulled him aside to tell him otherwise. Indignant, Elliott stormed into Shultz's office.

"I railed against [the CIA]. I had been out there [taking the heat] for two weeks . . . saying there were no U.S. Government connections, and now it seemed there were. The spooks were screwing it all up." Elliott was even more dismayed when Reagan appointed two more bodies to investigate: a congressional inquiry led by Senator John Tower and an office of independent counsel, with retired federal judge Lawrence Welsh at the helm. As a result, Elliott spend a good chunk of the second Reagan administration preparing for and testifying to various committees.

Elliott had made many enemies in his time at the State Department; now they feasted on his apparent downfall, and by extension, that of Reagan administration policies: a mixture of "hatred, pandering, cries of anti-Americanism, screwy logic, and jingoistic slogans," in the words of Derian. Aryeh Neier, then director of the human rights group America Watch weighed in: "The people I know have been referring to Abrams as Pinocchio for years." "I have rarely seen people react with so much relish to somebody's downfall." Senator Christopher Dodd crowed, "He's got some explaining to do," and Representative Sam Gejdenson quipped, "I wouldn't trust Elliott Abrams any further than I could throw Oliver North."

In a spate of articles written about Elliott's career at the time, reporters canvassed former schoolmates, and Tom Hurwitz and Steve Kelman in particular became favored go-to sources. "The interesting thing about Elliott, and a lot of neoconservatives of his age," Kelman observed to the *Washington Post*, "is that they're really still living in the 60s and they're still acting as if the SDS was about to take over the United States." For his part, Tom told the *Washington Post*, "I was sympathizing with the underdog in the world and he was sympathizing with that which identified him with what was powerful, dignified, in authority."

But Elliott had his own story to tell. He made himself available to the press and, as often as not, won them over with his charm. He told reporters how he had survived a radical high school that had produced Black Panthers and Weathermen and reminisced about founding the Ad Hoc Committee to Keep Harvard Open. It all made for good copy.

By the end of Reagan's second term in office, the careers of numerous Washington officials had been sidelined or ended by Iran-Contra. But through the endless third degrees, Elliott endured. On January 21, 1989, Elliott, soured on government service, secured a berth as senior Fellow at the Hudson Institute, one of the many neocon think tanks that had been established during Reagan's administration. There was no place for him, or indeed for practically any neocons, in the pragmatic White House of newly elected George H. W. Bush.

Elliott saw no future for himself in politics, an opinion that was shared by conservative pundits. "He's very bright," said William F. Buckley. "He'd be very good at running a foundation . . . as the president of a small college, and later on a larger college." Elliott's friend Charles Krauthammer, a conservative columnist, offered this sardonic farewell: "Maybe one day they'll name a square after him in a free Nicaragua. They could call it Plaza de Abrams."

CHAPTER SEVENTEEN

Epiphany

TOM HURWITZ, 1983–1999

In late summer 1983, thirty-year-old Margaret Klenck arrived at a film site in the Catskill Mountains, excited to be starring in her first feature-length movie. The daughter of a Methodist pastor, Klenck had studied acting at the prestigious ACT Academy in San Francisco. After moving to New York, her delicate features, expressive eyes and thick blonde hair helped her land a lead role on a popular soap opera, *One Life to Live*, playing the much-beleaguered Edwina Lewis. It was a lucrative gig, but not one that represented the career she had aspired to and trained for. But she was thrilled to be cast in an independent film, *Hard Choices*, featuring director John Sayles and Spaulding Gray. Klenck was to play the lead: a social worker who becomes involved with a young man accused of murder.

The production manager brought her to the shooting location—in a deep forest by a creek—and introduced her to the cast and crew. At one point, the director of photography emerged from a van and shook her hand. Every movement of her first day on the job was thrilling, but Klenck still noticed the particular current that ran between her and thirty-six-year-old Tom Hurwitz.

The next day, shooting began. The first scene involved two boys running into the creek escaping from the police. Klenck and the script girl watched as Tom ran along the bank of the stream with a handheld camera, keeping pace with the actors. Suddenly, Tom lost his footing and fell into the water, somehow keeping the camera aloft with one hand as he did so.

216

As he fell, Margaret gasped and stood up. "Right then, I knew there was something between you two," the script girl later told Margaret.

But Margaret was not interested in any new romances. This was her big break, and it was important that she conduct herself in a professional manner. Falling into bed with the DP, Margaret thought, would be less than politic. She tried to avoid Tom, but it was hard to ignore the chemistry between the two.

Two weeks into the shoot, Tom approached Margaret. "You're always disappearing on me," he said. "Can I book you to go for a walk Sunday?" It was Friday, and Tom was driving back to the city to spend time with his children. After the split with Barbara earlier that year, Tom had taken an apartment downtown. Barbara retained the 93rd street apartment and the summer home upstate. The two were engaged in a protracted and highly contentious divorce proceeding.

Caught off guard, Margaret agreed but immediately regretted her decision. "This is a really bad idea," she thought. Over the weekend, Margaret thought of little else but her upcoming rendezvous with Tom—and how to gracefully extract herself from it. She considered leaving Tom a note on the company bulletin board, but ruled that out as rude. She spent hours mentally rehearsing speeches telling Tom how inadvisable the walk would be. On Sunday, at the appointed hour, Tom strode through the door of her cabin.

"Ya ready?" he asked.

Margaret could summon none of her carefully prepared statements.

"Yep."

From that day on, Tom and Margaret were a couple. Tom's living quarters on the shoot were in in the main lodge with the rest of the crew but he spent all his time in Margaret's cabin. The lovers were careful to keep their romance secret from the rest of the company but they realized the futility of the ploy when Tom's call sheet for the next days' shoots started showing up under Margaret's door.

After *Hard Choices* wrapped, Tom moved into Margaret's East Village apartment. The movie, released the same summer as the Tom Cruise block-buster *Top Gun*, was a critical if not a commercial success, and Margaret received universally good reviews for her performance. Encouraged, in 1985 she left *One Life to Live* and moved to Los Angeles to try for film and regional theater work. Her hopes were frustrated, however, as her television-oriented agent booked her on one-off TV gigs. The money was good, but Margaret was miserable, living alone in L.A. and acting in what she considered to be sub-standard fare. Making matters worse was her separation from Tom, who, although he spent as much time as he could in her Venice Beach apartment, was often in New York with Maya and Mekea or on location.

The Zahm-Hurwitz divorce, now in its third year with no end in sight, was also a psychic and financial drain. Gradually, Margaret's dissatisfaction turned to sadness, her sadness into intense emotional pain. By 1986, Margaret was battling a debilitating depression. When Tom, who was shooting in New Mexico, flew up to see her he was shocked by the depth of Margaret's misery.

With Tom's support, Margaret's state of mind gradually improved to the point where she was able to take a leading role in a repertory production of Tom Stoppard's *The Real Thing* in San Diego. When the show closed, Tom and Margaret drove up the coast for a weekend at a bed and breakfast in Russian River, north of San Francisco. Tom was in a fine mood. It had been six months since Margaret's depression had reached a crisis point. Now, after her triumph in the play, Tom believed she was poised for a full recovery. But the very next day, the exhilaration of the play having worn off, Margaret had a serious setback. Tom had drawn heavily on his emotional reserves to support the woman he loved. Now, realizing that Margaret was far from well, he was gripped by a kind of despair. Together they took a walk on the cliffs overlooking the Pacific Ocean. Tom drifted away from Margaret. Standing at the edge of the cliff, he did something he had not done since he was a child: He prayed. He prayed for the strength to see Margaret through her crisis and for the wisdom to figure out what to do next. "Almost instantaneously, I was showered with grace," Tom recalled. "Peace, joy, clarity—an assurance that what I prayed for would be given and that I could do whatever I was called upon to do." The God that Tom had been looking for all his life had made himself known.

Tom and Margaret moved back to New York. Although he was now a successful cinematographer, Tom kept a hand in the political scene. In 1984, the political activism that had lain largely dormant at Columbia was revived as students rallied to demand that the university divest its holdings in South Africa. One rainy day, Tom came upon a protest in front of Hamilton Hall. He went up to one of the organizers and, identifying himself as one of the "old timers," asked if they'd like to hear what he had to say. Tom gave a rousing speech, recounting the weeklong occupation of the campus sixteen years earlier and tying it to the current protest. Concluding his impromptu remarks, Tom wished the students well in their demonstration, adding slyly, "But you know, it's drier in the building."

Years later, both Tom and Margaret became active in the divisive abortion debate. By the 1990s, the Religious Right had become a real power base in America, in part by adopting the grassroots politics-as-theater strategy of the New Left. In July 1992, the Democratic presidential convention came to New York for five days, and with it, Operation Rescue, a group known for blockading the entrances to abortion clinics, sometimes chaining themselves to the doors to bar access to women seeking abortions. Tom approached the leadership of Planned Parenthood, which was trying to thwart Operation Rescue by cordoning off the clinics before the anti-abortion people arrived, to see if he could be useful. "It was driving me crazy—them using our tactics," said Tom.

Soon after he approached Randall Terry, the leader of Operation Rescue, at their headquarters at a midtown Franciscan church. Trying not to lie outright, Tom told Terry that he was terribly upset about the abortion issue and wanted to do whatever he could to help. In the following days, Tom attended meetings and even participated in closing down some abortion centers. By gaining the trust of Terry and his people, Tom was able to learn which abortion clinics would be targeted, and he passed on the information to pro-abortion groups so that they could arrive first. Tom's plan was successful, but the scheme was more exciting in theory than in practice: The irony that he was now acting the part of the infiltrator—the same role that the FBI plants had played in his activist heyday—was not lost on him. On the last day of the convention, Tom, abandoning his guise, joined a huge pro-abortion march in midtown. Terry spotted Tom and confronted him furiously. "You're a Judas—you're going to burn in hell," he screamed.

———————

In the spring of 1987, Tom passed by the Cathedral of St. John the Divine. He had grown up less than half a mile away from the massive structure and had gone to college just blocks away from it; yet, he had never stepped inside. Now, he entered it and immediately realized that he had found his spiritual home. Tom told Margaret that he wanted to attend Easter service at the Episcopalian cathedral. Margaret, who was a practicing Christian, told Tom that if he wanted to go, he must do it right—attend all of the Holy Week services, starting with Palm Sunday. Tom was moved to tears at that service and decided to be baptized in the cathedral on Pentecost, fifty days after Easter.

Tom and Margaret were now living in a Riverside Drive apartment across the hall from Leo and his girlfriend, Nelly Burlingham, a former student of his who was a full forty years younger. By coincidence, Margaret and Burlingham had attended college together. The two couples saw each other almost daily. Tom and Leo had weathered many conflicts since Tom's return to New York, and their relationship had improved markedly. Leo, who had never gotten along with Barbara, was enchanted with Margaret. He was also intensely proud of the career Tom had carved out for himself as a cinematographer and of his continuing political work. But there was one barrier to a complete rapprochement between Leo and Tom: religion. In vain, Leo tried to explain how the Hurwitz family had struggled to throw off the shackles of Judaism, that being religious—in whatever denomination—went against everything the proud and intellectual Hurwitz family stood for; that religion was a force for evil that impeded the progress of civilization and had caused untold suffering throughout history. It was simply incomprehensible to Leo how a man of Tom's intellect could buy into such fairy tales. So it was with trepidation that Tom informed his father of his upcoming baptism. Leo took the news hard. He had known of Tom's epiphany on the cliffs of Russian River and that he had attended Holy Week services. But this baptism would be an irrevocable consecration of Tom's faith. The night before the ceremony, Leo had a dream: He was driving west across the George Washington Bridge, which connects upper Manhattan to New Jersey. Suddenly, the car in front of him shrieked to a halt. A young man emerged and leapt over the guardrail of the bridge, plunging headlong into the Hudson River. When Tom learned of the dream, its meaning was immediately clear to him: By being baptized, he had become an apostate. In the Jewish tradition, he had committed suicide.

In 1988, the divorce proceedings between Tom and Barbara were at last reaching an end, and Tom and Margaret were planning a May wedding. Leo agonized over whether to attend the nuptials at the cathedral—a formal affair with all the "smells and bells" of a high-church ceremony. Tom and Margaret assured Leo that they would not be upset if he decided not to attend, but in the end, he did—even buying a suit for the occasion and reading an e. e. cummings poem. After the wedding, Tom and Margaret moved uptown to Washington Heights, where their son Nicholas was born in 1989. Leo now became the doting grandparent he had never been with Mekea and Anya, taking the bus uptown every day to visit the infant.

The issue of religion continued to cause tremendous pain between father and son, but they never stopped trying to heal the wound. In true Hurwitz style, that process took the form of vigorous disputation. The two took to writing long letters to each other in an effort to explain their respective rationales and worldviews. But no amount of explication could resolve a dilemma essentially not rooted in intellect and reason but on emotion and faith. "The religion [issue] shredded Leo," said Margaret. "Leo was no longer God. When you were in his universe he would do anything for you but if you challenged assumptions—he would look away."

In 1990, Leo, at the age of eighty, was diagnosed with cancer. Leo soldiered on, unsuccessfully trying to get yet another project off the ground—this time a film about the life of the radical abolitionist John Brown. As his illness progressed, Leo was moved to a hospice, where he married his long-time companion, Nellie. Then, defiant to the last, he insisted on returning home. But although he was near death, Leo resisted signing his will, which appointed Tom, Nellie and Manny Kirshheimer as joint custodians of his work; such an act would be the ultimate capitulation to the universe. But finally, he did sign. Three days later, he died.

Looking back on his relationship with his father, Tom concluded that Leo never adjusted to his growing into adolescence and then into adulthood—becoming his own person. Leo never quite grasped how he had lost his purest disciple.

PART SIX

CHAPTER EIGHTEEN

The Man Who Named My Father

TOM HURWITZ, 1999

In the early hours of February 9, 1999, the actor Kevin Spacey, speaking from Los Angeles, announced the nominations for the year's Academy Awards. At 9 a.m. in New York the phone rang in Tom's Washington Heights apartment. "We're nominated!" said Matthew Diamond, director of the documentary *Dancemaker*. Tom, who had been the cinematographer of the film about Paul Taylor and his dance company, was thrilled. There had been word on the industry grapevine that the documentary might be nominated, but Tom had allowed himself to harbor only a small hope; movies about dance were rarely recognized, let alone by the Academy.

Since he had returned to New York twenty-six years earlier, Tom had worked on many award-winning films, including *Harlan County, USA* (1976); *Down and Out in America* (1986), which examined the lives of Americans devastated by the recession; *The Ten-Year Lunch* (1987) about the wits of New York's Algonquin Round Table; and *American Dream* (1990), also directed by Kopple, about a strike by the workers of a meat-packing plant in Austin, Minnesota. But this nod was especially sweet. Tom had grown up in dance studios watching his mother, Jane, work. *Dancemaker* had succeeded, he believed, in capturing the work of the greatest living choreographer while vividly illustrating the arduous process of choreographing a dance piece.

Tom's elation was dampened when a rumor making the rounds in the film community proved to be true: Elia Kazan, the legendary film and theater director, was slated to receive a Lifetime Achievement Award at the ceremony. In 1952, Kazan had named names—and plenty of them—in front the House Un-American Activities Committee. To be sure, he was not the only one who had done so, but Kazan's testimony was seen by many as the archetypal betrayal, coming as it did from a powerful man who had the clout to effectively resist, if not break, the Blacklist. Decades later, the mere mention of his name incited disgust and fury in New York artistic and intellectual circles. But for Tom, the anger was personal: He blamed Kazan in large part for the decade Leo had spent fruitlessly looking for work. "He ground Leo into the ground, now he's pissing on him," Tom fumed.

A few weeks before the ceremony, Tom learned that for the first time he would attend the awards ceremony; the producers of *Dancemaker* had arranged to fly him, Margaret and their ten-year-old son, Nick, to Hollywood. By this time a full-blown furor had erupted over the honorary award for Kazan. Hundreds of articles appeared in the media denouncing or defending the decision. Some thought Kazan had been right to testify, others that even if he was wrong, Kazan's artistic achievements should be separated from decisions made in his private life.

Those opposed, including those in the artistic community—many of them now in their eighties or nineties—and their children, who had been on the Blacklist, acknowledged Kazan's talent and his influence on theater and film. He had been a founding member of the radical Group Theater in the 1930s and of the hugely influential Actor's Studio in the 1940s. Kazan's directing credits include such seminal films as *A Streetcar Named Desire*, *Gentleman's Agreement*, *A Face in the Crowd* and *On the Waterfront*. Nevertheless, they argued that his betrayal of his colleagues disqualified him for the Academy's honor. It particularly rankled that Kazan was unrepentant. After his second appearance in front of HUAC giving his testimony, Kazan took out a full-page ad in the *New York Times* defending his position, and forty-seven years later, seemed just as invested in defending his behavior.

Kazan's masterpiece, *On the Waterfront*, released in 1954, was widely seen as a justification for his testimony in front of HUAC. In his autobiography, *A Life*, Kazan wrote: "When critics [of *On the Waterfront*] say I put my feelings on the screen to justify my informing they are right." In the film, Terry Malloy, a petty thug played by Marlon Brando, makes the dangerous decision to inform on the corrupt and violent bosses running the Hoboken longshoremen's union. In *Naming Names*, Victor Navasky summarizes the theme of the film as: "courageous stool pigeon frees sheep-like longshoreman from tyranny of corrupt union." Many on the Left were appalled at the comparison. "Terry Malloy's friends were killers, thugs, psychopaths," wrote a columnist. "The friends Kazan informed on were merely people with whom Kazan had once shared a proscenium, and an idea."

"Which Side Are You On?" the Old Left anthem that had resounded through the Hurwitz house when Tom was growing up, once again posed the question of the hour. As the day of the ceremony approached, the controversy gained momentum. Tom grew restless and agitated as he grappled with his desire to participate in the ceremony, and, at the same time, to boycott the travesty of the Kazan honor. Most of the time, Tom took a sanguine, if bitterly resigned view of the matter. Kazan was a devious little creep, thought Tom, but stupid moves by Hollywood involving dubious Cold War characters were nothing new. There are bad guys and there are good guys, he told himself. Sometimes the bad guys win one.

Tom had met Kazan only once, on a film set in 1982. "Your father hates my guts," Kazan said to him immediately after they were introduced. "That's right," Tom said, smiling, and walked away. Kazan was a mean, angry man who had always had it in for Leo and the Jewish intellectuals like him. But that battle had been fought long ago. Now, at the end of the twentieth century, it was not Tom's fight. Yet when film critic Richard Schickel wrote an article in *Time* magazine defending the Academy's decision, Tom felt he had to respond in a letter to the editor: "Kazan named my father, filmmaker Leo Hurwitz, before the House Un-American Activities Committee. Those who were named before the Committee as having been Communists had their careers ruined. Was Kazan a great director? Without a doubt. But should he be awarded a special Oscar? Although my father was not called before HUAC, the mention of his name by Kazan and others was enough to end his career in television and studio films for more than 10 years. Thousands of others were victimized by those with whom Kazan actively sided. What might their achievements have been had they not been named?"

A week before the ceremony, Tom learned there would be a picket line outside the Dorothy Chandler Pavilion, where the Oscars were being held, protesting the Kazan award. He discussed his options with his wife: Either stand outside with the protesters, or, as the Hollywood faction of protesters advocated, join the attendees who planned to "sit on their hands"—withhold applause—when Kazan was introduced. Tom felt, not for the first time, that he would lose all sense of himself if he made Leo's fight his fight. And after all, Tom thought, everyone who cares about the Blacklist is either dead or very old. It certainly was not an issue with his filmmaking contemporaries. He dearly wanted to be with his co-workers when the award was announced, but to do that he would have to sit there and watch Elia Kazan reap the rewards of a career that had in part been made possible by hobbling his father's career.

On the day of the ceremony, Tom in his tuxedo and Margaret, who had spent hours dressing and applying her makeup, left their room in the posh Four Seasons Hotel. In the lobby, the scene was one of controlled chaos. Frantic minions pushing racks of gowns across the cavernous lobby swerved to avoid colliding with one another. Masseuses carrying their folded massage tables rushed to soothe and ready their clients. Heavily made-up women staffed booths and gave away merchandise—sunglasses, scarves, anything that might be worn and recorded by television cameras at the ceremony. Outside a platoon of sleek elongated limousines circled the hotel as the doormen summoned them, one by one, via walkie-talkie, to collect their assigned passengers.

After picking up the director, the producers and the rest of the *Dancemaker* party, the group headed for the Dorothy Chandler Pavilion. Black limos packed the freeway; to Tom they looked like sharks swimming through an asphalt ocean. Occasionally a Lexus or an equally inferior vehicle—would make its way into the pack, but at the City Center exit the sharks peeled off, leaving the bottom feeders to their pitifully obscure fates.

As they pulled into the five-lane entrance of the pavilion, Tom caught sight of some 150 protesters. But this was not the anti-Kazan group. These were evangelical Christians holding up signs condemning the evils of Hollywood moviemaking. "Sodom and Gomorrah," one sign read. "Turn to Jesus," "Hollywood Full of Homosexuals" read two others. Farther on there were about sixty protestors supporting Kazin. "Thank God For Kazan," "Commies Shut Up," their signs proclaimed. The limo turned the corner, and there, finally, were the anti-Kazan protesters, five hundred-strong, stretched along the sidewalk behind wooden balustrades: "Don't Whitewash the Blacklist!" "Elia Kazan: Benedict Arnold." Until that moment, he had been unsure of what he would do. Now Tom made his decision. Kazan wasn't going to keep him from doing what he came to do, which was to be inside with his friends. Emerging from the limousine, Tom and his party were steered by ushers to a red carpet leading into the building. Walking toward the pavilion he could see celebrities—Demi Moore, Annette Bening and the rest of the "A"-list—walking alongside him, separated by a long pane of plexiglass, as if in a parallel universe. The glare from the enormous klieg lights bleached out all shadow, overwhelming and disorienting him. Tom had attended awards shows before, but nothing on this grand scale. He struggled to keep his mental and physical equilibrium. "Just take it slow," he thought as he gripped Margaret's hand.

The *Dancemaker* group was seated in the highest reaches of the balcony, dead center. The ceremony began, and went on and on. Tom didn't hold out great hopes of it winning the Oscar. It was, after all, up against *The Last Days*, a documentary about the Holocaust, a topic that was to be a perennial favorite with Academy voters. But as the hours passed, and the time for his category approached, Tom recognized the emergence of a familiar if ignoble feeling: an all-consuming desire to win.

Finally, the Best Documentary category was announced. The nominees were read as movie clips played on the screen. Finally, the presenter flicked the envelope open. It was *The Last Days*. As the crew for that film made their way to the stage to claim their trophies, Tom leaned back in his chair and applauded, relieved that the suspense was over.

No sooner had *The Last Days* winners been escorted off the stage than Martin Scorsese and Robert DeNiro appeared from the wings. Tom leaned forward. In the mounting anxiety about his potential win he had completely forgotten about the Kazan award. "He was the master of a new kind of psychological and behavioral truth in acting," DeNiro read off the teleprompter. Scorsese chimed in: "This poetic realist, this angry romantic . . . a ferociously gifted immigrant named Elia Kazan." The lights dimmed and a montage of clips from Kazan's movies appeared on a mammoth screen. Tom watched as scenes from Kazan's body of work flickered by. The finale featured the climactic scene from *On the Waterfront*, in which Karl Malden, playing the activist priest, and Malloy's girlfriend, portrayed by Eva Marie Saint, urge Malloy, who has been savagely beaten, to walk to the dock bay. If you can make it into the bay, Malden tells him, the workers will follow you, and the syndicate will be destroyed. Malloy, punch drunk, bloody and bruised, staggers to his feet and slowly, painfully, limps past the dockworkers lined on either side of him, gauntlet-like, to the bay. With a final effort of will, he enters the dock and the workers follow him. A metal gate lowers behind them.

As Tom watched, a horrible realization dawned upon him. In the penultimate scene of Leo's masterpiece, *Native Land*, made twelve years before *On the Waterfront*, a man is unmasked at a labor meeting as a spy. The union members want to beat him up, but instead he is made to walk a gauntlet, enduring the contempt and disgust of the workers he has betrayed. "It's a shot for shot steal," Tom thought, staring at the screen with growing amazement and rage. He had never put it together until now, though he must have seen *On the Waterfront* at least half a dozen times over the years. The truth hit him with physical force. Not only had Kazan copied the scene, but he had also transformed the reviled rat from Leo's film into a crusading hero. Kazan must have known it, Tom thought. The son of a bitch did this to say fuck you to Leo—not only did I name you, but I'm going to turn this scene from your masterpiece inside out and shove it in your face.

The montage ended and the lights came up. The applause began. Some in the audience sat on their hands as they had been urged to do by the anti-Kazan lobby. Most rose to their feet in ovation. Tom sat stock-still and watched as Kazan, ninety-years-old, tottered to the stage, supported by his wife. He lifted the Oscar above his head. "I want to thank the Academy for its courage and generosity," he said.

Yes, thought Tom, Kazan is a good director. He had staged this scene and cast himself as the star—a feeble old man, flanked by the giants of the next generation, finally getting his due. It was unbelievable. Forty-five years after Kazan had implicated his father, this corrupt, decaying filmmaker had gotten in one last swipe at Leo. The bad guys *had* won this round, and it mattered to Tom more than he ever imagined it would.

CHAPTER NINETEEN

The Next War

ELLIOT ABRAMS, 1989–2010

The years between 1980 and 1986 were heady ones for Elliott. He campaigned for the election of Ronald Reagan; married Rachel Decter, the daughter of Norman Podhoretz; joined the transition team for the incoming president; and became, at the age of thirty-two, the youngest assistant secretary of state in the twentieth century. From there, Elliott rapidly rose to assistant secretary of state for Human Rights and Humanitarian Affairs and then, with the backing of his new Beltway mentor, Secretary of State George Shultz, to assistant secretary of state for Inter-American Affairs.

But when the Iran-Contra scandal broke in October 1986, Elliott became one the main figures in the scandal. He spent a good portion of the next three years trying to keep his job while testifying about the extent of his knowledge about illegally diverted funds (to the Nicaraguan Contras) to three different groups charged with investigating the matter: joint hearings by the Senate and the House of Representatives; the Tower Commission, headed by Sen. John Tower; and a criminal investigation conducted by the Office of Independent Counsel. Despite the best efforts of his Democratic foes in Congress, Elliott, with the support of Shultz and by dint of his own savvy, had successfully remained at his post until the end of Reagan's presidency in January 1989.

Two and a half years later, in the summer of 1991, Elliott was well settled into his new life in the private sector. As a senior fellow at the Hudson

Institute, a Washington, D.C., think tank, Elliott was in the midst of writing what he hoped would be a major opus on the history and future of U.S. foreign policy. His eleven-year marriage to Rachel had produced three children: Jacob, Sarah and Joseph. The couple was a fixture in the neoconservative social scene and in the observant Jewish community.

By then, the Iran-Contra scandal had receded from the headlines, and two of the three bodies investigating it had completed their work. The Tower Commission's final report, issued in February 1987, took President Reagan to task for his lax oversight of the affair but declined to make any sweeping indictments.

The congressional committee then held televised hearings from May 5 to August 6, 1987, interrogating more than thirty-two witnesses including Caspar Weinberger; Secretary of State Shultz and his right-hand man Elliott; National Security Advisor John Poindexter, his Deputy National Security Advisor Robert McFarlane, who succeeded Poindexter as NSA chief, and their chief functionary, Oliver North; and CIA Deputy Director of Operations Clair George, and his Chief of the Central American Task Force (Elliott's opposite number in the CIA) Alan Fiers.

But despite months of testimony, no direct link to President Reagan emerged, and the committee ceased operation in the summer of 1987. That fall, the panel issued a report that also chided the president. But it went a step further, placing the majority of blame on a "cabal of zealots" who had disregarded "fundamental processes of governance" and who had "subverted" the rule of law. A minority report issued by Republicans on the committee, including Wyoming senator Dick Cheney, however, found "mistakes in judgement and nothing more" and took aim at the "hysterical conclusions" reached by Democrats on the committee.

Still, one investigatory body stayed doggedly on the case: the Office of the Independent Counsel (OIC), headed by Lawrence Walsh. A retired federal judge, Walsh had been appointed Independent Counsel on December 19, 1986. The office itself had been created in reaction to the Watergate scandal—specifically, to the "Saturday Night Massacre" of October 1973, in which a scandal-plagued President Nixon ordered Attorney

General Elliot Richardson to fire Watergate Special Prosecutor Archibald Cox. Richardson resigned rather than do so, as did his subordinate. In 1978, legislation followed to prevent such politically motivated maneuvers in the future, allowing for the appointment of an investigator who could be fired only by the attorney general. The investigator's office was to be given virtually unlimited funds and an open time frame in which to complete its work.

By 1991, well into the fifth year of his investigation into the Iran-Contra matter, Walsh, now nearly eighty years old, and his eleven-member staff, had achieved several significant convictions: McFarlane, who had pleaded guilty to four misdemeanor counts of withholding information from Congress; North, for three of the sixteen felony counts brought against him; North's associate Richard V. Secord, who pleaded guilty to one felony count of making false statements to Congress; and Poindexter, who was convicted on five felony counts on April 7, 1990.

But since then, Walsh's team had suffered significant reversals when the convictions of North and Poindexter were overturned. Despite pressure from Congressional Republicans, most notably Speaker of the House Bob Dole, to wind up its investigation, Walsh decided to press on. The OIC appealed the overturned convictions. In May 1991, when the Supreme Court declined to review North's case, Walsh redoubled his efforts.

In his memoir of the investigation, *Firewall: The Iran-Contra Conspiracy and Cover-Up*, Walsh wrote, "The reversal of Oliver North's conviction forced us into a new race with Congress, a race for public opinion. I had to outrun a determined political effort by North's supporters, George Bush's administration, and congressional critics [who wanted] to shut down my office. Public support was waning, and many negative editorials and columns appeared as our expenditures approached the $25 million mark in September 1990. . . . Without any political constituency of my own, I depended on the news media to help me reach the public and explain why, after spending so much money only to have the man at the center of the scandal go free, I now planned to expand the scope of my investigation."

Despite Walsh's persistence, by the beginning of 1991 Elliott believed he had nothing to fear from the OIC. After the congressional hearings had wrapped up in 1987, he had testified three times in front of a grand jury convened by the OIC and had been interviewed several times by one of Walsh's chief assistants and by a young lawyer on the staff named Jeffrey Toobin. In early 1988, according to Elliott, the OIC had informed his lawyer, W. DeVier Pierson, that it was satisfied with his testimony. Elliott had not heard from the committee since then.

Part of his sanguine attitude was also due, somewhat counter-intuitively, to the recent publication of *Opening Arguments*, Toobin's chronicle of the time he spent working with the OIC. As a teenager, Toobin had been transfixed by watching crusading lawyers bring down the corrupt Nixon administration on the televised Watergate hearings, so the opportunity to be part of this new crusade was thrilling. "We would take on Reagan and all the President's men, with their contempt for the Constitution, disdain for the Congress, and hostility to the truth," he wrote. "We had nothing less than a blank check to uncover and rectify the misdeeds of a corrupt and dishonorable administration. We wouldn't stop until we reached the top."

Among the "president's men," Elliott Abrams particularly excited Toobin's interest. He volunteered to work on the Abrams case exclusively, a task he undertook "with an enthusiasm that bordered on the unseemly. . . . The prosecution of Abrams would serve as a warning to all those who thought they could dispense truth like charity on a chosen few. Getting the bad guys—this was what being a prosecutor was all about."

Elliott's sense of satisfaction upon reading Toobin's book in January 1991was twofold. First, *Opening Arguments* plainly made nonsense of the OIC's stance as a disinterested seeker of justice. "Its members were primarily liberal and Democratic, and motivated by a nasty mix of personal ambition, ideology, and animus," Elliott wrote. "They were after scalps and had only very reluctantly concluded they could not get mine."

Walsh himself was dismayed by Toobin's gleefully partisan tone. "Never having broken a case, or even tried one, but professing to speak for all 'prosecutors,' [Toobin] characterized McFarlane specifically and all accomplices who testified against their confederates as 'scumbags,'" he wrote in *Firewall.* "A chapter was devoted to his own shallow investigation of Elliott Abrams."

But Elliott's sense complacency was marred when he learned that Walsh's staff was questioning his friends and former White House colleagues. Then, on July 9, 1991, Fiers, with whom he had testified side by side in front of the House Intelligence Committee in July 1991, reached an agreement with the OIC to avoid prosecution, pleading guilty to two misdemeanor counts of withholding information from Congress. "Oh yes, my heart had skipped a beat when we read in the papers . . . about Alan Fiers' guilty plea," Elliott wrote. "But the more I read the more I relaxed. . . . He had, according to his statement, known of the arms sales to Iran and the diversion of money to the Contras early in the game, and had been ordered by a superior officer to leave it out of his testimony. I had learned of it, with everyone else, when the story broke."

When Elliott returned to Washington with his family from a summer vacation, he found the investigation still very much in play. On September 6, Clair George, Fiers' boss at the CIA, was indicted by a grand jury and charged with ten felonies after refusing to strike a plea bargain with the OIC. And on September 10, Elliott's lawyer called him with the news that the OIC had said there was "movement" in the case against Elliott and that he was, indeed, still a target of the investigation. That movement was prompted by a specific urgency on the OIC's part: Walsh had determined that their best case against Elliott was to charge him with perjury for his testimony to the House Intelligence Committee given on October 10, 1986. Due to the five-year statute of limitations on perjury charges, the OIC had only weeks to make its move.

Despite Fiers' plea bargain and George's indictment, Elliott remained confident that OIC would not be able to do him any real damage. At the very worst, he thought, he could appear before a grand jury, a move that would expose the weakness of Walsh's case against him. "I wasn't scared of their 'evidence.'" Elliott wrote in his account of his travails with the OIC, *Undue Process.* I was confident I would impress them as a credible person and a powerful witness. Either they would believe me and drop their case, or they would conclude that they would lose their case if they brought it to trial. They'd see that they could never convince a jury beyond a reasonable doubt that I had known North was running the private network or, for that matter that he was doing anything illegal. Two hours on the stand, and this terrible business would be over."

Elliott's lawyers deflated his bravado, and he began to appreciate the precariousness of his position. Indictment was a real possibility, and with it, ruinous legal fees, the possible loss of his reputation and livelihood and—most terrifying of all—the prospect of going to prison. While Elliott's lawyers tried to arrange a meeting with Walsh to find a way to make the situation go away, Elliott contacted Schultz, asking him to write a letter of support. Schultz demurred, saying he had made an enemy of Walsh and that his support would do Elliott more harm than good.

On September 26, two weeks before the statute of limitations on Elliott's testimony was set to expire, Pierson met with Walsh and laid out Elliott's position: That he had been kept ignorant of the extent of North's illegal activities in funding the Contras, and was completely unaware of the arms-for-hostages scheme in Iran. Later that day, Pierson told Elliott that Walsh's team had no intention of dismissing the matter. Knowing that George had just been indicted for refusing to plead to a lesser charge, Elliott realized that Walsh was not bluffing. On his way home that night, Elliott, distraught, had a brief urge to drive his car off the road. At home, Rachel, whose combative nature rivaled Elliott's own, urged him to fight. "They can go to hell," she said. "We'll fight this. We'll win."

Fortified by his wife's support, Elliott met with his lawyers the next day and told them he would make no plea and would take his chances at trial. Another option was floated: Elliott himself would meet with Walsh and his staff to make his case. The next day he and Pierson met with Walsh and his new executive assistant Craig Gillen in the OIC office. The day-long summit failed to move Walsh, but Elliott at least had the satisfaction of delivering an impassioned defense to his inquisitors. He recalls saying: "Look, I spent my time in the government doing my job following the President's and Secretary's instructions. I did not feather my nest. I spent zero time, zero, setting up future clients, meeting with bankers, investors, future employers, because that was not right. Then came this scandal and I have been paying and paying and paying." Elliott's oration elicited only a noncommittal "I understand" from Walsh. Still, he left the office on an emotional high, feeling he had scored a moral victory.

At home that evening, Elliott, still determined to go to trial, called his children together and explained the situation, delivering perhaps his most frank rationale of the events that had brought him to this point.

"When I was in the State Department I knew a lot of secrets. Lots and lots, and I wasn't allowed to tell anyone," he recalls saying. "You remember Nicaragua, and the Contras, and how they were fighting the Communists in Nicaragua? Well, I knew lots and lots of secrets about that, and Secretary Shultz and President Reagan didn't want me to tell. Now, some people are saying, you should have told Congress. You had to tell. When they asked you, you had to tell, and not telling is a crime. And I am saying, no it isn't. So we may have a court case, where they accuse me, they say I did something wrong, and I say, No I didn't. And it might take a year. And if it happens, there will be lots of TV cameras around for a day or so. But then, life will be pretty normal, and you don't have to worry about it. Instead of going to my office, to write my book, I'll go to court. But for you, for us, life will really be the same after the first day or two."

Elliott then recalls his son, Jacob, asking, "If they are accusing you, what about Ronald Reagan? What about George Bush? Why didn't they get accused too?" It was a question that tapped into the particular bitterness and sense of betrayal Elliott felt toward the men he had served for eight years. When he was being regularly grilled by Congress, taking hits for the team, Reagan had not once reached out to him. It was the least he could have done, Elliott thought. He was incredulous at the way Reagan had immediately caved in to congressional pressure to appoint the Tower Commission. After becoming president in 1988, George H. W. Bush had been similarly unhelpful.

As the September days passed, Elliott toggled back and forth between his determination to tough it out—a stance still fervently backed by Rachel—and his desire to make the situation go away by making some sort of a plea—a course of action devoutly wished for by his mother and brother. Elliott's greatest fear about a plea was the perception by his friends and colleagues that he had informed upon his former colleagues in order to obtain it, as Fiers was presumed to have done when he reached his agreement with the OIC. "Everyone would assume I had also incriminated someone in any plea I made, would assume I was an informant, a stoolie. 'Cooperating with the investigation,' 'Turned state's evidence.' Disgusting." The fact that the record of any such discussion or testimony would be sealed, he thought, would only incite speculation.

Just days before the October 10 deadline, Elliott relented, agreeing to plead guilty to two misdemeanor counts of withholding information from Congress. In exchange, Elliott agreed to attend a proffer conference at which he would be required to submit to close questioning about his activities in the Iran-Contra affair—and those of his colleagues. Despite maintaining that he had no incriminating information to offer, Elliott was repelled not only by the idea that he would be "asked to ruin the life of a former colleague but by the odd Communist Chinese quality of the process. This was not only prosecution but 'reeducation' as well." Elliott wrote that during the two-hour meeting with the OIC lawyers, he "learned that collaborationism was possible, was possible in America, was possible for me. I tasted the temptation to burn my friends to save myself; and I wanted for a moment, to do it. The feeling was literally sickening."

Any irony to be found in Elliott undergoing an ordeal similar to that of some of the parents of his high school friends who had been the targets of the McCarthy hearings was lost on Elliott.

On Monday morning, October 7, Elliott watched the televised opening session of congressional hearings against Supreme Court nominee Clarence Thomas, who was accused by a former assistant, Anita Hill, of sexual harassment. "Think of it," he thought. "Here is a man who is having a worse day than I am, and I am pleading guilty today." In court later that day, he pled guilty to two counts of withholding information from Congress.

Elliott received his sentence a few weeks later: two years probation, one hundred hours of community service and a nominal fine. Outside the courthouse, he read a statement to the press: "I take full responsibility for my actions, for my failure to make full disclosure to Congress in 1986. I am proud to have given twelve years serving the United States government and of the contribution I made in those years and am very glad to have this entire matter—at long last—behind me." As he and Rachel made their way down the court steps the reporters shouted out questions: "Did you lie to Congress?" "Don't you feel repentant?" "Is that all you're going to say?" "Won't you apologize?"

"Screw you," Elliott thought.

He felt no need to apologize. Looking back, Elliott blamed himself only for his inexperience and naïveté in failing to be more proactive in pressing Fiers and North for information. "I had been new. I had not been a career operative, a career diplomat, a career soldier, and I had to learn the hard way," he wrote.

But other than that, Elliott blamed everyone else with a sense of rage and ill use almost Nixonian in its scope. He blamed Reagan, who, instead of backing up the men carrying out his policies, took the "cowardly" route and appointed a special prosecutor. He blamed the Democrats who hated him for giving as good as he got when he testified in front of them; the CIA who had "misled, fooled, bamboozled, tricked and deceived him" and the backstabbing culture of Washington. While watching the Clarence Thomas hearings, Elliott had felt the urge to call him and say "[This kind of thing] doesn't happen in America. Only here, in this cesspool. Welcome to your nation's capital." And he hated Walsh's committee, "miserable, filthy bastards . . . bloodsuckers . . . trying to build a career over my bleeding body."

In a wider sense, Elliott blamed left-wing politicians and pundits who harbored an "undying, undimmed hatred" of him. Why? "For having been smart enough to know better . . . being better at fighting them than the others in the Administration, and being unrepentant." Most galling to his enemies, Elliot thought, was the fact that he was openly unrepentant for his service in the Reagan administration.

Once he had harbored hopes of returning to government service in a future administration. No more. "For the first time I realized I would really, seriously tell a young man or woman interested in politics to stay home. To tend their own gardens . . . Stay out of Washington."

On Christmas Eve 1992, before leaving with his family for Camp David, outgoing President George H. W. Bush signed the pardons of six architects of the Iran-Contra scandal: Caspar Weinberger, Alan Fiers, Clair George, Robert McFarlane, Duane Clarridge and Elliott Abrams.

By the time Walsh delivered his final report on the Iran-Contra affair in 1993, eleven officials had been convicted of crimes committed during their participation the scandal. Most of those crimes, however, had been pled down to lesser offenses or were rendered moot by the Bush pardons. Only one low-level CIA operative received jail time.

After Elliott's plea in October 1991, the D.C. Bar Board on Professional Responsibility moved to suspend him from the practice of law. Elliott fought the move. It was 1995 when a District of Columbia appeals court finally ended the threat to his professional standing by ruling that Bush's presidential pardon "blots out the existence of guilt, so that in the eye of the law, the offender is an innocent as if he had never committed the offense."

———————

On June 3, 2000, most of the original thirty-two graduates of the Little Red School House and Elisabeth Irwin High School Class of '65 gathered at the school for their thirty-fifth reunion.

After a cocktail party in the courtyard of the lower school on Bleecker Street, the classmates, now in their mid-fifties, walked the five short blocks downtown to the high school for the official dinner and awards presentation. Afterward, the old friends took another stroll in the warm, late spring evening, this time to a spacious, loft-like apartment on West 12th Street, formerly the home of their classmate Lisa Fein Gilford. Lisa's mother, Madeline, answered the door dressed as a Gypsy fortuneteller, a kerchief wrapped around her cropped white hair, her round face thick with costume makeup.

"Welcome, welcome!" she cried in a theatrical Transylvanian accent. Her performance was a nod to Halloweens past, when the students, their orange cardboard UNICEF containers heavy with coins after a night of

trick-or-treating, would adjourn to the Gilfords' apartment. Lisa's late father, Jack Gilford, had been a celebrated character actor on stage, in television and in film. Both Jack and Madeline were Little Red parents who had
been blacklisted through the 1950s and had appeared before the House
Un-American Activities Committee as unfriendly witnesses.

Milling about in the expansive sunken living room as a CD of 1960s
protest songs by Pete Seeger, Paul Robeson and the Weavers played in
the background, the classmates caught each other up on their lives. Rob-
bie Meeropol, with his brother Michael (Elisabeth Irwin class of '60), the
sons of Julius and Ethel Rosenberg, had started a foundation for the
children of parents targeted for their political activities. Fred Feinstein
had recently finished a stint as general counsel of the National Labor Relations Board under President Bill Clinton. Jeff Melish, whose family
had hosted Angela Davis in their Brooklyn townhouse when she attended Elisabeth Irwin, was a lawyer who did pro bono work for the
poor. Robert Miller, son of playwright Arthur Miller, was a film producer who had brought his father's play *The Crucible* to the screen a few
years before.

At some point, as it always did at these gatherings, the talk turned to an
absent classmate. It had been nine years since Elliott had pled guilty to
misleading Congress, and some in the group were not above crowing
about his fall from power.

"He got what he deserved," said Madeline Gilford, chuckling about Elliott's $10 million misadventure with the Sultan of Brunei. A classmate rose
wryly to Elliott's defense. "Well, none of us were ever any good at math."

Long before his Iran-Contra troubles began in 1986, Elliott had
stopped attending reunions. He found it tiresome to rehash the same old
ideological fights and to be cast, as always, in the role of the reactionary. "I
remember going to a reunion [in 1968] and people saying, 'Are you for
[Eugene] McCarthy?' And I said no. And I started to be abused for being
for [George] McGovern. . . . And when I said, 'No, no, that's not it, I'm for
Humphrey,' there was absolute silence. People thought for a moment then
they realized it was a joke. It was a very funny joke. . . . And I said, 'No it's
not a joke.' That was when they realized I was truly hopeless."

His last contact with the school had been in 1992, when the high school solicited alumni reminiscences for a publication celebrating the school's fiftieth anniversary. Among the fond, nostalgic memories submitted by other alumni, Elliott's entry stood out in sharp relief.

"The EI I attended in the 1960s had a reputation for social and political activism, but it was in precisely these areas that it failed its students," he wrote. "The political bias, not only among the students but much worse in the actual teaching of history and 'social studies,' was pronounced, even scandalous. We were taught hypercritical thinking when it came to the United States, and uncritical acceptance of the pieties of the Left. But EI was spectacular when it came to the humanities and the teaching of culture. . . . EI taught us French, introduced us to theater, started us writing. . . . Here in the humanities, every advantage of a small, independent school was manifest. I hope the old Leftism has departed now, with the Cold War, leaving EI to nurture an appreciation of Western Culture and independent thinking about politics."

The inclusion of Elliott's remarks in the booklet sparked an uproar from his fellow alumni, most of whom were appalled by the part he had played in making policy in Latin America in the 1980s.

"I do not understand what 'balance' you thought you were achieving with the inclusion of the 'opinions' of Elliott Abrams," one alumnus wrote. "Most faculty and students in the school that I attended would have been embarrassed if it were revealed that the 'Albert Speer' of our age and country had spent his high school years in Charlton Street. I do not object to Mr. Abrams expressing his opinion in whatever forum. I would have hoped that it was unthinkable for EI's 50th Anniversary Album to be sullied by three paragraphs by this architect of the Reagan Administration's bloody anti-democratic campaign in Latin America. I guess the faculty can feel proud that they had as few spectacular failures as Elliott Abrams. . . . I am still embarrassed by this graduate's inability to learn any of the important lessons taught at EI. Why aren't you?"

Other alumni missives expressed themselves far less politely—one of them in scatological terms. Decades after Elliott left EI, he still had the power to render his schoolmates apoplectic with rage.

But in the Gilford apartment in the year 2000, Elliott's name evoked a tamer, if condescending reaction from the class of 1965—he was not powerful or threatening enough now to inspire his classmates' passionate agitation. In 1992, twelve years of Republican governance had come to an end with the election of William Jefferson Clinton as president. Although Clinton's working-class Southern upbringing was alien to the classmates, he was still one of their own: an idealistic baby boomer who had protested the war in Vietnam and who had been an enthusiastic participant in the counterculture revolution of the 1960s and '70s. Now the country was prospering and at peace. If, as seemed likely, Vice President Al Gore won the presidency in November, the Reagan years diminish into a reactionary blip. With the Cold War over, it seemed Elliott and his neoconservative brethren had had their day.

By midnight, the group was sitting in a circle in the living room, taking stock of the '60s and its aftermath. It was no longer clear that their generation would live to see a world in which social and economic justice was the norm. And they noted with disappointment that the current crop of college students—their own children among them—were not imbued with the same sense of mission they had possessed.

But if the revolution hadn't turned out quite the way they had planned, it seemed that at least, at the start of this new century, the country was again on the right track—and for that the classmates took some small portion of credit. "Little Red changed the world," one of them told a *New York Times* reporter who was on hand. "Big revolutions are made by little places."

Elliott had kept a low public profile through the 1990s after his plea bargain. From the Hudson Institute, he had moved in 1996 to the Ethics and Public Policy Institute, another D.C. think tank whose mission was to "enforce the bond between the Judeo-Christian moral tradition and the public debate over domestic and foreign policy issues." He wrote three books: *Undue Process: A Story of How Political Differences Are Turned into Crimes* (1993); *Security and Sacrifice: Isolation, Intervention, and American Foreign Policy* (1995); and *Faith or Fear: How Jews Can Survive in a Christian America* (1997), and had co-written several more.

Although much of the outside world thought he had fallen from his high perch, Elliott's status in the tightly knit neoconservative community, already high by virtue of being Norman Podhoretz's son-in-law and his service in the Reagan State Department, had only been burnished by his bruising encounter with the Office of Independent Counsel.

The neocons as a group were not much heard from through the 1990s as they sought to retool their philosophy to fit the new world order. With the end of the Cold War, they found themselves in a dilemma similar to that of the New Left when the Vietnam War ended in 1975—the foe they had initially rallied around to vanquish no longer existed. Without that focus, the neocons faced the worst fate imaginable: irrelevance.

When George H. W. Bush became president in 1989, he surrounded himself with pragmatic, old-school Republicans like his secretary of state James Baker and his national security advisor Brent Scowcroft. The neocons were nominally represented in the new administration, most notably by Elliott's second-generation contemporaries Paul Wolfowitz, Richard Armitage and I. Lewis "Scooter" Libby—all of whom worked under Secretary of Defense Dick Cheney—and by William Kristol, who served as Vice President Dan Quayle's chief of staff. But these men had limited influence over Bush, who associated them with the Iran-Contra disaster.

Written off by liberals and mainstream Republicans, the neocons patiently set about quietly expanding their spheres of influence through think tanks, through their berths in Ivy League universities and in Georgetown social circles.

In January 1991, the void left by the collapse of the U.S.S.R. was filled when President Bush launched Operation Desert Storm with a coalition of thirty-four countries to liberate the Middle Eastern kingdom of Kuwait, which had been invaded by Iraq, led by its dictator Saddam Hussein. The neocons were elated when Kuwait was liberated in a matter of weeks, with minimal loss of American lives. Now all that was left to do, in their eyes, was to march the troops into Baghdad and depose Hussein. But to their dismay, Bush, taking the more measured course recommended by Scowcroft and Baker, declined to do so. That decision sparked what many would come to see as an obsessive desire by neocons to finish the job—to effect regime change in Iraq and remove Saddam Hussein from power.

If the neocons had been sparsely represented in the Bush administration, they were virtually banished in Clinton's. But they continued to present their ideas, and the neocon message began to surface not only through established conduits like conservative radio talk shows like *The Rush Limbaugh Show* but also in mainstream conservative media outlets such as the *Washington Times*, the *Wall Street Journal* and even in perceived liberal bulwarks like the *New York Times* and the *Washington Post*.

Although his involvement in Iran-Contra had scuttled any hope of a position on the Bush administration, Elliott worked diligently to keep the neoconservative message alive. He was a founding member of some if its key committees, notably the Committee on U.S. Interests in the Middle East, founded in 1991 to challenge what they considered to be faint support for Israel by the administration. In 1997, Elliott, along with neocon luminaries including Dick Cheney, Norman Podhoretz, Midge Decter, I. Lewis Libby, Dan Quayle, Donald Rumsfeld and Paul Wolfowitz, founded the Project for a New American Century. One of the organization's main goals was regime change in Iraq. In an open letter to President Clinton in 1998, the group stated that it was necessary to eliminate "the possibility that Iraq will be able to use or threaten to use weapons of mass destruction. In the near term, this means a willingness to undertake military action as diplomacy is clearly failing. In the long term, it means removing Saddam Hussein and his regime from power. That now needs to become the aim of American foreign policy."

As the Clinton administration wound down, the neocons were divided on which Republican candidate to back in 2000: Arizona Senator John McCain or Texas Governor George W. Bush. Many, including William Kristol and Jeane Kirkpatrick, backed McCain, fearing that the younger Bush would continue his father's policies. But a few, including Perle, Wolfowitz, and Stephen Hadley, an assistant secretary of defense in the George H. W. Bush administration, lined up behind the younger Bush. Candidate George W. Bush's chief foreign affairs advisor, Condoleezza Rice, put them to work building up his rudimentary knowledge of foreign affairs. When

Bush won the election, they and other neocons were appointed to positions in the Defense Department under Donald Rumsfeld, in the State Department under Colin Powell and in the National Security Council (NSC) under Rice.

By this time, Elliott had reconsidered his vow never to return to public service. In 1999, he had accepted a presidential appointment to the United States Commission on International Religious Freedom; in the spring of 2001, he became chairman of the commission. Now that his colleagues had gained a foothold in the new administration, Elliott began to chart his own course back to power.

"The latest whisper on the diplomatic grapevine concerns Elliott Abrams, that whipping boy of liberals still angry over the Iran-Contra affair. . . . Reaganites think it is time for Abrams to be rehabilitated after running afoul of the Iran-Contra inquiries," read a gossipy May 2001 item in the conservative *Washington Times*.

Elliott was also reportedly approaching old colleagues on Capitol Hill, testing the waters to see if he had the votes to be confirmed to a position in the administration. If not contrite, Elliott portrayed himself as having been tempered by his experiences in office under Reagan, even, according to one staffer, admitting that he judged some of his adversaries in the human rights community too harshly. "He said he'd come to believe that he was wrong about some things—that some human-rights groups had been right in certain instances," a staffer told the *New Yorker*. "He said some people whom he had identified as his enemies he now believed had been playing a legitimate role—but he had lumped them all together as evil because they were opposing him."

His groundwork paid off. On June 28, the White House announced that Elliott, now fifty-three, had been named special assistant to the president and senior director for democracy, human rights, and international operations at the NSC. The announcement was met by howls of outrage from liberal policy makers and pundits. "I consider this one of the most bizarre appointments imaginable," said Larry Birns, director of the Council on Hemispheric Affairs. A subsequent comment on the organization's website read: "A self-confessed perjurer conceivably should be in jail rather than on the NSC."

Liberal columnist and journalist Mary McGrory summed up the anti-Elliott sentiment in the *Washington Post*: "Abrams was the pit bull for the [Reagan] administration's 'better dead than red' policy on Central America. Despite his record, George W. Bush is giving him another chance. . . . The appointment signifies a step beyond Bush's in-your-face selections for Latin America. This one is in your eye, a signal to the right wing that there is nothing he will not do for it. Choosing Abrams makes laughable Bush's promise of increased civility and bipartisanship. Ditto his claims of being 'a uniter, not a divider.'"

The position, by virtue of its NSC umbrella, needed no confirmation from Congress. Elliott was back in.

On the morning of September 11, 2001, Elliott was in his White House office preparing for the daily NSC briefing conducted by Rice, when one of his deputies pointed to the surreal and terrifying events playing out on the television.

"My immediate thought was, a plane had once crashed into the Empire State building, you know, the pilot must be a fool or something," Elliott later recalled. "During the staff meeting, Condi was called away—because the second plane had hit. Getting back to the office, I looked at the TV and saw a second plane had hit and it was obvious this was a terrorist attack. And we were then evacuated from the White House grounds."

In the immediate aftermath of the World Trade Center attack, Elliott became indispensible to Rice. "In the turmoil at the NSC after September 11, Abrams stood out as a problem solver—focused, quick, and decisive, unburdened by doubt," wrote Connie Bruck in an extensive article about Elliott that appeared in the *New Yorker* in December 2003. Rice valued him not just as a manager, but as a skilled strategist, a colleague of Rice's told the *New Yorker*. She put him in charge of co-ordinating humanitarian relief efforts when the United States invaded Afghanistan in October 2001 and, in March 2003, Iraq.

Having proved himself invaluable to his new mentor, Elliott embarked on a familiar trajectory. In December 2002, he was elevated to the position of special assistant to the president and senior director for Near East and North African Affairs, becoming the key official in charge of all Middle

East affairs, including Iran and Iraq. In 2005, he was promoted again, to the post of deputy assistant to the president and deputy national security adviser for global democracy strategy.

With the War on Terror in full force, Elliott and his fellow neocons were once again on ideological terra firma. "I feel young again! I love all these battles—they're so familiar to me," he told a friend.

In January 2008, Elliott left the White House after eight years of service to return to private life. As in the Reagan years, he had outlasted a majority of his colleagues, many of whom had been forced out as a result of the debacle that was the very short war in, and very long occupation of, Iraq. He took up residence at the Council on Foreign Relations in Washington, D.C. as senior fellow for Middle Eastern Studies. This time, however, the organization was a non-partisan one whose members include news anchor Brian Williams, contributing editor for *Time* magazine Fareed Zakaria and actress and activist Angelina Jolie.

In March 2010, sixty-two-year-old Elliott cordially escorted a reporter from the well-appointed Council on Foreign Relations conference room to the elevator after an interview. As the two made small talk, Elliott's assistant walked over and spoke a few words into his boss's ear. Energized, Elliott strode quickly away, calling happily over his shoulder, "I've got to go—we're doing a lunch on whether there will be a third intifada."

CHAPTER TWENTY

Occupy Everywhere

ANGELA DAVIS, 1972–2012

On February 19, 2012, Angela joined hundreds of past and present members of the Communist Party USA to pay tribute to the late Henry M. Winston on what would have been his 100th birthday. Winston, or Winnie, as he was universally called by those who knew him, served as national chairman of the CPUSA for decades, the only African American to hold that post. Born in Mississippi in 1933, he joined the party at the age of twenty-two. After serving in World War II, Winston returned to the United States where he was arrested and tried with other party members for violating the Smith Act of 1940, which made it illegal to advocate violent overthrow of the U.S government. Upon being convicted, Winston went underground, then turned himself in and served nearly a decade in prison. Winston died in 1986.

Angela had tremendous affection for Winston. They first met in 1970, shortly after her arrest, in the visiting room at New York's House of Detention, Winnie had calmed her with his gentle manner and with his assurance the party would devote all of its resources to freeing her. Now, when Angela took the podium and recounted the events that had propelled her onto the public stage.

"When I think back on that period, I find it hard to believe that so much happened within a relatively short period of time," she said. "I had been a member of the Communist Party for less than a year when I accepted a position at UCLA. During the summer prior to the semester I was scheduled to teach, Kendra Alexander and I joined a delegation to Cuba. We returned to discover that I had been made the target of a raging anti-communist attack headed by Governor Ronald Reagan."

Angela spoke of her friend Charlene Mitchell's run for president on the CPUSA ticket in 1968. It was the first time the party had put forward a candidate since the beginning of the Blacklist and Mitchell was the first African American to run for president on a third-party ticket. Angela had accompanied Mitchell on campaign stops from state to state.

After Angela's trial and acquittal in June 1972, she returned to her life as an academic and activist in California. In 1980, Mitchell and other party members approached Angela about running for president. Although it was a symbolic run—no third party had ever won the presidency in modern times—Mitchell was convinced that Angela, a nationally known figure with youth and charisma, could revitalize the CPUSA, which was experiencing growing internecine tensions, many of them revolving around race and gender equality. Angela categorically refused to run for president, but she was persuaded to run for vice president with General Secretary Gus Hall at the top of the ticket. Now, it was Mitchell's turn to accompany Angela on campaign stops, noting that where she, Mitchell, more than a decade before, had encountered indifference, if not outright hostility, Angela commanded standing-room-only crowds. Angela ran again for vice president on the CPUSA ticket in 1984.

When Angela's old nemesis Ronald Reagan became president in 1980, the need for new thinking and new leadership in the CPUSA became even more pronounced, as Reagan chipped away at progressive advances made in the 1960s and '70s. In the summer of 1981, Reagan fired thirteen thousand striking air traffic controllers, effectively breaking their union. But American Communists saw an opportunity to rally around emerging populist movements on the international scene, including the Solidarity movement in Poland and the anti-apartheid crusade in South Africa, which were gaining traction worldwide.

At the same time, the world's leading exporter of Communist ideology, the U.S.S.R., was in irreversible decline. The CPUSA's seemingly endless capacity for denial rendered it incapable of grasping the democratization of the Soviet Union taking place throughout the 1980s.

Winston lived to see the beginning of the end of Soviet Communism under General Secretary Mikhail Gorbachev but died before the defection of his closest comrades from the CPUSA. Throughout the 1990s, a growing number of members became increasingly alienated by the racism, sexism and homophobia prevalent within the leadership of the party under Gus Hall. By 1991, Angela, Mitchell, the Alexanders, James Jackson, Bettina Aptheker and her father, Herbert, had come to believe, in Mitchell's words, that the CPUSA's "devotion to sterile dogmas were driving the Party into sectarianism, isolation and irrelevance."

On December 5, 1991, days before the formal dissolution of the Soviet Union, hundreds of CPUSA delegates arrived at the Sheraton Hotel in Cleveland for the party's national convention and were shocked to discover a strong police presence in the meeting hall. The leadership of the CPUSA had asked for their help to guard against demonstrations from dissident party members. In anticipation of the convention, those members had drafted a document and petition called "Unite and Renew the Party," advocating reform and democratization. When told they would not be allowed to speak at the convention or to run for office, the Unite and Renew contingent held its own convention across the street. Angela, who was in California with a former student and friend who was dying of AIDS, did not attend.

In the weeks after the conference, nearly a third of the party's 2,700 members resigned in protest, including virtually the entire Communist Party of Northern California. In February 1992, that contingent released a scathing document declaring that the convention had been illegitimate and fraudulent and calling the resolutions it had adopted a "cult-like exposition of dogma." The atmosphere of the convention, it continued, was "racist, sexist and intimidating with veteran Communists, women and people of color treated with contempt."

In quitting the party, Angela and her comrades had not relinquished their Marxist beliefs. Under Mitchell's leadership, the Committees of Correspondence for Democracy and Socialism was created—named after Revolutionary War–era groups struggling against British rule—in order to more democratically pursue "the development and application of Marxism-Leninism."

"Our members are activists in all the social movements of our country—of labor, civil rights, immigrant rights, women, peace, international solidarity, gay and lesbian rights, environment, youth and students, seniors, and religion," its mission statement read. "We have come together to help shape a clear-cut alternative to the destructive, mean-spirited corporate drive for profit above all else. We seek constructive solutions to the problems of poverty and unemployment, racism, sexism, health, education, and housing."

At age forty-eight, Angela severed her connection with the CPUSA, an organization to which she had belonged for most of her adult life, with reluctance. "I kept saying that I wouldn't have, at that point, left the party had not it been for the fact that we were basically prohibited from running for office," she later said. It was a point of pride for Angela that the Committees of Correspondence did not become involved in the vitriolic conflicts with the CPUSA. Her presence at Winston's posthumous birthday celebration in 2012, sponsored by the CPUSA, was proof of that.

Angela continued her speech. "I cannot reflect on the life of Henry Winston without also remembering Kendra and Franklin Alexander, who loved Winnie with all their hearts. It was the two of them, along with Charlene Mitchell, who recruited me into the Communist Party."

Weeks after her acquittal in the summer of 1972, Angela, accompanied by Franklin and Kendra, embarked on a victory tour of Cuba, Chile, East Germany and the Soviet Union, the communist countries that had supported her during the trial. From the time she stepped onto the tarmac in Moscow, Angela was greeted as a hero. She received bouquets from school children, accepted a Lenin Centenary medal from a middle-aged party apparatchik and addressed thousands in an outdoor rally in Moscow, where she was welcomed by cosmonaut Valentina Vladimirovna Teresh-kova, the first woman in space. The three friends placed floral tributes at Lenin's tomb and at the monument of the Siege of Leningrad. From the shop floor of a Kirov factory, Angela praised the workers for not using "products of labor [to fuel the] irrational drive for capitalist profits as it is used in our country." As she left the country, Angela gave the cheering crowd at the airport in Moscow the Black Power salute as she said, "Long live the friendship of our two peoples and long live the science of Marxism-Leninism."

In 1980, Angela, now thirty-six, married Hilton Braithwaite, a photographer and fellow professor in the University of California system. Mitchell, who was herself getting remarried that summer, drove from New York to Birmingham to attend Angela's nuptials in the Davis family home. Although Angela and Hilton had dated for a year, Mitchell was surprised to hear of the engagement. "I'd never seen her in a relationship where she was ready to do that," she said. Arriving shortly before the ceremony, Mitchell greeted Sallye and Frank, with whom she had grown close over the months of Angela's imprisonment and trial. Mitchell then helped Angela, who was "scampering around" in a bit of a tizzy, prepare for the ceremony.

Somewhat improbably, the wedding was covered by *People* magazine. Under the headline "Angela Davis, Sweetheart of the Far Left, Finds Her Mr. Right." "A pianist played 'We've Only Just Begun' and then the traditional *Lohengrin* wedding march as the couple came down the stairs," the story ran. The groom wore tails and Davis, radiant in a peach-colored gown, carried a bouquet of flowers complete with baby's breath. Then they exchanged simple gold bands and vows they wrote themselves, including a plea for world peace and a commitment to separate identities. The only party line in evidence was the usual one at the reception held a block away at her mother's church." The story identified Frank as "a gas station owner" and Sallye as "a retired schoolmarm." Sallye had acquired multiple degrees in education by that time, and Frank, although his career choices had been constrained in the Jim Crow South in which he came of age, had a bachelor's degree and had done graduate work at Fisk University.

Despite its promising beginning, the marriage quietly ended in divorce a few years later.

But Angela's extended family of friends remained in place. Among the closest of them were Franklin and Kendra, whose marriage had endured. Living in the Berkeley house they had owned for decades, the Alexanders continued their activism in northern California. In 1993, Kendra was serving as a legislative aide to a Berkeley city councilwoman. Franklin worked with union groups and led African Americans Against the War in the Middle East, which he founded when the United States invaded Iraq in 1991.

On May 23, 1993, Kendra was talking on the telephone with Franklin in the upstairs bedroom when she smelled smoke. She ran downstairs and found the source of the fire: a quilt that had been set ablaze by the smoldering cigarette butt of a houseguest. Kendra threw the quilt out the back door and returned upstairs. Franklin, still on the line, told her to call 911. Minutes later, there was an explosion. By the time Angela, living in nearby Oakland, received a call from a distraught Franklin, the house was engulfed in flames and Kendra could not be found. After the fire was brought under control, her body was found in the bedroom.

Somehow, Franklin blamed himself for the tragedy. "He never recovered from the depression that accompanied Kendra's death," said Angela. "He felt in a sense responsible and I don't think he ever forgave himself for that, although we tried to convince him that it was not his fault." On the anniversary of Kendra's death, several years later, Franklin committed suicide.

In 2009, Mitchell suffered a debilitating stroke that left the right side of her body paralyzed. Angela cleared her schedule to accompany him to Cuba for several weeks so that Mitchell, having exhausted the physical therapy allowance under Medicare, could receive an intensive regimen of physical therapy. As a result, although still suffering from aphasia and partial paralysis, Mitchell is able to walk with assistance and to live in her Harlem home.

Angela has been consistent in maintaining a wall of privacy around her personal life. In a 1993 keynote address at the annual conference of the National Black Lesbian and Gay Leadership Forum, she tacitly came out as a lesbian, or so many believe, saying that gay and lesbian issues were "informed by both my personal and political life." But Angela has then and since declined to speak directly about own sexual orientation. Being a lesbian is "something I'm fine with as a political statement," she told *Out* magazine in 1998, "but I still want a private space for carrying out my relationships." Despite a life overflowing with dramatic events, she remains "unwilling to render my life as a personal adventure."

Angela was initially displeased with the rise of identity politics, in which groups organize around shared life experiences as opposed to an overarching philosophy. "The personal is not political; the *political* is political," she believed. But the AIDS epidemic of the 1980s caused her to rethink that stance. "In the 1970s, nobody would have imagined it possible to build a huge movement around an illness."

Whatever the vicissitudes of her personal life, Angela's public life remains remarkably consistent. By 2000, despite the regents' best efforts, she had been a professor in the University of California system for three decades, a tenured professor in the History of Consciousness Department at UC Santa Cruz. She has published many books on a range of topics concerning oppressed peoples, feminism, African American studies, critical theory and Marxism.

Angela continues to maintain a punishing schedule of personal appearances and interviews and to speak at numerous universities around the country. The focus of that activism is the U.S. prison system. When Angela was herself in prison, she vowed "that if I was ever free, I would use my life to uphold the cause of my sisters and brothers behind walls." In 1998, Angela founded the Critical Resistance, a national grassroots organization dedicated not to the reform but the abolishment of the "Prison Industrial Complex."

Her most sustained and well-known work in this arena has been the decades-long campaign to free Mumia Abu-Jamal. In 1982, the African American activist and journalist was convicted of murdering a Philadelphia policeman and sentenced to death. Angela helped to spearhead the international "Free Mumia" movement. Like George Jackson, Abu-Jamal wrote a best-selling book in prison, *Live from Death Row*. Also like Jackson, Abu-Jamal, regardless of his guilt or innocence, has become a symbol of the disproportionate and growing percentage of African American men in the U.S. prison system.

"He's been in prison for so, so long," Angela told students in 2009. "You don't have a current mobilization in the U.S. [but] in Germany and France ordinary people everywhere know his name and there are streets named after him and he was made an honorary citizen of Paris." In 2012, Abu-Jamal was removed from death row; he is now serving a life sentence without parole.

Angela's framing of prison issues in the broader contexts of race, class and corporate greed has slowly made its way into mainstream dialogue. In her signal work on the subject, *Are Prisons Obsolete?*, published in 2003, Angela sought to show how the growing population of men and women in American prisons affects the wider population. "In Alabama and Florida, once a felon, always a felon, which entails the loss of status as a rights-bearing citizen," she wrote. "One of the grave consequences of the powerful reach of the prison was the 2000 (s)election of George W. Bush as president. If only the black men and women denied the right to vote because of an actual or presumed felony record had been allowed to cast their ballots, Bush would not be in the White House today. And perhaps we would not be dealing with the awful costs of the War on Terrorism declared during the first year of his administration."

———

On September 11, 2001, Angela had just returned from a conference on racism and xenophobia in South Africa when she learned of the attacks on the World Trade Center and the Pentagon. In the following weeks, at scheduled speaking engagements at campuses around the country, she voiced a controversial opinion: "The United States significantly contributed to conditions that lead to the violence on September 11."

At Keene State College in New Hampshire, Angela said: "I've been told, 'You've expressed how I've been feeling, but I've been afraid to express it.' That, to me, is more frightening than anything else, the idea that we're

afraid to discuss these issues. I find it bizarre, if freedom is being defended, that it is necessary to curtail freedom in order to defend freedom."

At Wellesley, in late October: "So many people are swept up in this odd
patriotism and think all they need to do is wave a flag to become part of a
protected community called the nation. But I don't feel comfortable, considering the leaders of the nation." Nationalism, Angela continued, "cre-
ates fear in those who aren't a part of the nation and in those who might
want to express dissenting ideas."

And at Northwestern University on October 31, 2001: "We have to realize that things have not fundamentally changed. We will no longer be able
to harbor the illusion that the United States is invulnerable, but September
11 did not change the history of this country."

Angela credits her resiliency and optimism in the face of continual set-
backs to Sallye. "My mother always told us children that things would not
always be the same as they were. She always invited us to live in a world in
which there was not that kind of rigid racial segregation. She said over
and over 'this may be the way things are today but they will not be this way
in the future.' She actually trained us to use our imaginations in order not
to feel so totally ensconced in a racist society that we were destroyed by it."

But Angela, like many other Americans, found it hard to be optimistic
during the 2000s, as 9/11 was followed by the invasions of Iraq and Afghanistan, the government's calamitously slow response to the victims
of Hurricane Katrina and the growing disparity between the rich and the
poor. In 2008, however, Angela was heartened as she watched a grassroots
movement encompassing Americans of all races and socioeconomic situ-
ations emerge to support Barack Obama's bid to become America's first
African American president. The two have characteristics in common:
Both are academics; both are blessed with good looks, charm and a gift for
oratory; both have spent their lives trying to reconcile their places in the
white and African American communities. In the run-up to the election,
although Angela was not involved in the campaign, many thought of her
when the cover of the September 21, 2008, issue of the *New Yorker* featured an illustration of Obama in Muslim garb and his wife, Michelle, in
battle fatigues, an AK-47 slung over her shoulder, wearing a tall Afro. That

hairstyle, much to Angela's frustration, has become enduringly associated with her as the only female Black Power figure of the 1960s known by name to the general public.

But after the election, Angela was saddened to see the coalition that elected Obama disperse. "What we didn't do . . . is that we didn't keep that movement going," she said in 2010. "We went back home. We became individuals. We let Obama become an individual again. . . . It's our responsibility. We are the ones we've been waiting for."

———————

On a raw October day in 2011, Angela stepped onto a concrete bench in Washington Square Park in Greenwich Village to address the hundred or so young men and women bundled up against the late autumn chill. Angela, now sixty-seven, wore a black leather coat, a long scarf, knee-high boots and rimless glasses, A light wind blew through her hair, a softened and highlighted version of the trademark Afro of her youth. Referring to notes on her iPhone, she began to speak.

"It is truly an honor to be among you this afternoon."

Immediately, and with gusto, the crowd, in one voice, repeated her words in unison:

"It is truly an honor to be among you this afternoon!"

Angela smiled broadly, appearing touched by the young people's earnestness, while at the same time amused by the absurd aspect of the scenario. For weeks now, Occupy Wall Street protestors had been camping on the concrete ground of Zuccotti Park, an open space in the center of financial district, and had been holding rallies around New York. Similar actions were taking place around the country and around the world. The economic devastation brought on by the worldwide financial collapse of 2008 had again mobilized diverse constituencies who, with their cry of "We are the 99%," had taken to the streets. Since New York City had banned the use of amplifying devices at such demonstrations, the protestors had developed the "human microphone" method of relaying a speaker's address to the back of the crowd.

Angela continued:

"For you are reinventing our political universe."
"For you are reinventing our political universe!"
"You have renewed our collective passion."
"You have renewed our collective passion!"
"You have reminded us that it is still possible to build communities of resistance.
"You have reminded us that it is still possible to build communities of resistance!

Bouyed by her listener's enthusiam, Angela rhetorically leaned in to the call and response cadence of the exchange, visibly drawing energy from her audience as she did so.

And so (And so!)
We say no (We say no!)
To Wall Street (To Wall Street!)
We say no (We say no!)
To big banks (to big banks!) . . . to corporate executives . . . to student debt . . . to eviction . . . We say no (We say no!) to police violence . . . global capitalism . . . to the prison industrial complex [a flurry of wiggling fingers conveyed particular approval of that sentiment] . . . to racism . . . class exploitation . . . homophobia . . . transphobia . . . ableism . . . to the devastation of the environment . . . military occupation . . . to war.

With each call and response, Angela seemed to grow younger, more elated, more carefree.

"We say yes (we say yes!)
To hope (to hope!)
Yes to creativity (Yes to creativity!)
And Yes to the future (Yes to the future!)

Angela finished triumphantly:

"Occupy everywhere!"

On that day, within sight of the jail to which she'd been taken in hand-cuffs forty years earlier and just blocks from the high school she had ten-tatively entered as a teenager, Angela seemed radiantly happy. Despite all the losses, despite the heartbreaking reverses that had followed many gains, nothing had robbed her of the power to imagine a more perfect world. Whether or not such a reality ever came to pass, it was worth spending a lifetime fighting for.

ACKNOWLEDGMENTS

My first thanks must go to the protagonists of this book: Tom Hurwitz, Elliott Abrams and Angela Davis, for sharing their extraordinary life stories with me.

I wish to acknowledge the HistoryMakers; the Schomburg Center for Research in Black Culture; Madeline Ford of Medgar Evers College, CUNY; and the Allen Room of the New York Public Library for allowing me access to their collections and facilities. At Little Red School House and Elisabeth Irwin, thanks to director Phil Kassen and the alumni and development department for their making the school's archives available to me. I particularly extend my gratitude to Sasha Abramsky, who allowed me access to extensive interviews he conducted with Tom Hurwitz, his family and his friends.

I am also happily indebted to Constance Rosenblum, Linda Harvey, John Jones, John V. O'Leary, Melissa Tiers and, as ever, Sandra Roche, for their help and support. My great thanks to Judith Caplan Inglese, Little Red and Elisabeth Irwin class of 1961, and Tullio Inglese. Their recollections and insights informed and enriched this book immeasurably.

I extend my insufficient but heartfelt gratitude to Betsy Lerner of Dunow, Carlson & Lerner Literary Agency and to Lisa Kaufman of PublicAffairs for their skillful guidance and unflagging championing of this long-gestating project. I am also thankful for the thoughtful editorial contributions of Mindy Werner, Ann Delgehausen, and Melissa Totten. My thanks also to Collin Tracy and Melissa Raymond at PublicAffairs.

Finally, I must try to express my inexpressible gratitude to Professor Samuel G. Freedman of the Columbia Graduate School of Journalism, without whose faith this book would simply not exist. Through his Book Seminar, Sam has inspired, nurtured and shaped a generation of non-fiction authors. It is my privilege to count myself among their number.

NOTES

8 **"I gave them nothing,"** interview with Milt Unterman

9 **"street guide to Moscow,"** interview with Victor Navasky

12 **Picketing Woolworth's was an "unofficial requirement at EI,"** Nadelson, *Who is Angela Davis?*, 68

19 **"We had marched, picketed, and petitioned for years,"** Tom Hurwitz, Elisabeth Irwin High School yearbook, 1965, 44

Chapter 2 • Transplant from Birmingham Angela Davis, 1943–1961

21 **"open and guarded,"** Davis, *Angela Davis: An Autobiography*, 20

21 **"setting up a cot at the 42nd Street library,"** interview with Harold Kirshner

22 **"Wish I was a bird,"** Nadelson, *Who Is Angela Davis?* 32

22 **"archaic pot-bellied stove in the corner,"** *Angela Davis: An Autobiography*, 99

24 **"[Communism] threatens not only intellectual integrity,"** Melish Defense Committee, *The Melish Case* pamphet, 32

24 **"Certainly, the test of a man's faith is what he is willing to risk for it,"** Melish Defense Committee, *The Melish Case* pamplet, 48

25 **"She was very pleasant,"** interview with Ed Suvanto

25 **"Davis was . . . hard to penetrate,"** interview with Ellen Fried Sklar

25 **"tough, intellectual, cynical, and with-it,"** quoted in Nadelson, *Who Is Angela Davis?*, 63

26 **"White liberal New Yorkers were faced with a problem in Angela,"** Nadelson, *Who Is Angela Davis?*, 64

26 **"tendency to be over solicitous of their few Black acquaintances,"** Davis, *Angela Davis: An Autobiography*, 106

27 **"I had no idea what they were doing outside of the school,"** interview with Judy Jackson

27 **"It must have been because you sent your picture in,"** interview with Judy Jackson

28 **"It would be interesting to invite members from the Harlem Lords,"** interview with Harold Yates

29 **"We went into a bar and I saw a transvestite,"** interview with Bridget Leicester

30 **"It hit me like a bolt of lightning,"** Davis, *Angela Davis: An Autobiography*, 110

30 **"Two, four, six, eight, Woolworth's doesn't integrate,"** quoted in Nadelson, *Who Is Angela Davis?*, 68

32 **Looking back, Angela believes Van Dyke's casting her in the one "racialized" role in the play,** interview with Angela

Chapter 3 • The Contrarian: Rlliott Abrams, 1948–1965

35   **"The culture is dominated by right-wing politics,"** interview with Elliott

36   **"It would be going too far to call it a sneer,"** Grove, "The Contrary Evolution of Elliott Abrams," *Washington Post*

36   **"He was very facile, funny and bright,"** Grove, "The Contrary Evolution of Elliott Abrams," *Washington Post*

37.   **"If you didn't agree with the political mantra,"** interview with Cathy Michaelson

37   **"For me, it was like growing up in the Midwest,"** interview with Sara Fishko

37   **"generous, kind, funny and insanely smart,"** interview with Lisa Fein Gilford

37   **"I called him and said 'I need your help,'"** interview with Lisa Fein Gilford

38   **"He used to stand at the window of his father's law office,"** Grove, "The Contrary Evolution of Elliott Abrams," *Washington Post*

38   **"half in jest, wholly in earnest,"** Grove, "The Contrary Evolution of Elliott Abrams," *Washington Post*

38   **"All of us thought it was a reprehensible, bizarrely radical position,"** interview with Sara Fishko

PART TWO

Chapter 4 • The Making of a Revolutionary: Angela Davis, 1961–1969

45   **"interested in the fact that the people of Cuba were in terrible jeopardy,"** Davis, *An Autobiography*, 119

46   **"Carole . . . Cynthia,"** Davis, *An Autobiography*, 129

46   **"It's too bad it had to happen,"** Davis, *An Autobiography*, 129

46   **"How many of them had shed tears,"** Davis, *An Autobiography*, 132

48   **"There wasn't the slightest trace of fear in my father,"** Davis, *An Autobiography*, 137

50   **"Negroes have been walking down a dream street,"** Carmichael, "Black Power"

50   **"Because the masses of white people harbor racist attitudes,"** Davis, *An Autobiography*, 150–51

52   **"Hey, take off your glasses and get some new rags,"** Nadelson, *Who Is Angela Davis?*, 129

52   **Mitchell had become politicized at an early age,** interview with Angela

52   **"the black power movement was strong,"** interview with Charlene Mitchell

53   **"hip young lady,"** interview with Charlene Mitchell

53   **"The Black Party of Self Defense demands,"** Davis, *An Autobiography*, 164

53   **"I knew that if I were ever stopped by the police and searched,"** Davis, *An Autobiography*, 164–65

54   **"Guilty! Guilty! Guilty!"** Davis, *An Autobiography*, 174

54   **"Death to the pig!"** Davis, *An Autobiography*, 175

54   **"an amorphous sense of guilt fell upon me,"** Davis, *An Autobiography*, 176

55   **"matriarchal coup d'etat,"** Davis, *An Autobiography*, 181

55   **"purged of any traces of Marxist and Communist ideology,"** Davis, *An Autobiography*, 185

56   **"red diaper baby,"** Richards, *Black Heart*, 203

56   **"Her hatred of cultural commodification,"** Richards, *Black Heart*, 203

56   **"[Angela] seems to be torn between the old line theory and her friendship with black people,"** Brown, *Writing the Black Revolutionary Diva*, 130

57   **"If I still retained any of the elitism,"** Davis, *An Autobiography*, 192

57   **"for the benefit of the other members of the class,"** Davis, *An Autobiography*, 190

58   **"Filled with hate?"** Nadelson, *Who Is Angela Davis?*, 129

Chapter 5 • Propaganda of the Deed: Tom Hurwitz, 1965–1969

62   **"I thought, this is the end of Israel,"** interview with Tom

62   **"*Amerikanish gonniff* culture,"** interview with Tom

63   **Hoffman and Rubin began the theatrical centerpiece of the event,** Rosenfeld, "Stew Albert–Original Yippie," *San Francisco Chronicle*

64   **"It is this type of spirit and this type of love,"** King, *Where Do We Go From Here*

65   **"propaganda of deed,"** Marcuse, "Repressive Tolerance," *A Critique of Pure Tolerance*, 95–137

66   **"The three weeks we spent in Cuba were dominated by this military action,"** Rudd, *Underground*, 39

67   **"Something has got to happen in the spring,"** Interview with Tom

67   **"I don't do political groups,"** interview with Tom

67   **"Anything we want to do,"** interview with Tom

67   **"The SDS intended to sit politely,"** Rudd, *Underground*, 44

68   **"Colonel, you've gotten your just desserts,"** Rudd, *Underground*, 46

68   **"unserious and terroristic,"** Rudd, *Underground*, 45

69   **"that the bloody experience of Vietnam is to end in a stalemate,"** Walter Cronkite in unidentified film clip, 1968

70   **"gym crow"** Avorn et al, *Up Against the Ivy Wall*, 51

71   **"We could see the flames of dozens of fires,"** Rudd, *Underground*, 49

71   **"Dr. Truman and President Kirk are committing a moral outrage,"** Rudd, *Underground*, 52

71   **"Grayson, I doubt if you will understand any of this,"** Rudd, *Underground*, 56

72   **"We're going to have a demonstration today,"** interview with Tom

72   **scruffy and somewhat scary lot,** Abramsky interview with Deborah Robison

73   **"Send Rudd back to Vietnam"** . . . "Order is Peace," Rudd, *Underground*, 59

73   **"Did we come here to talk, or did we come here to march to Low?"** interview with Tom

74   **"IDA must go! IDA must go!"** Columbia University seminar, "Columbia 1968 + 40"

74   **"Seize Hamilton!"** Rudd, *Underground*, 63

74   **"Suddenly, all heads turned toward the main entrance,"** "Protestors Crowd Into Hamilton Hall" *Columbia Daily Spectator*

75   **"Now we've got the Man where we want him,"** Rudd, *Underground*, 64

75   **We've gone from a pie in the face to taking a hostage in six weeks,** interview with Tom

75   **"protestors' hotel,"** "Protestors Crowd Into Hamilton Hall" *Columbia Daily Spectator*

76   **"Halt construction on the gymnasium,"** Rudd, *Underground*, 66

76   **"six black men, community people, moved toward Dean Coleman's door,"** Rudd, *Underground*, 67

76   **"We want to make our stand here,"** Rudd, *Underground*, 69

78   **"We've got ourselves another dean!"** interview with Tom

80   **"It's painful to remember how subservient and passive the women were."** Abramsky interview with Susan Brown

81   **"bullshit,"** Avorn et al, *Up Against the Ivy Wall*, 140

81   **"Kirk must go!"** . . . **"Up against the wall, motherfuckers!"** Avorn et al, *Up Against the Ivy Wall*, 193

82   **"the fifty-nine-year-old took off at a sprint"** Kirschheimer, "A Few Minutes About Leo On the Day of His Memorial, March 30, 1991," provided by Sasha Abramsky

83   **"What are you proposing on building?"** interview with Tom

84   **"The Midwestern SDS was just fabulous,"** interview with Tom

85   **"printing presses running twenty-four hours a day,"** interview with Tom

86   **Susan was miserable,** Abramsky interview with Susan Brown

86   **"Tom had a huge heart and a great sense of humor,"** Abramsky interview with Josh Robison

86   **"we would have realized that you can't always be in charge of events,"** interview with Tom

88   **"The world was faced with a huge crime that was going on in Vietnam,"** interview with Tom

90   **"A revolutionary mass movement is different,"** "Neighborhood-Based Citywide Youth Movement" in "You Don't Need A Weatherman To Know Which Way The Wind Blows," *New Left Notes,* June 18, 1969

90   **"The strategy of the [revolutionary youth movement] for developing an active mass base,"** "Neighborhood-Based Citywide Youth Movement," *New Left Notes,* June 18, 1969

91   **"hamburger joints and schoolyards, talked about 'kicking ass,'"** Gitlin, *The Sixties,* 377

91   **"but to totally destroy this imperialist and racist society,"** Gitlin, *The Sixties,* 378

Chapter 6 • Paper Airplanes: Elliott Abrams, 1965–1969

94   **"for centuries, men at Harvard wore a coat and tie to breakfast,"** interview with Elliott

95   **"the strongest Boston accent Elliot had ever heard,"** interview with Elliott

95   **"That was life,"** interview with Elliott

95   **"Not being radicals hampered sex lives,"** interview with Dan Hastings

95   **"At Wellesley you'd sit in the lobby and the girls would come down the stairs,"** interview with Elliott

95   **"Elliott was the best informed man I ever met,"** interview with Dan Hastings

95   **"He was a skillful debater,"** interview with Dan Hastings

96   **"hereditary radicals,"** Kelman, *Push Comes to Shove,* 145

96   **"I remember [journalist] Eric Sevareid in one of his broadcasts,"** interview with Elliott

96   **"We were so worried about the idea of a Vietcong victory,"** interview with Steven Kelman

97   **"I remember one fine fall day, coming from an anti-war demo,"** interview with Daniel Pipes

97   **"How will we convince young people in the rest of the world,"** Abrams, "The Sky Is Falling," *New Leader*

97   **"They were very good debates as I recall them,"** interview with Elliott

98   **"When McNamara comes out, everyone lock arms so he can't leave!"** Kelman, *Push Comes to Shove,* 57

98   **"[The difference is] I was tougher and I was more courteous,"** Kelman, *Push Comes to Shove,* 60–61

99   **"New Left had now become the same old totalitarian Left,"** Kelman, *Push Comes to Shove,* 130

100   **"The only time I got a whiff—literally—of it,"** interview with Elliott

100   **This had little effect on Elliott,** interview with Elliott

100   **"fast bust or no bust,"** Rosenblatt, *Coming Apart*, 14

100   **when students received no response from inside the darkened house,** Rosenblatt, *Coming Apart*, 30

101   **"Mainly the atmosphere was fun,"** Rosenblatt, *Coming Apart*, 17

101   **"The bust is on!"** Abrams, "Cambridge Patterns," *New Leader*

101   **"an uncharacteristic fit of bravery,"** Abrams, "Cambridge Patterns," *New Leader*

101   **"The effect they created that misty morning was not merely terrifying but grotesque,"** Abrams, "Cambridge Patterns," *New Leader*

102   **"Those police were brutal!"** Kelman, *Push Comes to Shove*, 266

102   **One of his proudest moments,** Grove, "The Contrary Evolution of Elliott Abrams," *Washington Post*

102   **"He gave an impassioned plea for why universities should never close—ever,"** interview with Elliott

103   **"Harvard seems headed back to normality,"** Abrams, "Cambridge Patterns," *New Leader*

PART THREE

Chapter 7 • The Belly of the Beast: Angela Davis, 1969–1970

108   **"reserved for the sons and daughters of the wealthy,"** Davis, *An Autobiography*, 204

108   **"A widely accepted falsehood about Cuba,"** Davis, *An Autobiography*, 207

109   **"While I think this membership requires no justification,"** Nadelson, *Who Is Angela Davis?*, 149

110   **"Carrying Ronald Reagan's racist, anti-Communist policies to the extremes,"** Davis, *An Autobiography*, 223

111   **"Before I proceeded to lecture today,"** *ABC News*, May 23, 1969. http://www.youtube.com/watch?v=AI4U-q2o2cg&feature=related

111   **"For students she was a model of what a teacher should be,"** Nadelson, *Who Is Angela Davis?*

112   **Found guilty, Jackson was sent to the California Youth Authority in Paso Robles,** Liberatore, *The Road to Hell*, 15

113   **"George was too casual about killing people,"** Carr, *Bad*, 153

113   **"It weighed two pounds and would go right through Jack Fox,"** Carr, *Bad*, 138–39, 171

113   **"They redeemed me,"** Interview with Paul Liberatore in *Day of the Gun*, KRON Channel 4, http://www.youtube.com/watch?v=oT-apgRlJlQ

113   in tiny print in order to fit as much text as possible on two sides of the
       8½ x 11 ruled sheet of paper, Jackson, *Soledad Brother*, 50

114   "I should be out of here this year," Jackson, *Soledad Brother*, 47

114   "You could start writing letters to the Adult Authority now," Jackson,
       Soledad Brother, 47

114   "I have at least another fourteen or eighteen months to do," Jackson,
       Soledad Brother, 98

114   "and this made him the best proselytizer for revolution on the yard,"
       Eric Cummings in *Day of the Gun*, KRON Channel 4

114   "The project he took on was to [transform] those who were behind
       bars," Angela Davis in http://www.youtube.com/watch?v=RqhoZdgYpd
       Q&NR=1

115   The study group evolved into a revolutionary brotherhood, Liberatore,
       The Road to Hell, 19

115   "I don't prefer anything as mild as pen and paper," Jackson, *Soledad
       Brother*, 307

115   "serene and strong," Davis, *An Autobiography*, 250

115   "exposing and challenging Ronald Reagan," Davis, *An Autobiography*, 255

116   "George looked more vibrant than I had imagined," Davis, *An Autobiog-
       raphy*, 264

116   "a determination began to swell immediately," Davis, *An Autobiogra-
       phy*, 254

116   "Dearest Angela, I hope you have discovered that I love you deeply,"
       Jackson, *Soledad Brother*

117   "They couldn't get George one way," Aptheker, *The Morning Breaks*, 15

117   "Jon is a young brother and he is just a little withdrawn," Jackson,
       Soledad Brother, 287

117   "He is at that dangerous age," Davis, *An Autobiography*, 278

117   "racists and reactionaries who might try and make [Angela] a martyr,"
       Davis, *An Autobiography*, 269

117   "Academic freedom does not include attacks on faculty members,"
       http://www.youtube.com/watch?v=AI4U-q2o2cg&feature=related

118   "long series of repressive and genocidal measures," Charlton, "F.B.I.
       Seizes Angela Davis in Motel Here," *New York Times*

118   "the greatest threat to the internal security of the country," *A Huey P.
       Newton Story*, directed by Spike Lee

119   At 10:45 a.m. Jonathan Jackson quietly entered the courtroom, Libera-
       tore, *The Road to Hell*, 89

119   Minutes later, Jonathan stood up holding a Browning 380 pistol, Liber-
       atore, *The Road to Hell*, 90

119   **"All right gentlemen,"** Aptheker, *The Morning Breaks*, 188
119   **even gently, talking Jonathan out of choosing an infant and an elderly woman as hostages,** Liberatore, *The Road to Hell*, 90
120   **"Stop firing! Please stop firing!,"** Liberatore, *The Road to Hell*, 91
120   **"was to reveal to the world the dimensions of George's ordeal,"** Aptheker, *The Morning Breaks*, 16
120   **exchange for George and the plane would be flown either to Cuba or to Algeria** Liberatore, *The Road to Hell*, 93
121   **"Jonathan was to have had the assistance of the Black Panther Party,"** Liberatore, *The Road to Hell*, 93
121   **"Jonathan Jackson was deserted,"** Liberatore, *The Road to Hell*, 93

Chapter 8 • Tommy Takes Charge: Tom Hurwitz, 1969–1971

123   **"Isn't anybody here?"** **Abramsky** interview with Susan Brown
124   **"tighten their stranglehold on the throats of the people,"** "Kick the Ass of the Ruling Class," *Movement*, September 1969
126   **"We were vigorously non-violent,"** interview with Kent Hudson
127   **"We're going to destroy what we've built here,"** interview with Tom
127   **"We were the object lesson that organizing worked,"** interview with Tom
128   **"we were against the war . . . using guns was no way to win,"** interview with Kent Hudson
130   **"Someone called in saying there's a bomb,"** interview with Tom
130   **"Gimme a second,"** interview with Tom
130   **"All of a sudden there was Tommy at the microphone talking to the crowd,"** interview with Leland Lubinsky
130   **"Once again, welcome to People's Armed Forces Day,"** interview with Tom
130   **"A bomb threat has been called in,"** interview with Tom
131   **"hypnotized the audience,"** interview with Leland Lubinsky
131   **"Congratulations,"** . . . **"You're a People's Army,"** interview with Tom
132   **"'I'm hit!' yelled Corporal Jesse Woodard,"** interview with Tom
133   **"At that point I was free of the movement,"** interview with Tom
133   **"'How could you do this? How could you humiliate me?'"** interview with Tom
134   **"What have I done with you that you haven't done with me?"** interview with Tom
134   **Utterly demoralized, Tom caught a ride back East,** interview with Tom; Abramsky interview with Josh Robison
135   **They did a simultaneous double take**, interview with Tom

136   **"It's dangerous work. But if you want to stay there's a lot of work we can do,"** Abramsky interview with Barbara Zahm

137   **"In my gut, I didn't think we'd be able to make it,"** Abramsky interview with Barbara Zahm

Chapter 9 • The Family: Elliott Abrams, 1969–1972

139   **"Thurgood Marshall made third-rate knee-jerk decisions,"** interview with Elliott

139   **"From a liberal point of view they got to the right place,"** interview with Elliott

140   **"One of the most remarkable features of the neoconservative movement is the filial piety that pervades it,"** Heilbrun, *They Knew They Were Right*, 107

142   **"After the Jewish state's lightning victory in 1967,"** Heilbrun, *They Knew They Were Right*, 80

142   **"It was a pivotal moment in the emergence of the neoconservative movement,"** Heilbrun, *They Knew They Were Right*, 81

142   **"He was a very impressive figure,"** interview with Elliott

143   **"I remember the last line of the article [said],"** interview with Elliott

143   **to become a "facsimile WASP,"** Podhoretz, *Making It*, 49

143   **"an instinct for the jugular,"** Heilbrun, *They Knew They Were Right*, 75

143   **"success was the supreme, even the only, American value,"** Podhoretz, *Making It*, xv

144   **"clear signal to the Democratic Party to return to the great tradition,"** Heilbrun, *They Knew They Were Right*, 114

PART FOUR

Chapter 10 • "Angela Is Welcome in Our House": Angela Davis, 1970–1971

148   **Angela reasoned, she would have the support of her family, friends and the movement,** Davis, *An Autobiography*, 12

149   **"Are you Angela Davis? Are you Angela Davis?"** Davis, *An Autobiography*, 15

149   **"Would you like a cigarette Ms. Davis?"** Davis, *An Autobiography*, 16

149   **"A lot of officers here—the black officers—have been pulling for you,"** Davis, *An Autobiography*, 20

150   **"Free Angela Davis!" "Free all political prisoners!"** Davis, *An Autobiography*, 23

151 **"Mickey—the mice that infested the dilapidated building,"** Davis, *An Autobiography*, 49

152 **"Good night" to each other, their voices ringing up and down the corridors,"** Davis, *An Autobiography*, 59

152 **"We must fight for your life as though it was our own, which it is,"** Baldwin, "An Open Letter To My Sister Angela Y. Davis"

152 **"'I have the money,' Franklin said,"** Davis, *An Autobiography*, 78

153 **"This was the first time I had seen male guards in the House of D,"** Davis, *An Autobiography*, 68

155 **"The pigs killed him, Angela,"** Davis, *An Autobiography*, 316

156 **"female army,"** Jackson, *Soledad Brother* 325

157 **"All right gentlemen. This is it. I'm taking over now,"** Aptheker, *The Morning Breaks*, 16

158 **"It's me they want,"** Liberatore, *The Road to Hell*, 155

159 **"For me, George's death has meant the loss of a comrade,"** Davis, *An Autobiography*, 74

Chapter 11 • Politics of the Purge: Tom Hurwitz, 1971–1972

162 **"We were sort of sucked into the Red Guard mentality,"** Abramsky interview with Leland Lubinsky

162 **"You could give out 500 leaflets [at any given time] and get fifteen hundred to your demonstration,"** Abramsky interview with Leland Lubinsky

162 **"It had been four years of nonstop action . . . "** interview with Tom

163 **"Tommy and I were very attached and work very well together,"** Abramsky interview with Barbara Zahm

163 **"meeting after meeting after meeting . . . "** Abramsky interview with Leland Lubinsky

163 **"Brook no excuses,"** interview with Tom

164 **"It's not going to work out with you staying here,"** interviews with Leland Lubinsky and Tom

164 **"commandist,"** interview with Tom

Chapter 12 • The State of California vs. Angela Y. Davis: Angela Davis, 1972

167 **"This is the one day I wouldn't mind being on San Quentin's Death Row,"** Davis, *An Autobiography*, 331

167 **"What kind of a bail hearing?"** Davis, *An Autobiography*, 331

167 **"Angela, the death penalty has been abolished,"** Davis, *An Autobiography*, 331

167   **"Knowing the deep personal pain they had suffered,"** Davis, *An Auto-biography*, 341

168   **"After dinner, when I had finished one glass of champagne,"** Davis, *An Autobiography*, 344

169   **"The basic motive for the crime was the same motive underlying hundreds of criminal cases,"** Davis, *An Autobiography*, 359

169   **"the creation of a movement encompassing millions of people,"** James, *The Angela Y. Davis Reader*, 336

170   **"run out of things to say,"** http://www.eleanorslegacy.com/news/ms-magazine-celebrates-its-40th-anniversary

171   **"I was convinced with good reason that I needed some sort of protection,"** Davis, *An Autobiography*, 355

171   **"The evidence will show that I had good reason to make myself unavailable,"** James, *Angela Y. Davis Reader*, 342

171   **"Members of the jury [w]hen you have sat patiently, almost to the point of exhaustion,"** James, *Angela Y. Davis Reader*, 346

172   **"The night after I saw you in court for the first time in months, I dreamt we were together,"** Anspacher, "Setback for the State in Angela Trial," *San Francisco Chronicle*

172   **"barbarous capitalist society,"** Aptheker, *The Morning Breaks*, 209

172   **"to translate the 'be a good boy' syndrome into a 'take the sword in hand' attitude,"** Aptheker, *The Morning Breaks*, 211

172   **"Women's liberation in the revolution is inseparable from the liberation of the male,"** Aptheker, *The Morning Breaks*, 211

172   **"Jonathan and I have made a truce,"** Davis, *An Autobiography*, 86

172   **"instantly and unexpectedly fallen in love,"** Aptheker, *The Morning Breaks*, 283

172   **"high tides of unanticipated joy,"** Aptheker, *The Morning Breaks*, 212

172   **"Something inside you has managed to smash through the fortress I long ago erected around my soul,"** Aptheker, *The Morning Breaks*, 214

173   **"We have learned from our revolutionary,"** Davis, *An Autobiography*, 370

173   **"Accepting the murder of a comrade in struggle is not easy,"** DeLeon, "A Revealing Report," *Jet*

173   **"Frustrations, aggressions cannot be repressed indefinitely,"** Davis, *An Autobiography*, 37

174   **the defense team decided to present a "pin point" defense,** interview with Bettina Aptheker

175   **"There's been a hijacking,"** Davis, *An Autobiography*, 389

177   **"Ms. Timothy, had the jury reached a verdict?"** Aptheker, *The Morning Breaks*, 237

Chapter 13 • The Fact Book: Tom Hurwitz, 1972–1973

178   **"Have you been following the Gary Lawton case?"** interview with Tom
179   **"good little local,"** interview with Tom
179   **"I was sick and tired of relying on the movement for my identity . . . "** interview with Tom
180   **"We're in real trouble,"** interview with Tom
180   **"Wait a minute—haven't the Angela Davis people been supporting you?"** interview with Tom
180   **"We're leaving in a week but I know some lawyers in L.A,"** interview with Tom
181   **"Look, we're weeks from trial. This woman's husband is going to go to jail . . . "** interview with Tom
181   **"She was one of our greatest assets,"** Abramsky interview with Barbara Zahm
181   **"The first thing Epstein did was to visit the crime scene with Hurwitz,"** Bradlee, *Ambush Murders*, 258
182   **"blunt, intensely proud, uncompromising,"** Bradlee, *Ambush Murders*, 94
182   **"blown away a couple of pigs,"** Bradlee, *Ambush Murders*, 112
183   **"If you really read the transcripts,"** Abramsky interview with Barbara Zahm
183   **"It was amazing,"** Abramsky interview with Barbara Zahm
184   **"Things like this just don't happen in cases,"** interview with Tom

Chapter 14 • The Prince: Elliott Abrams, 1972–1980

185   **"If you're running for president again in '76,"** interview with Elliott
185   **"These people don't even read *Commentary*,"** Heilbrun, *They Knew They Were Right*, 175
186   **"Dorothy Fosdick, who was his chief foreign policy advisor,"** interview with Elliott
186   **"I said OK—it wasn't my line of work,"** interview with Elliott
187   **"Quiet everybody, we're going to hear from Charles and Elliott,"** interview with Elliott
187   **"We're standing with our backs to the fireplace and there's this crowd waiting to hear,"** interview with Elliott
188   **"Wow, she's gorgeous,"** interview with Elliott
188   **"Why don't I marry someone like Elliott Abrams,"** interview with Elliott
189   **"We went out Labor Day weekend and we got engaged at Thanksgiving,"** interview with Elliott
189   **"We thought the invasion was a wakeup call for Carter,"** interview with Elliott

189   **"We had about twenty minutes with Mondale first,"** interview with Elliott

190   **"We were really treated quite badly by the Democratic Party,"** Heilbrun,
       They Knew They Were Right, 155

191   **"closest thing to an arranged marriage that the modern world allowed,"**
       Unger, *The Fall of the House of Bush,* 163

PART FIVE

Chapter 15 • Family Man: Tom Hurwitz, 1973–1983

195   **Maybe, Tom speculated, the guilt she felt growing up,** interview with
       Tom

196   **"The left was shattered but the community was cooking,"** interview with
       Tom

196   **"He needed people to sit at his feet,"** Abramsky interview with Barbara
       Zahm

196   **"Barbara experienced Leo's cerebral style as being cold,"** interview with
       Tom

197   **"He was just being Leo,"** interview with Tom

197   **Just months ago, Tom had been instrumental,** interview with Tom

197   **"The film was ostensibly about Peggy,"** interview with Tom

197   **"My ego began to disappear,"** interview with Tom

198   **"Hey," he thought. "I love this,"** interview with Tom

198   **"Everyone was carrying guns,"** interview with Tom

199   **"In the sixties I tried to make myself believe,"** Abramsky interview with
       Barbara Zahm

200   **"I was as much a director and a producer as he was,"** Abramsky inter-
       view with Barbara Zahm

200   **"It would have been nice and loving to do so,"** interview with Tom

200   **"But Tom wanted his own career,"** Abramsky interview with Barbara Zahm

200   **"I don't think Tom was sure,"** Abramsky interview with Barbara Zahm

200   **"It was tough, painful and productive,"** interview with Tom

Chapter 16 • The King of Latin America: Elliott Abrams, 1980–1989

201   **It was the beginning of what he would call the "worst single day,"**
       Welch, "Abrams Contradicts Documents," *Associated Press*

201   **"Why didn't the president know [about] providing arms to Iran,"**
       http://www.reagan.utexas.edu/archives/speeches/1986/112586a.htm

202   **"Were you then in the fundraising business?" the Senator demanded.**
       http://www.fas.org/irp/offdocs/walsh/chap_25.htm

202 **"I would say we were in the fundraising business. I take your point,"** http://www.fas.org/irp/offdocs/walsh/chap_25.htm

202 **realizing that Elliott had not been sworn in for that round of testimony,** http://www.fas.org/irp/offdocs/walsh/chap_25.htm

202 **"Oh, Elliott, you're too damn smart not to know,"** "Eagleton-Abrams Row Detailed in Documents." *Houston Chronicle News Service*

203 **"He's so young—do you realize how young he is?"** interview with Dan Hastings

204 **"You asked me to think about candidates,"** Grove, "The Contrary Evolution of Elliott Abrams," *Washington Post*

204 **"Compared with the International Organizations Bureau, it was smaller,"** Abrams, *Undue Process,* 4

204 **"The Abrams attempt to undercut the 'moral superiority,'"** Alterman, "Elliott Abrams, The Teflon Assistant Secretary," *Washington Monthly*

205 **"secret" liberal,** Weintraub, "Reagan's Human Rights Chief," *New York Times*

205 **"They thought I was a liberal mole hidden in the Reagan administration,"** Weintraub, "Reagan's Human Rights Chief," *New York Times*

205 **"We consider anticommunism to be a human rights policy,"** Heilbrun, *They Knew They Were Right,* 177

205 **But Elliott drew some of his strongest criticism for his policy on El Salvador,"** Heilbrun, *They Knew They Were Right,* 177

206 **"They have essentially abandoned human rights,"** Patricia Derian quoted in Weintraub, "Reagan's Human Rights Chief," *New York Times*

206 **In promulgating this theory, the administration often gave two examples: Iran and Nicaragua,** Madison, "Abrams, State's Human Rights Chief," *National Journal*

207 **"Elliott was a member of the administration,"** Grove, "The Contrary Evolution of Elliott Abrams," *Washington Post*

207 **On the floor of the Senate he declared the move "painfully stupid,"** Goldstein, "They Kept Her Out to Protect the American People," *Christian Science Monitor*

207 **a member of the Columbian terrorist organization M19,** Grove, "The Contrary Evolution of Elliott Abrams," *Washington Post*

208 **"There is a word for Elliott Abrams: coward,"** Lewis, "Action by Abrams Regrettable," *Palm Beach Post*

208 **"It's still going on now—except that Elliott's doing it,"** Franklin said. Grove, "The Contrary Evolution of Elliott Abrams," *Washington Post*

208 **"manage the emergence of Elliott Abrams as King of Latin America,"** http://jewishcurrents.org/elliott-abrams-on-the-settlement-obsession-6714 http://www.fas.org/irp/offdocs/walsh/chap_25.htm

209   **"body and soul,"** Congressional Committee Investigating Iran Contra (The Iran-Contra Report), http://www.presidency.ucsb.edu/PS157/assignment%20files%20public/congressional%20report%20key%20sections.htm

210   **"It was clear the others kept a good deal from me,"** Abrams, *Undue Process*, 57

211   **"No one mentioned it to me,"** Abrams, *Undue Process*, 89

212   **"We had . . . taken a walk in Hyde Park,"** Abrams, *Undue Process*, 89

212   **"a ne'er-do-well 'kicker,'"** Abrams, *Undue Process*, 85

214   **"hatred, pandering, cries of anti-Americanism,"** Patricia Derian in Alterman, "Elliott Abrams," *Washington Monthly*

214   **"The people I know have been referring to Abrams as Pinocchio,"** Plummer, "Elliott Abrams Must Now Face the Music," *People*

214   **"He's got some explaining to do,"** Plummer, "Elliott Abrams Must Now Face the Music," *People*

214   **"I wouldn't trust Elliott Abrams any further than I could throw Oliver North,"** Plummer, "Elliott Abrams Must Now Face the Music," *People*

214   **"The interesting thing about Elliott, and a lot of neoconservatives of his age,"** Grove, "The Contrary Evolution of Elliott Abrams," *Washington Post*

214   **"I was sympathizing with the underdog in the world,"** Grove, "The Contrary Evolution of Elliott Abrams," *Washington Post*

215   **"He's very bright,"** Grove, "The Contrary Evolution of Elliott Abrams," *Washington Post*

215   **"Maybe one day they'll name a square after him in a free Nicaragua,"** Grove, "The Contrary Evolution of Elliott Abrams," *Washington Post*

Chapter 17 • Epiphany: Tom Hurwitz, 1983–1999

217   **"You're always disappearing on me,"** interview with Margaret Klenck

217   **"Ya ready?"** interview with Margaret Klenck

219   **Tom came upon a protest in front of Hamilton Hall,** interview with Tom

219   **"But you know, it's drier in the building,"** interview with Tom

221   **"smells and bells" of a high-church ceremony,** interview with Tom

PART SIX

Chapter 18 • The Man Who Named My Father: Tom Hurwitz, 1999

227   **"When critics [of *On the Waterfront*] say I put my feelings on the screen,"** Kazan, *A Life*, 500

227   **"courageous stool pigeon frees sheep-like longshoreman,"** Navasky, *Naming Names*, 338

227   **"Terry Malloy's friends were killers, thugs, psychopaths,"** Navasky, *Naming Names*, 209

227   **Kazan was a devious little creep,** interview with Tom

227   **Yet when film critic Richard Schickel wrote an article in *Time* magazine,** Schickel, "An Oscar for Elia," *Time*

227   **"Kazan named my father, filmmaker Leo Hurwitz, before the House Un-American Activities Committee,"** Hurwitz, "Letters," *Time*

228   **"sit on their hands,"** Goldstein, "Many Refuse to Clap as Kazan Receives Oscar," *Los Angeles Times*

229   **"The limo turned the corner, and there, finally, were the anti-Kazan protesters,"** Goldstein, "Many Refuse to Clap as Kazan Receives Oscar," *Los Angeles Times,* and "Praise and Silent Protest Greet Kazan's Oscar," *The Guardian*

230   **"He was the master of a new kind of psychological and behavioral truth in acting,"** Robert DeNiro, 71st Academy Awards© telecast, 1999, http://www.youtube.com/watch?v=3YziNNCZeNs

231   **"I want to thank the Academy for its courage and generosity,"** Elia Kazan, 71st Academy Awards© telecast, 1999, http://www.youtube.com /watch?v=3YziNNCZeNs

Chapter 19 • The Next War: Elliott Abrams, 1989–2010

233   **"cabal of zealots,"** Schafer, "Iran-Contra Panels Went Beyond Tower Commission Probe," *Associated Press*

234   **"The reversal of Oliver North's conviction forced us into a new race with Congress,"** Walsh, *Firewall,* 263

235   **"We would take on Reagan and all the President's men,"** Toobin, *Opening Arguments,* 17

235   **"with an enthusiasm that bordered on the unseemly,"** Toobin, *Opening Arguments,* 76

235   **"Its members were primarily liberal and Democratic,"** Abrams, *Undue Process,* 12

235   **"Never having broken a case, or even tried one, but professing to speak for all 'prosecutors,'"** Walsh, *Firewall,* 273

236   **"Oh yes, my heart had skipped a beat when we read in the papers,"** Abrams, *Undue Process,* 15–16

236   **And on September 10, Elliott's lawyer called him with the ominous news,** Abrams, *Undue Process,* 19

236   **"I wasn't scared of their 'evidence,'"** Abrams, *Undue Process,* 26

237   **"They can go to hell,"** Abrams, *Undue Process,* 65

237   **"Look, I spent my time in the government doing my job,"** Abrams, *Undue Process,* 78

238   "When I was in the State Department I knew a lot of secrets," Abrams, *Undue Process*, 80

239   "Everyone would assume I had also incriminated someone," Abrams, *Undue Process*, 100

239   "asked to ruin the life of a former colleague," Abrams, *Undue Process*, 147

239   "I tasted the temptation to burn my friends to save myself," Abrams, *Undue Process*, 147

239   "Here is a man who is having a worse day than I am," Abrams, *Undue Process*, 158

239   "I take full responsibility for my actions," Abrams, *Undue Process*, 165

249   "Screw you," Abrams, *Undue Process*, 165

240   "I had been new. I had not been a career operative," Abrams, *Undue Process*, 104

240   Elliott blamed left-wing politicians and pundits who harbored an "undying, undimmed hatred" toward him, Abrams, *Undue Process*, 140

240   Most galling to his enemies, Elliot thought, was the fact that he was openly unrepentant, Abrams, *Undue Process*, 140

241   "blots out the existence of guilt, so that in the eye of the law, the offender is an innocent," http://caselaw.findlaw.com/dc-court-of-appeals/1280741.html

241   "Welcome, welcome!" she cried in a theatrical Transylvanian accent, Hampton, "Little Red Radicals," *New York Times*

242   "I remember going to a reunion [in 1968] and people saying, 'Are you for [Eugene] McCarthy?'" Grove, "The Contrary Evolution of Elliott Abrams," *Washington Post*

243   "The EI I attended in the 1960s had a reputation for social and political activism," Abrams, "Elisabeth Irwin High School at 50," Little Red and Elisabeth Irwin Archives

243   "I do not understand what 'balance' you thought you were achieving with the inclusion of the 'opinions' of Elliott Abrams," letter from Peter Orris, LREI class of '62, August 19, 1992, Little Red and Elisabeth Irwin Archives

246   "the possibility that Iraq will be able to use or threaten to use weapons of mass destruction," Project for a New American Century website, http://www.newamericancentury.org/

247   "The latest whisper on the diplomatic grapevine concerns Elliott Abrams," *Washington Times*

247   "He said he'd come to believe that he was wrong about some things," Bruck, "Back Roads: How Serious Is the Bush Administration about Creating a Palestinian State?" *New Yorker*

247   **"I consider this one of the most bizarre appointments imaginable,"** "White House Names Perjurer Abrams to National Security Council," *EFE News Service*

247   **"A self-confessed perjurer conceivably should be in jail,"** "White House Names Perjurer Abrams to National Security Council," *EFE News Service*

248   **"Abrams was the pit bull,"** McGrory, "Bush Brings Back Iran-Contra Affair," *Charleston Gazette*

248   **"My immediate thought was, a plane had once crashed into the Empire State building,"** Tauber, "Defending Bush's Mideast 'Freedom Agenda,'" *Jerusalem Post*

248   **"In the turmoil at the NSC after September 11, Abrams stood out as a problem solver,"** Bruck, "Back Roads: How Serious Is the Bush Administration about Creating a Palestinian state?" *New Yorker*

248   **"She put him in charge of co-ordinating humanitarian relief efforts,"** Woodward, *Plan of Attack*, 276

249   **"I feel young again! I love all these battles,"** Bruck, "Back Roads: How Serious Is the Bush Administration about Creating a Palestinian state?" *New Yorker*

Chapter 20 • Occupy Everywhere: Angela Davis, 1972–2012

250   **"When I think back on that period,"** Davis, "A Tribute to Henry Winston," *Political Affairs*

252   **"cult-like exposition of dogma,"** Rubin, "Lessons From the Past and Our Choice of Direction"

253   **"I kept saying that I wouldn't have, at that point, left the party,"** interview with Angela

254   **"products of labor [to fuel the] irrational drive for capitalist,"** *Our Friend Angela* 1972

254   **"Long live the friendship of our two peoples,"** *Our Friend Angela*

254   **"I'd never seen her in a relationship where she was ready to do that,"** interview with Charlene Mitchell

254   **"A pianist played 'We've Only Just Begun,'"** "Angela Davis, Sweetheart of the Far Left, Finds Her Mr. Right," *People*

255   **"He never recovered from the depression that accompanied Kendra's death,"** interview with Angela

256   **"something I'm fine with as a political statement,"** Miles, "Angela Davis at Our Table," *Out*

256   **"unwilling to render my life as a personal 'adventure,'"** Davis, *An Autobiography*, xvi

256   **"In the 1970s, nobody would have imagined it possible,"** Miles, "Angela Davis at Our Table," *Out*

256   **"that if I was ever free, I would use my life to uphold the cause of my sisters and brothers behind walls,"** Davis, *An Autobiography*, 328

257   **"In Alabama and Florida, once a felon, always a felon,"** Davis, *Are Prisons Obsolete?*, 38

257   **"The United States significantly contributed to conditions that led to the violence on September 11,"** Seitz, "Angela Davis Shares Views at KSC" *The Union Leader*

257   **"I've been told, 'You've expressed how I've been feeling, but I've been afraid to express it.'"** Seitz, "Angela Davis Shares Views at KSC" *The Union Leader*

258   **"So many people are swept up in this odd patriotism,"** Noonan, "Still Fighting a War Angela Davis Urges Less Nationalism, More International Concern," *The Boston Globe*, October 28, 2001

258   **"We have to realize that things have not fundamentally changed,"** Gupta, "Activist, Former Black Panther, Speaks at Northwestern University on Patriotism" *Daily Northwestern*

258   **"My mother always told us children,"** interview with Angela

259   **"What we didn't do . . . is that we didn't keep that movement going,"** Angela Davis speaking at "Be Good To Women Day," March 2010 http://www.youtube.com/watch?v=vldq1bi4GqI

259   **"It is truly an honor to be among you this afternoon,"** Angela Davis speaking at Occupy Wall Street, Washington Square Park, http://www.youtube.com/watch?v=HlvfPizooII

BIBLIOGRAPHY

A Huey P. Newton Story. Directed by Spike Lee. Forty Acres and a Mule Film-
    works and Luna Ray Films. 2001. See also http://www.pbs.org/hueypnewton
    /people/people_hoover.html.
"Angela Davis and Her New Husband." *Jet.* July 24, 1980.
"Angela Davis, Sweetheart of the Far Left, Finds Her Mr. Right." *People.* July 21,
    1980.
"The Angela Davis Case," *Newsweek.* October 26, 1970.
Abrams, Elliott. "Black Capitalism and Black Banks." *New Leader.* March 17, 1969.
Abrams, Elliott. "Cambridge Patterns." *New Leader.* April 28, 1969.
Abrams, Elliott. "Liberalism on Campus." *New Leader.* January 20, 1969.
Abrams, Elliott. "The Sky Is Falling." *New Leader.* February 12, 1968.
Abrams, Elliot. *Undue Process: A Story of How Political Differences Are Turned
    into Crimes.* Free Press. 1993.
Abramsky, Sasha. *Marching Toward Eden.* Interviews, book proposal, sample
    chapter drafts.
Alterman, Eric. "Elliott Abrams: The Teflon Assistant Secretary." *Washington
    Monthly.* May 1987.
Anspacher, Carolyn. "Setback for the State in Angela Trial." *San Francisco Chronicle.*
    April 26, 1972.
Aptheker, Bettina F. "The Angela Davis Case: A Brief Summary," in *Angela Davis
    Case Collection.* Oceana. 1974.
Aptheker, Bettina F. *Intimate Politics: How I Grew Up Red, Fought for Free Speech
    and Became a Feminist Rebel.* Seal Press. 2006.
Aptheker, Bettina F. *The Morning Breaks: The Trial of Angela Davis.* International.
    1975.
Aptheker, Herbert. *Racism, Imperialism & Peace: Selected Essays by Herbert
    Aptheker.* Eds. Marvin J. Berlowitz and Carol E. Morgan. Studies in Marxism
    21. Marxist Educational. 1987.
Arguing the World. Produced, directed and written by Joseph Dorman. Riverside
    Films Productions for Thirteen/WNET. 1997. Distributed by First Run Features.
Avorn, Jerry L., with Andrew Crane, Mark Jaffe, Oren Root Jr. Paul Starr, Michael
    Stern, Robert Stulberg of the staff of the *Columbia Daily Spectator. Up Against*

the Ivy Wall: A History of the Columbia Crisis. Ed. and Intro. by Robert Freid-
    man. Atheneum. 1969.

Baldwin, James. "An Open Letter to My Sister Angela Y. Davis." *New York Review
    of Books*. November 19, 1970. Also in Angela Davis, *If They Come in the
    Morning*. http://www.historyisaweapon.com/defcon1/itcitmbaldwin.html.

Bernstein, Walter. *Inside Out: A Memoir of the Blacklist*. Knopf. 1996.

Bradlee, Ben, Jr. *The Ambush Murders: The True Account of the Killing of Two
    California Policemen*. Dodd, Mead. 1979.

Braudy, Susan. *Family Circle: The Boudins and the Aristocracy of the Left*. Knopf.
    2003.

Brown, Kimberly Nichele. *Writing the Black Revolutionary Diva: Women's Sub-
    jectivity and the Decolonizing Text*. Indiana University Press. 2010.

Bruck, Connie. "Back Roads: How Serious Is the Bush Administration about Cre-
    ating a Palestinian State?" *New Yorker*. December 15, 2003.

Budhos, Marina. "Angela Davis Appointed to Major Chair." *Journal of Blacks in
    Higher Education*. Spring 1995.

Buhle, Mari Jo, Paul Buhle, and Dan Geogakas, eds. *Encyclopedia of the American
    Left*. Garland. 1990.

Burch, Philip H.. *Research in Political Economy, Supplement 1*. Jai Press. 1997.

Carmichael, Stokely. "Black Power." *SoJust: A Primary Source History of Social Jus-
    tice*. http://www.edchange.org/multicultural/speeches/stokely_carmichael
    _blackpower.html.

Carr, James. *Bad: The Autobiography of James Carr*. Herman Graf Associates.
    1975.

Castellucci, John. *The Big Dance: The Untold Story of Weatherman Kathy Boudin
    and the Terrorist Family that Committed the Brink's Robbery Murders*. Dodd,
    Mead. 1986.

Charlton, Linda. "F.B.I. Seizes Angela Davis in Motel Here." *New York Times*. Octo-
    ber 14, 1970. http://www.nytimes.com/books/98/03/08/home/davis-fbi.html.

Collier, Peter, and David Horowitz. *Destructive Generation: Second Thoughts
    About the Sixties*. Encounter Books. 1989.

Columbia University seminar, "Columbia 1968 + 40: War, Race, Activism, and the
    University. An Intergenerational Dialogue." April 24–27, 2008.

Cotj, Lawrence V. "The Facts Behind the Angela Davis Case." *Human Events*. June
    17, 1972.

Cronkite, Walter. February 27, 1968. *http://www.hark.com/clips/fbtgscsymj-for-it
    -seems-now-more-certain-than-ever-that-the-bloody-experience-of-vietnam
    -is-to-end-in-a-stalemate*.

Dash, Samuel. "Final Report of the Independent Counsel for Iran/Contra Mat-
    ters." Carnegie Endowment for International Peace, Foreign Policy Report.
    September 22, 1994.

Davis, Angela Y. *Angela Davis: An Autobiography*. International. 1974.

Davis, Angela Y. *Are Prisons Obsolete?* Seven Stories. 2003.

Davis, Angela Y. *Blues Legacies and Black Feminism*. Pantheon. 1998.

Davis, Angela Y. *If They Come in the Morning: Voices of Resistance*. Signet/New American Library. 1971.

Davis, Angela Y. "Rhetoric vs. Reality," written in May 1971 from Marin County Jail. *Ebony*. July 1971.

Davis, Angela Y. "To Save Our Nation." *Freedomways*. 20. 1980.

Davis, Angela Y. "A Tribute to Henry Winston." *Political Affairs* blog. February 23, 2012. http://politicalaffairs.net/tribute-to-henry-winston.

Davis, Angela Y. *Women, Race and Class*. Vintage. 1983.

Day of the Gun. Produced by Belva Davis. KRON Channel 4. 2001. Eric Cumming interview. http://www.youtube.com/watch?v=oT-apgRlJlQ.

De Lima, Agnes, and the Staff of the Little Red School House. *The Little Red School House*. Macmillan. 1942.

DeLeon, Robert A. "A New Look at Angela Davis." *Ebony*. April 1972.

DeLeon, Robert A. "A Revealing Report." *Jet*. November 8, 1971.

Dewey, John. *American Education Past and Future*. University of Chicago Press. 1931.

Dewey, John. *The School and Society*. McClure, Phillips. 1900.

Dewey, John. *Schools of To-Morrow*. Dutton. 1915.

Dialogue With A Woman Departed. Directed by Leo Hurwitz. 1981.

Dorman, Joseph. *Arguing the World: The New York Intellectuals in Their Own Words*. The Free Press. 2000.

Dougan, Andy. *Untouchable: A Biography of Robert De Niro*. Thunder's Mouth. 1996.

Draper, Theodore. *A Very Thin Line*. Hill & Wang. 1991.

"Eagleton-Abrams Row Detailed in Documents." *Houston Chronicle News Service*. June 10, 1987. http://www.chron.com/CDA/archives/archive.mpl/1987 _468331/eagleton-abrams-row-detailed-in-documents.html.

Elisabeth Irwin High School at 50. 1992. Published by the school's alumni and development department, with photographs from the Little Red and Elisabeth Irwin Archives.

"Fed: Racism Boosts PM's Popularity, Says Activist." *AAP Newsfeed*. November 28, 2001.

Fischer, Klaus P. *America in White, Black, and Gray: The Stormy 1960s*. Continuum. 2006.

Fowler, Glenn, "Leo Hurwitz, 81, Blacklisted Maker of Documentaries." *New York Times*. January 19, 1991.

Gardner, Fred. *Unlawful Concert: An Account of the Presidio Mutiny Case*. Viking. 1970.

Gerdes, Louise I., ed. *The 1930s.* Greenhaven. 2000.

Gillon, Steven M. *Politics and Vision: The ADA and American Liberalism, 1947–1985.* Oxford University Press. 1987.

Ginger, Ann Fagan. "Annotated Procedural Guide and Index," in *Angela Davis Case Collection.* Ed. Ann Fagan Ginger. Meiklejohn Civil Liberties Institute. 1974.

Gitlin, Todd. *The Sixties: Years of Hope, Days of Rage.* Revised version. Bantam. 1993.

Goldstein, Eric. "They Kept Her Out to Protect the American People." *Christian Science Monitor.* October 23, 1986. http://www.csmonitor.com/1986/1023/elara.html.

Goldstein, Patrick. "Many Refuse to Clap as Kazan Receives Oscar," *Los Angeles Times.* March 22, 1999. http://www.writing.upenn.edu/~afilreis/50s/kazan-protest.html.

"GOP Minority Report Rips Iran-Contra Panel Findings." *Houston Chronicle News Service.* November 17, 1987. http://www.chron.com/CDA/archives/archive.mpl/1987_503323/gop-minority-report-rips-iran-contra-panel-finding.html.

Gray, Christopher. "The Little Red School House at 196 Bleecker Street; Progressive Education in a Onetime Mission Church." *New York Times.* October 29, 1998.

Grove, Lloyd. "The Contrary Evolution of Elliott Abrams: From Counterculture Encounters to Conservative Affairs of State." *Washington Post.* January 14, 1987.

Gupta, Rani. "Activist, Former Black Panther, Speaks at Northwestern University on Patriotism." *Daily Northwestern.* October 31, 2001.

Hampton, Dina. "Little Red Radicals." *New York Times.* June 25, 2000.

Hayden, Tom. *Reunion: A Memoir.* Collier. 1989.

Heilbrun, Jacob. *They Knew They Were Right: The Rise of the Neocons.* Doubleday. 2008.

Huffman, Nicole. "History: Worker's Film and Photo League: 1930–1935." *New Frontiers in American Documentary Film.* University of Virginia. 2001. http://xroads.virginia.edu/~ma01/huffman/frontier/history.html.

Hurwitz, Tom. "Letters." *Time.* March 29, 1999.

Irwin, Elisabeth A. *Truancy: A Study of the Mental, Physical, and Social Factors of the Problem of Non-Attendance at School.* Public Education Association of the City of New York. 1915.

Irwin, Elisabeth A., and Louis A. Marks. *Fitting the School to the Child: An Experiment in Public Education.* Macmillan. 1924.

Jackson, George. *Blood in My Eye.* Random House. 1972. Reprinted, Black Classic Press. 1990.

Jackson, George. *Soledad Brother: The Prison Letters of George Jackson.* Coward-McCann. 1970. Reprinted, Chicago Review Press. 1994. See also http://www.youtube.com/watch?v=apbkX_1bpQE&feature=related.

James, Joy, ed. *The Angela Y. Davis Reader.* Blackwell. 1998.

Josephson, Hannah. *Biographical Study of Katherine Anthony and Elisabeth Irwin*. Little Red and Elisabeth Irwin Archives. Unpublished.

Kaplan, Judy, and Lynn Shapiro, eds. *Red Diapers: Growing Up in the Communist Left*. University of Illinois Press. 1998.

Kazan, Elia. *A Life*. De Capo. 1997.

Kelman, Steven. "The Contented Revolutionists." *New Leader*. April 28, 1969.

Kelman, Steven. *Push Comes to Shove: The Escalation of Student Protest*. Houghton Mifflin. 1970.

Kindig, Jessie. "GI Movement: Antiwar Soldiers at Fort Lewis, 1965–1973." *Antiwar and Radical History Project–Pacific Northwest*. Pacific Northwest Labor and Civil Rights Projects, University of Washington. http://depts.washington.edu /antiwar/gi_history.shtml.

King, Martin Luther, Jr. *Where Do We Go From Here: Chaos or Community?* Beacon. 1968.

Kirschheimer, Manny. "A Few Minutes About Leo on the Day of His Memorial, March 30, 1991." Sasha Abramsky Collection.

Kisselgoff, Anna, "Jane Dudley, Modern Dancer and Teacher, Is Dead at 89." *New York Times*. September 22, 2001.

Kunen, James Simon. *The Strawberry Statement: Notes of a College Revolutionary*. Random House. 1968.

Last Summer Won't Happen. Directed by Peter Gessner and Tom Hurwitz. Icarus Films. 1968.

Lekachman, Robert. "The Brighter Side." *New Leader*. April 28, 1969.

Lewis, Anthony. "Action by Abrams Regrettable." *Palm Beach Post*. December 3, 1986.

Liberatore, Paul. *The Road to Hell: The True Story of George Jackson, Stephen Bingham and the San Quentin Massacre*. Atlantic Monthly. 1996.

Lind, Michael. "A Tragedy of Errors." *The Nation*. February 5, 2004.

Little Red School House & Elisabeth Irwin High School: A Chronicle of 75 Years: As Told by the Alumni. 1997. Published by the alumni and development department, with photographs from the Little Red and Elisabeth Irwin Archives.

Little Red Schoolhouse & Elisabeth Irwin High School Directory. Bernard C. Harris Publishing Company. 1997.

Madison, Christopher. "Abrams, State's Human Right's Chief, Tries to Tailor a Policy to Suit Reagan." *National Journal*. May 1, 1982.

Mailer, Norman. *Armies of the Night*. Plume. 1995.

Manis, Andrew M. *A Fire You Can't Put Out: The Civil Rights Life of Birmingham's Reverend Fred Shuttlesworth*. University of Alabama Press. 1999.

Marcuse, Herbert. "Repressive Tolerance." *A Critique of Pure Tolerance*. Beacon Press. 1969. See also http://www.marcuse.org/herbert/pubs/60spubs/65repressive tolerance.htm.

Margolick, David. *Strange Fruit: Billie Holiday, Café Society and an Early Cry for Civil Rights*. Running Press. 2000.

Marx, Karl, and Federick Engels. *The Communist Manifesto*. International. 1948.

McGrory, Mary. "Bush Brings Back Iran-Contra Affair." *Charleston Gazette*. July 10, 2001.

McLellan, Scott. *What Happened*. Public Affairs. 2009.

Meeropol, Robert and Michael. *We Are Your Sons: The Legacy of Ethel and Julius Rosenberg*. University of Illinois Press. 1986.

Melish Defense Committee. *The Melish Case: A Challenge to the Church* pamphlet. 1949. http://www.amazon.com/Melish-Case-Challenge-Classic-Reprint/dp /B00930BBCO.

Menaker, Daniel. *The Old Left*. Knopf. 1982.

Mertus, Julie A. *Bait and Switch: Human Rights and Foreign Policy*. Routledge. 2004.

Miles, Sara. "Angela Davis at Our Table." *Out*. February, 1998.

Miller, James. *Democracy in the Streets: From Port Huron to the Siege of Chicago*. Harvard University Press. 1994.

Mishler, Paul C. *Raising Reds: The Young Pioneers, Radical Summer Camps and the Communist Political Culture in the United States*. Columbia University Press. 1999.

Morrison, James. "Embassy Row: Religious Envoy." *Washington Times*. May 4, 2001.

Mostel, Kate, and Madeline Gilford, with Jack Gilford and Zero Mostel. *170 Years of Show Business*. Random House. 1978.

Movement. September 1969.

Nadelson, Regina. *Who is Angela Davis? The Biography of a Revolutionary*. Wyden. 1972.

Navasky, Victor S. *Naming Names*. Penguin. 1980.

"Neighborhood-Based Citywide Youth Movement" in "You Don't Need A Weatherman To Know Which Way The Wind Blows" *New Left Notes*. June 18, 1969. *http://archive.org/stream/YouDontNeedAWeathermanToKnowWhichWay TheWindBlows_925/weather#page/n17/mode/2up*.

Noonan, Erica. "Still Fighting a War Angela Davis Urges Less Nationalism, More International Concern." *The Boston Globe*. October 28, 2001.

"Occupy Everywhere." *Democracy Now!* Pacifica. November 25, 2011.

Oral Histories: The HistoryMakers Video Oral History with Angela Yvonne Davis. April 3, 2004. Courtesy of the Schomburg Center for Research in Black Culture. http://www.thehistorymakers.com.

Our Friend Angela. Directed by Yolande du Luart. New Yorker Films. 1972.

Parker, J. A. *Angela Davis: The Making of a Revolutionary*. Arlington House. 1973.

Plummer, William. "Elliott Abrams Must Now Face the Music on Nicaragua and Congress Is Calling the Tune." *People*. June 8, 1987. http://www.people.com /people/archive/article/0,,20096460,00.html.

Podhoretz, Norman. *Ex-Friends.* Encounter Books. 2000.

Podhoretz, Norman. *Making It.* Random House. 1967.

"Praise and Silent Protest Greet Kazan's Oscar." *The Guardian.* March 22, 1999.

"Protestors Crowd Into Hamilton Hall for All Night Vigil," *Columbia Daily Spectator.* April 24, 1968.

Radosh, Ronald. *Commies: A Journey Through the Old Left, the New Left and the Leftover Left.* Encounter. 2001.

Radosh, Ron. *Divided They Fell: The Demise of the Democratic Party.* Simon & Shuster. 1996.

Radosh, Ronald, and Joyce Milton. *The Rosenberg File.* Second edition. Yale University Press. 1997.

Ravich, Diane. *The Great School Wars: New York City, 1805–1973: A History of the Public Schools as Battlefield of Social Change.* Basic. 1974.

Reitman, Valerie, and Mitchell Landsberg. "40 Years Later." *Los Angeles Times.* August 11, 2005. *http://articles.latimes.com/2005/aug/11/local/me-watts11.*

Richards, Phillip M. *Black Heart: The Moral Life of Recent African American Letters.* Peter Lang. 2006.

Rose, David. "The Gaza Bombshell." *Vanity Fair.* April 2008. http://www.vanityfair.com/politics/features/2008/04/gaza200804.

Rosenblatt, Roger. *Coming Apart: A Memoir of the Harvard Wars of 1969.* Little, Brown. 1997.

Rosenfeld, Seth, "Stew Albert–Original Yippie at Heart of 1960s Idealism," *San Francisco Chronicle.* February 1, 2006.

Rubin, Danny. "Lessons from the Past and Our Choice of Direction." History of the Communist Party and the Future of the COC. See also *http://www.nathannewman.org/EDIN/.left/CoC/.aboutCoC/.general/whereto.dr.html.*

Russell, Corigan. "Angela Davis' Moving Eloquence." *About Time.* March 1997.

Rudd, Mark. *Underground: My Life with SDS and the Weather Underground.* William Morrow. 2009.

Sanders, Charles L. "The Radicalization of Angela Davis." *Ebony.* July 1971.

Schafer, Susan M. "Iran-Contra Panels Went Beyond Tower Commission Probe." *Associated Press.* http://www.apnewsarchive.com/1987/Iran-Contra-Panels-Went-Beyond-Tower-Commission-Probe/id-4c3e1d066a9988b618b40a32faf6f4c6.

Schickel, Richard. *Elia Kazan, A Biography.* Harper Collins. 2006.

Schickel, Richard. "An Oscar for Elia." *Time.* Volume 153/Issue 9. March 8, 1999.

Seitz, Stephen. "Angela Davis Shares Views at KSC." *The Union Leader.* October 21, 2001.

Shuttlesworth, The Rev. Fred L. "Birmingham Revisited." *Ebony.* August 1971.

Sir! No, Sir! A Film by David Zeiger. Displaced Films. 2005. http://depts.washington.edu/antiwar/gi_links.shtml.

Stern, Sol. "The Campaign to Free Angela Davis and Ruchell Magee." *New York Times*. June 27, 1971. http://www.nytimes.com/books/98/03/08/home/davis-campaign.html?_r=1.

Strange Victory. Directed by Leo Hurwitz. Target Films. 1948.

Swain, Martica, and Floyd Skloot. *Robert De Niro, Sr. (1922–1993)*. Salander-O'Reilly Galleries. 1995.

Tauber, Daniel. "Defending Bush's Mideast 'Freedom Agenda.'" *Jerusalem Post*. August 27, 2012.

Timberg, Robert. *The Nightingale's Song*. Touchstone. 1995.

Timothy, Mary. *Jury Woman: The Story of the Trial of Angela Y. Davis*. Limited ed. Glide Publications/Emty Press. 1974.

Toobin, Jeffrey. *Opening Arguments: A Young Lawyer's First Case, United States v. Oliver North*. Viking. 1991.

Unger, Craig. *The Fall of the House of Bush*. Scribner. 2007.

"Unpardonable: Bush Pardons Iran-Contra Defendants." Editorial. *The Progressive*. Februrary 1, 1993.

Vibrations for a New People: A Conversation with Angela Davis. CBS 5, KPIX-TV. January 1972. See also https://diva.sfsu.edu/collections/sfbatv/bundles/190044.

Waitt, Alden. *Katherine Anthony: The Evolution of a Butterfly into a Chrysalis*. Master's Thesis. Undated. Little Red and Elisabeth Irwin Archives.

Waldron, Arthur N. "A Quest for Seriousness." *New Leader*. April 18, 1969.

Wallechinsky, David. *The People's Almanac Presents the Twentieth Century: History with the Boring Parts Left Out*. Little, Brown. 2001.

Walsh, Lawrence E. *Firewall: The Iran-Contra Conspiracy and Cover-up*. Norton. 1997.

The Weather Manifesto submitted by Karin Asbley, Bill Ayers, Bernardine Dohrn, John Jacobs, Jeff Jones, Gerry Long, Home Machtinger, Jim Mellen, Terry Robbins, Mark Rudd and Steve Tappis.

Weintraub, Bernard. "Reagan's Human Right's Chief: No 'Liberal Mole.'" *New York Times*. October 19, 1982.

Welch, William M. "Abrams Contradicts Documents and Oral Testimony of Others with AM-US-Iran-Contra Rdp." *Associated Press*. June 2, 1987. *http://www.apnewsarchive.com/1987/Abrams-Contradicts-Documents-And-Oral-Testimony-Of-Others-With-AM-US-Iran-Contra-Rdp/id-bd51d7e626db526 ca99e455046b20d45*.

Wetzsteon, Ross. *Republic of Dreams: Greenwich Village: The American Bohemia, 1910–1960*. Simon & Schuster. 2002.

"White House Names Perjurer Abrams to National Security Council." *EFE News Services*. June 29, 2001.

Woodward, Bob. *Bush at War*. Simon & Schuster. 2002.

Woodward, Bob. *Plan of Attack*. Simon & Schuster. 2004.

Woodward, Bob. *State of Denial.* Simon & Schuster. 2006.

Woodward, Bob. *The War Within: A Secret White House History 2006–2008.* Simon & Schuster. 2009.

YouTube clip for Davis quotation, ABC News. May 23, 1969. http://www.youtube .com/watch?v=AI4U-q2o2cg&feature=related.

YouTube clip for DeNiro, Scorsese, Kazan quotations, 71st Academy Awards© telecast. 1999. *http://www.youtube.com/watch?v=3YziNNCZeNs.*

Interviews

Elliott Abrams
Bettina Aptheker
Greta Berman
Walter Bernstein
Will Bruder
Richard Caplan
Teresa Caplan
Judith Caplan Inglese
Grace Cohen
Angela Davis
Ellen Fried Sklar
Peter Gallway
Lisa Fein Gilford
Sara Fishko
Dan Hastings
Tom Hayden
Kent Hudson
Tom Hurwitz
Tullio Inglese
Fred Feinstein
Arthur Kaufman
Peter Knobler
Judith Jackson
Anne Jackson Johnson
Harold Kirshner
Judith Jackson Inglese
Steven Kelman
Margaret Klenck
Bridget Leicester
Leland Lubinsky
Andrew McLaren

Robert Meeropol
Jeff Melish
Cathy Michaelson
Robert Miller
Charlene Mitchell
Victor Navasky
Daniel Pipes
Daniel Prince
Sandra Roche
Jill Z. Rubin
Mark Rudd
Amy Saltz
Dave Sarlin
Stephanie Stroud
Ed Suvanto
Milt Unterman
Mary Van Dyke
Andrew Weiss
Betty Wolder
Harold Yates
Barbara Zahm
Julian Zukmann

Interviews by Sasha Abramsky

Susan Brown
Jane Dudley
Tom Hurwitz
Leland Lubinsky
Deborah Robison
Josh Robison

INDEX

Credit: Donnah Welby.

Dina Hampton is a graduate of the Columbia Graduate School of Journalism and has worked for more than a decade as a reporter and editor for publications including the *New York Times* and the *Daily News*. She is a late 1970s graduate of Little Red and later served as its alumni director. She lives in New York City.

PublicAffairs is a publishing house founded in 1997. It is a tribute to the standards, values, and flair of three persons who have served as mentors to countless reporters, writers, editors, and book people of all kinds, including me.

I. F. STONE, proprietor of *I. F. Stone's Weekly*, combined a commitment to the First Amendment with entrepreneurial zeal and reporting skill and became one of the great independent journalists in American history. At the age of eighty, Izzy published *The Trial of Socrates*, which was a national bestseller. He wrote the book after he taught himself ancient Greek.

BENJAMIN C. BRADLEE was for nearly thirty years the charismatic editorial leader of *The Washington Post*. It was Ben who gave the *Post* the range and courage to pursue such historic issues as Watergate. He supported his reporters with a tenacity that made them fearless and it is no accident that so many became authors of influential, best-selling books.

ROBERT L. BERNSTEIN, the chief executive of Random House for more than a quarter century, guided one of the nation's premier publishing houses. Bob was personally responsible for many books of political dissent and argument that challenged tyranny around the globe. He is also the founder and longtime chair of Human Rights Watch, one of the most respected human rights organizations in the world.

•   •   •

For fifty years, the banner of Public Affairs Press was carried by its owner Morris B. Schnapper, who published Gandhi, Nasser, Toynbee, Truman, and about 1,500 other authors. In 1983, Schnapper was described by *The Washington Post* as "a redoubtable gadfly." His legacy will endure in the books to come.

Peter Osnos, *Founder and Editor-at-Large*